Adriaen van de Velde

Dutch Master of Landscape

Adriaen van de Velde

Dutch Master of Landscape

Bart Cornelis

Marijn Schapelhouman

DULWICH
PICTURE
GALLERY

RIJKS MUSEUM

PAUL HOLBERTON PUBLISHING

First published to accompany the exhibition

Adriaen van de Velde *Dutch Master of Landscape*

at the Rijksmuseum, Amsterdam
24 June – 25 September 2016

AND

at Dulwich Picture Gallery, London
12 October 2016 – 15 January 2017

The grant from the American Friends of Dulwich Picture Gallery Inc. was made possible through the generosity of the Arthur and Holly Magill Foundation and Arturo and Holly Melosi.

**DULWICH
PICTURE
GALLERY**
REDISCOVERING OLD MASTERS:
THE MELOSI SERIES

ISBN 978 1 907372 96 4 (hardback)
ISBN 978 1 911300 06 9 (paperback)

British Library Catalogue in Publishing Data
A CIP record of this publication is available from the British Library

Produced by Paul Holberton Publishing
89 Borough High St, London, SE1 1NL
www.paul-holberton.net

Designed and typeset by Laura Parker

Translation of Marijn Schapelhouman's entries by Beverley Jackson

Proofreading by Sophie Kullmann

Printed by Gomer Press Ltd, Llandysul

FRONT COVER Detail of cat. no.5, *The beach at Scheveningen*, 1658. Museumslandschaft Hessen Kassel, Gemäldegalerie Alte Meister, inv. no.GK 374

BACK COVER (HARDBACK): Detail of cat. no.51, *Herdsman and herdswoman with livestock by a stream*. Teylers Museum, Haarlem, inv. no.R 043

FRONTISPIECE Detail of cat. no.2, *A farm with a dead tree*, 1658. The National Gallery, London, inv. no.NG867

Contents

Directors' foreword

The landscapes of Adriaen van de Velde are among the very best that the Dutch Golden Age produced, showing great variety and superb draughtsmanship, depicting meadows, Italianate views, beaches, dunes, forests, winter scenes, and portraits in landscape settings. The short-lived artist's work was greatly appreciated in the eighteenth and nineteenth centuries, highly sought after by collectors in Germany, France and England. Despite that fame and the exquisite quality of Adriaen van de Velde's output, this exhibition marks the first time that a substantial body of his work has been assembled.

The artist made figure and animal studies in seductive red chalk and compositional studies in pen and ink in preparation for his paintings, making it possible to follow very precisely the various phases in his creative process – perhaps more so than is possible for any other Dutch artist of the period. For this reason, and because of their exceptional quality, drawings form a major part of our exhibition and are reunited for the first time with the paintings for which they were studies.

The Rijksmuseum, Amsterdam, and Dulwich Picture Gallery, London, are proud to be collaborating on this exhibition which will thus offer not only a survey of the artist's oeuvre, but also a fascinating insight into the working methods of a seventeenth-century Dutch landscape painter: one can, as it were, look over the shoulder of an artist at work.

The exhibition has been expertly curated by Bart Cornelis, Deputy Editor of *The Burlington Magazine*, London, in collaboration with Marijn Schapelhouman, Senior Curator of Drawings at the Rijksmuseum. On behalf of both institutions we are grateful to them for the dedication and enthusiasm demonstrated at every stage of the tour and for the illuminating texts found in this publication. Our thanks to Paul Holberton and Laura Parker at Paul Holberton Publishing for producing this beautiful catalogue.

We are deeply grateful to the great many lenders – the museums, organizations and private collectors who agreed to part with their work for the duration of the tour so visitors to our institutions can enjoy and discover the artist through an extremely careful selection of exquisite works.

The exhibition has been a happy collaboration between the Rijksmuseum and Dulwich Picture Gallery. At Dulwich Picture Gallery our thanks go to Dr Xavier Bray, Chief Curator, for his expert guidance, and we are grateful to Phoebe Newman, Exhibitions and Displays Coordinator, for the exhibition and catalogue arrangements with Clare Simpson, Head of Exhibitions. A word of thanks is due to Head of Exhibitions Tim Zeedijk, Project Coordinator Suzanne Plaum and Registrars Wobke Hooites and Lindy de Heij of the Rijksmuseum for making the Amsterdam venue possible.

For Dulwich Picture Gallery, special thanks must be given to Arturo and Holly Melosi; they are enlightened and generous supporters who, through the Arthur and Holly Magill Foundation and the American Friends of Dulwich Picture Gallery, sponsor the 'Melosi Series' of exhibitions entitled Rediscovering Old Masters. The Rijksmuseum owes special thanks to its founder Philips and main sponsors Bankgiro Loterij, ING and KPN, whose generous support makes ambitious projects of this nature possible.

WIM PIJBES
General Director, Rijksmuseum

IAN A.C. DEJARDIN
The Sackler Director, Dulwich Picture Gallery

Authors' acknowledgements

No exhibition happens in isolation, and this show is no exception. While researching the work of Adriaen van de Velde and writing the catalogue, we have benefitted from the help of many friends and colleagues. At the risk of forgetting someone who has in fact been particularly helpful, we would like to thank the people mentioned below, all of whom have in one way or another helped bring this exhibition and its catalogue to fruition. A special word of thanks is due to Ian Dejardin, who enthusiastically welcomed the idea of an exhibition devoted to Adriaen van de Velde. We are very grateful to Stijn Alsteens, Christopher D.M. Atkins, Sir Nicholas Bacon, Colin B. Bailey, Christopher Baker, Charles Beddington, Holm Bevers, Jonathan Bikker, Albert Blankert, Malin Borin, Xavier Bray, William Breazeale, Christopher Brown, Hans Buijs, Edwin Buijsen, the Trustees and staff of The Burlington Magazine, Quentin Buvelot, Hugo Chapman, Jan and Lotte Cornelis, Remmelt Daalder, Sara van Dijk, Blaise Ducos, the staff of Dulwich Picture Gallery, Frits Duparc, Xander van Eck, Rudi Ekkart, Caroline Elam, Jan Piet Filedt Kok, Ton Geerts, Hans de Gier, Emilie Gordenker, George Gordon, Johnny van Haeften, Michael Hall, Anne Harmssen, Peter Hecht, Paul Holberton, Wobke Hooites, Bastiaan Ingen Housz, Paul Huys Janssen, Beverley Jackson, Guido Jansen, Erik Jurgens, Larry Keith, Stephan Kemperdick, David Kirkham, Bram de Klerck, Felix Krämer, Sophie Kullmann, Alastair Laing, Deborah Lambert, Friso Lammertse, Justus Lange, Christophe Leribault, Nadine Loach, Ger Luijten, Pauline Lunsingh Scheurleer, Jan Gorm Madsen, Maria del Mar Borobia, Jane Martineau, Helen van der Meij, Arturo and Holly Melosi, Norbert Middelkoop, Carmen Mladin, Dana Mokaddem, Jane Munro, Uta Neidhardt, Phoebe Newman, Jan Nicolaisen, Jolanda van Nijen, Petria Noble, Eva Nygårds, Laura Parker, Sheldon Peck, Viola Pemberton-Pigott, Henry Pettifer, Barbara Pezzini, Suzanne Plaum, Michiel Plomp, Elizabeth Rabineau, Paul Raison, Sophie Renouard de Bussièrre, Robert-Jan te Rijdt, the staff of the Rijksmuseum, the staff of the RKD – Netherlands Institute for Art History, William W. Robinson, Martin Royalton-Kisch, Gregory Rubinstein, Francis Russell, Peter Schatborn, Robert Schillemans, Frits Scholten, David Scrase, Christian Tico Seifert, Desmond Shawe-Taylor, Richard Shone, Clare Simpson, Maria Smit, Anthony Speelman, Marja Stijkel, Cécile Tainturier, Louis van Tilborgh, Hayley Tomlinson, The Hon. Kate Trevelyan, Jane Turner, Gabri van Tussenbroek, Ige Verslype, Adriaan Waiboer, Amy Walsh, the staff of the Warburg Library, Henrietta Ward, Matt and Susan Weatherbie, Gregor Weber, Catherine Whistler, Sir Christopher White, Betsy Wieseman, Alan Wintermute, Gerdien Wuestman and Tim Zeedijk, and those who wish to remain anonymous.

Detail of cat. no.48, *Summer landscape with wheatfield*, 1662. Kupferstichkabinett, Staatliche Museen zu Berlin, inv. no.kdz 2424

Reintroducing Adriaen van de Velde

BART CORNELIS

Anyone who leafs through an early eighteenth-century auction catalogue will notice how covetable Dutch paintings of the Golden Age were among collectors soon after the seventeenth century had come to a close. The artists responsible for the works listed in these catalogues were already considered 'Old Masters', and it was evident to connoisseurs that the preceding century had been one of exceptional artistic achievement.[1] Today few would disagree, and most of the names that we encounter in these catalogues sound reassuringly familiar. There was, in other words, already an established canon, and one that largely resembles the canon we recognize today, even if there were obvious exceptions: Johannes Vermeer was not yet a household name, and Frans Hals was not nearly as famous as he is now, while at the other end of the spectrum we come across names of artists who were then held in high esteem but whose star later waned, only to be rediscovered in more recent times. But by and large the canon that existed then was still more or less in place when, between 1828 and 1842, the London art dealer John Smith (1781–1855) compiled his magnum opus – the nine-volume *Catalogue raisonné of the works of the most eminent Dutch, Flemish, and French painters*, a reference work that remains an important port of call today. It formed the basis of the *Beschreibendes und kritisches Verzeichnis der Werke der hervorragendsten holländischen Maler des XVII. Jahrhunderts nach dem Muster von John Smith's catalogue raisonné*, published in ten volumes between 1907 and 1928 by the Dutch art historian Cornelis Hofstede de Groot (1863–1930),[2] who made only some minor changes to Smith's selection of artists whose works should be catalogued, adding, among others, the oeuvres of Vermeer and Hals.

There was no question in the minds of either Smith or Hofstede de Groot that their volumes should include the works of Adriaen van de Velde, the landscape artist who is the subject of this exhibition, just as there would have been no question in the minds of serious eighteenth-, nineteenth- and early twentieth-century collectors that their collections should include at least one example by the artist. A brief glance at the provenances listed in this exhibition catalogue makes clear just how desirable Van de Velde's works were; they read like a roll-call of the great and the good, from royals and aristocrats to members of banking dynasties, all of whom were prepared to part with significant sums of money to own a fine example of his work.

Most of the artists whose paintings were catalogued by Smith and Hofstede de Groot have received ample attention in modern monographs or monographic exhibitions, but, even though Adriaen van de Velde's work has always been held in high esteem, there has never been an exhibition devoted exclusively to it, while only very recently has there been an attempt to compile

Detail of fig. 27, *The Migration of Jacob*, 1663.
The Wallace Collection, London, inv. no. P80

11

a new catalogue of his paintings.[3] Van de Velde was also a phenomenal draughtsman. His drawings have fared a little better, frequently featuring in exhibitions devoted to seventeenth-century Dutch drawings. They have also been discussed in important articles by William W. Robinson.[4]

With this exhibition, we draw renewed attention to the superbly refined paintings of this "aristocrat among Dutch landscape painters", as he was once dubbed.[5] The intrinsic quality of his paintings is such that it is hoped that the exhibition will be a revelation to visitors on that count alone, but the emphasis of the show is as much on his drawings, for Van de Velde's paintings and drawings are inextricably intertwined. This dual approach is meant to bring the artist's oeuvre to life, as there is perhaps no other seventeenth-century Dutch artist whose working methods can be followed so closely. Van de Velde meticulously – one might even say obsessively – prepared his paintings through preliminary drawings that, even if they served a specific function, are nevertheless beautiful works of art in their own right. Not all his drawings will have survived, but luckily many have. They would once have lived in a book or folder in Van de Velde's studio so that he could use them when he composed a picture. A good number of them have been brought together here for the first time, like long-lost siblings. Van de Velde's drawings were and remain highly collectable and are now scattered around the world, but some are temporarily reunited in this show, once more rubbing shoulders not only with each other but in a few cases also with the paintings that were made with their help. Van de Velde also made more finished drawings that were most probably intended to be sold as independent works of art, and examples from that category are included in this exhibition as well.

Like many of his contemporaries, Van de Velde was also active as a printmaker. His etched oeuvre comprises 28 prints, many of which show the same motifs as are found in his paintings, with a few exceptions in isolation rather than as part of an elaborate composition. As this exhibition concentrates on the artist's paintings and drawings, his prints are not shown in its Amsterdam or Dulwich installation and are not catalogued in this publication; they occupy a very definite place in the canon of prints produced by Dutch *peintres-graveurs* and were superbly catalogued as early as 1803 by Adam Bartsch,[6] and more recently in the Hollstein series, the standard reference work for Dutch, Flemish and German printmaking.[7]

Life and work

Although there are quite a few archival documents relating to Adriaen van de Velde, they present many small nuggets of information and do not necessarily add up to a biography. The bare facts are straightforward enough. Adriaen's grandfather, Willem Willemsz van de Velde, born c.1572 in Oostwinkel in Flanders, earned his living as a merchant and as a bargemaster in inland shipping. His family had most likely converted to Calvinism, which brought severe consequences once the main cities in Flanders had returned to the control of Catholic Spain. He and his family fled north to Leiden, probably around 1584, where around 1611 Adriaen's father, Willem van the Velde (the Elder), was born and in 1631 married Judith van Leeuwen (they divorced in 1662). In 1633 their son Willem van de Velde (the Younger) was born in Leiden. Not long afterwards, the family moved to Amsterdam, where on 20th November 1636 Adriaen was baptized in the Oude Kerk. Quite how his father came to be a marine artist is unclear, although the Van de Velde family's connection to inland shipping is surely significant in this respect. While Adriaen's brother Willem chose to become a marine painter, like his father, and continued to collaborate with his father throughout his career, Adriaen pursued an independent career as a landscape painter.[8]

The two brothers probably received their initial training from their father. It is likely that around the end of the 1640s Willem moved to Weesp to study under Simon de Vlieger (c.1601–1653),[9] but we have no documentary evidence to tell us whether Adriaen received any further training, and if so, who was his master. It is probable that after their training both worked in their father's Amsterdam studio for a while.

Most seventeenth-century Dutch artists specialized in one particular genre, as this gave them the best chance to be successful in a highly competitive market in a country where the Church's role as a patron of the arts had significantly diminished. Artists catered instead for an affluent merchant class, making paintings not on commission but to be sold on the open market. Adriaen van de Velde was no exception, although in addition to landscapes he also painted some religious works. As far as we know, he never left his native country and his presence in Amsterdam is documented for every year from 1657 onwards.[10]

Although born into a Protestant family, in 1657 Adriaen married a Catholic woman, Maria Pietersz Ouderkerck. The couple's five children were all baptized in various clandestine Catholic churches in Amsterdam, while, not long before his death, Van de Velde declared in a statement "that he was Catholic",[11] so he must have converted to Catholicism: this is relevant for an entirely different strand in Van de Velde's oeuvre, his religious work.

Van de Velde died young in January 1672,[12] only thirty-five years old, leaving an oeuvre of over 170 paintings, 28 etchings and a large number of drawings. In the same year, also known as the *rampjaar* (the 'disaster year') because it saw the start of the Franco-Dutch War (1672–78), his father and brother decided to move to England, presumably because they expected better prospects there than in a country that was under attack from many sides and had suffered a severe economic downturn.[13] The fact that Adriaen had died earlier that year may well have been a contributing factor in their decision. In England they greatly benefited from the patronage of Charles II and his brother James, Duke of York. Both Willems remained in England for the rest of their lives. Willem van de Velde the Elder died in London in 1693, and Willem van de Velde the Younger died there in 1707.

In Arnold Houbraken's biography of Adriaen van de Velde in his *Groote schouburgh der Nederlantsche konstschilders en schilderessen* (1718–21), our chief early source of information for seventeenth-century Dutch painters,

FIG.1
Adriaen van de Velde, *Two cows*. Signed and
dated, lower left: *A.v.Velde.f. 1656*. Oil on canvas,
66 × 58 cm. Wachtmeister Collection, Wanås

FIG.2
Paulus Potter, *Two cows and a young bull beside
a fence in a meadow*. Signed and dated, on the
fence: *Paulus.Potter.f. / 1647*. Oil on panel,
49.5 × 37.2 cm. Art Institute of Chicago,
inv. no.1997.336

we read that the author had been in contact with Adriaen's daughter
Judith. She had made it clear to him that her father had been considered
something of a *Wunderkind*, who "from an early age, through an inherited
inclination, was driven to the art of drawing and painting, and, still a school
boy, sneakily managed to get hold of his brother Willem's drawing pens,
brushes and paints, drawing and painting on everything he could find, even
the headboard of his cupboard bed, on which he … painted a dairy farmer in
colours, so curious for his age, and without any training, that it was treasured
long afterwards. This I have been told by his daughter, the wife of the broker
Sodyn in Amsterdam."[14] Whether this anecdote is true or not is a moot
point; what matters is that Adriaen was evidently considered a child prodigy,
something that is not difficult to believe in light of the fact that he painted a
masterpiece such as *The beach at Scheveningen* (cat. no.5) at the age of twenty-
two, when many artists of that age would still be trying to find their way into
their profession. Even in the seventeenth century, when artists often received
their training in their mid teens, it is a remarkably precocious achievement.

Sadly, although Houbraken managed to speak to the artist's daughter,[15]
his biography of Van de Velde is dismally brief. Apart from this anecdote, all
he provides is some information about the artist's training, that he kept up
his habit of making sketches outside in the countryside until the end of his
life (a passage that is quoted ad nauseam in the literature on Van de Velde),
and that, in addition to landscapes with animals, he painted some
religious works.

Because Houbraken's short biography is probably based on information
supplied by the artist's daughter, one might expect that the few facts that
he provides would be reliable, but his statement that Van de Velde received
his training from the landscape painter Jan Wijnants (1631/32–84) is

almost certainly incorrect. If this information indeed came from the artist's daughter, she may well have misremembered the situation, because in the 1660s Van de Velde and Wijnants certainly collaborated, with the former frequently adding the staffage to landscapes by the latter, who from at least 1660 also lived in Amsterdam. That Van de Velde was Wijnants's pupil is repeated in the literature to this day, although some have rightly treated it with caution.[16] Among the several good reasons to doubt it the most obvious is that there is not a trace of Wijnants's style in Van de Velde's earliest works. Then there is the very small difference in age between the two artists: Wijnants was Van de Velde's senior only by five years at most. Van de Velde is likely to have received his training at some point in the early 1650s, between the ages of fourteen and eighteen, when Wijnants himself would have been aged nineteen to twenty-three. It is highly unlikely that Wijnants would have taken an artist under his wing who was practically of his own generation and at a time when his own style had not yet fully developed; the very few dated paintings by Wijnants from before 1656 show farmhouses in the style of Emmanuel Murant, furnished with poultry by Dirck Wijntrack.[17] There is the added complication that, although Wijnants was from Haarlem, which is relatively close to Amsterdam, in 1653 he is recorded as living in Rotterdam,[18] and therefore at that point could not have taken on pupils in Haarlem.

The artist who undoubtedly exerted the greatest influence on young Van de Velde was Paulus Potter (1625–1654), so much so that one may legitimately wonder whether there was some kind of pupil–teacher relationship. Potter spent the last two years of his life, from 1652 to 1654, in Amsterdam, the years in which Van de Velde would have received his training, but there is no documentary evidence for Van de Velde's apprenticeship, so the idea must be treated with caution.[19] The visual evidence can seem compelling, but it is not as straightforward as it may appear at first sight. A comparison between Van de Velde's painting in the Wachtmeister Collection in Wanås, Sweden (fig.1), reliably dated 1656,[20] and Potter's *Two cows and a young bull beside a fence in a meadow* of 1647 (fig.2) speaks volumes, but then this is Van de Velde at his

FIG.4
Adriaen van de Velde, *Meadow with cattle*.
Signed and dated, lower left: *A.v.d.Velde / 1654*.
Oil on canvas, 25 × 21 cm. Present whereabouts
unknown

FIG.5
Adriaen van de Velde, *Meadow with cattle*.
Signed and dated, lower right: *A.v.Velde f. 1658*.
Oil on panel, 27 × 22 cm. Gemäldegalerie,
Staatliche Museen zu Berlin, inv. no.903A

most Potteresque.[21] Two earlier pictures, *Meadow with a horn-blower* of 1655 (fig.3)[22] and Van de Velde's earliest dated painting, his *Meadow with cattle* of 1654 (fig.4),[23] certainly show Potter's influence, but especially the latter has a quality that is already entirely Van de Velde's own, principally in its much softer handling of paint and superb command of aerial perspective, neither of which are particularly Potteresque qualities. In his survey of Dutch landscape painting of 1966, Wolfgang Stechow memorably described the 1654 picture as "a small gem of crystalline clarity and lucidity, a harbinger of that Mozartian serenity, harmony and composure which was to become the hallmark of the finest works of this lovable artist (who died at the same age as Mozart)".[24] It may seem somewhat peculiar that two years later Van de Velde should return to such a straightforwardly Potteresque mode in his painting in Sweden (fig.1), only to revert to the more independent style of his 1654 picture in a beautiful panel preserved in Berlin (fig.5),[25] which is dated 1658, the same year as *A farm with a dead tree* in London (cat. no.2). The last two pictures show the influence of Potter but at the same time also show Van de Velde taking his very own "crystalline clarity" to new heights, in the latter in a far more elaborate composition. It is in this same year that he painted his unforgettable beachscape in Kassel (cat. no.5), which shows no trace of Potter's influence at all. The small gem-like *View of an estuary* from Leipzig (cat. no.3) also stems from this year and equally has little to do with Potter. In other words, it is clear that Van de Velde chose to be a 'disciple' of Potter

FIG.6
After Paulus Potter, *Herders with cattle*.
Inscribed and dated, lower left: *Paulus Potter.f
1651*. Oil on canvas, 81 × 97.5 cm. Rijksmuseum,
Amsterdam, inv. no.SK-A-318

FIG.7
Paulus Potter, *Herders with cattle*. Signed and
dated, lower left: *Paulus Potter: f: 1651*. Oil
on canvas, 82 × 89.5 cm. The Woburn Abbey
Collection

FIG.8
Adriaen van de Velde, *St Jerome*. Signed and
dated, lower right: *A.v.Velde.f.1668*. Oil on panel,
75.5 × 65.1 cm. Staatliches Museum, Schwerin,
inv. no.G115

to varying degrees. There was no straightforward linear development, with
Potter as its starting point, and this makes it very doubtful that his debt to
Potter can be the result of a pupil–teacher relationship. Van de Velde was
well acquainted with Potter's work, however, and while technical evidence
for the way the paint layers are built up suggests that he is not the author of a
faithful copy (fig.6) of Potter's *Herders with cattle* (fig.7), it is understandable
that this was considered a possibility once it was established that the work
could not be by Potter himself. In this case the idea was reinforced by the
fact that Van de Velde used a compressed version of the background in
Potter's *Herders with cattle* for his *St Jerome* of 1668 (fig.8), demonstrating
just how familiar he was with Potter's work.[26]

Another factor to take into consideration in this respect is that Van de
Velde's earliest dated works are a number of etchings of 1653 that show the
influence of prints by Potter and Karel Dujardin (1622–1678), and Simon de
Vlieger for that matter, an artist who is less often mentioned in this context
but whose etched oeuvre is equally relevant. All these artists, including Van
de Velde himself, were evidently familiar with the etchings of Pieter van
Laer (1599–c.1642). Although livestock and other animals were roaming
freely in early seventeenth-century Dutch landscapes, it was Van Laer's
paintings and his series of etchings of 1636 that put such subjects firmly on
the map of seventeenth-century Dutch art.[27] The influence of Pieter van Laer
is best demonstrated by comparing Van de Velde's etching of a *Shepherd
and shepherdess with their animals* (fig.10) with Van Laer's 1636 etching of
Spinning woman with boar and donkeys (fig.9).[28] But Van de Velde seems to
have been just as keen on the etchings of Karel Dujardin.[29] It is difficult

to overstate the importance of prints in this respect, which by their very nature were readily available to artists.[30] The point here is that young Van de Velde could be eclectic, effortlessly moving from one example to another, perhaps too much so to be able to identify any one artist as his master. Van de Velde soon turned to the example of Dujardin in his paintings as well. His uncanny ability to assimilate various styles is borne out by his Dujardinesque *Horseman at a ford, asking the way of a herdswoman* of 1659 (fig.11),[31] in which he takes his cue from paintings such as Dujardin's *Young peasants crossing a ford* (fig.12),[32] only a year after having painted such a Potteresque work as *A farm with a dead tree* of 1658 (cat. no.2).

This is not to say that Van de Velde was merely an eclectic follower of other artists. Although there is no doubt that he turned to their work for certain motifs, his paintings are highly individual in their refined and balanced compositions, perfect integration of figures and staffage into the landscape, clarity of tone and superb use of aerial perspective. His aptitude for assimilating various influences also partly accounts for the tremendous variety in his early works.

Dujardin's work remained a source of inspiration throughout Van de Velde's career, more so perhaps than that of Potter, whose influence did not disappear but waned as Van de Velde's later works became more Arcadian and Italianate. It must be added that in the case of Dujardin and Van de Velde it is not always entirely clear who was looking at whom. There must have been a fair amount of artistic emulation between the two artists. As is discussed under cat. no.11, Dujardin, who was older, on occasion took inspiration from his younger colleague; this seems to be true for his *Italianate landscape with cattle* (fig.14),[33] which probably dates from a few years after Van de Velde's *Meadow with horses and cattle*, dated 1660 (fig.13).[34]

What characterizes the early works and pictures such as those discussed under cat. nos.1–10 is that the figures and animals are relatively small and a warm light permeates the landscapes, with only mild contrasts between light and dark, while Van de Velde was clearly keen to try his hand at all sorts of subjects – landscapes with animals (cat. no.2), river landscapes (cat. no.3 and

FIG.11
Adriaen van de Velde, *A horseman at a ford, asking the way of a herdswoman*. Signed and dated, lower right: *A. v. Velde / 1659*. Oil on canvas, 54 × 47 cm. The Royal Collection / HM Queen Elizabeth II, inv. no.RCIN 400941

FIG.12
Karel Dujardin, *Young peasants crossing a ford*. Signed, lower left: *K. DV. IARDIN. fe*. Oil on canvas, 49.5 × 45.5 cm. The State Hermitage Museum, St Petersburg, inv. no.792

FIG.13
Adriaen van de Velde, *Meadow with horses and cattle*. Signed and dated, lower left: *A.V.Velde. f. 1660*. Oil on canvas, 44.5 × 41 cm. Statens Museum for Kunst, Copenhagen, inv. no.KMS3608

FIG.14
Karel Dujardin, *Italianate landscape with cattle*. Oil on panel, 41 × 37 cm. Signed: *K.DU.IARDIN. fec*. Mauritshuis, The Hague, inv. no.1095

FIG.15
Adriaen van de Velde, *The edge of a wood, with a sleeping shepherd, sheep and goats*. Signed and dated, lower right: *A.v.Velde.f / 1658*. Oil on panel, 27.7 × 38.1 cm. The National Gallery, London, inv. no.NG982

FIG.16
Adriaen van de Velde, *Landscape with collapsed bridge*. Signed, in the middle, on the bridge. Oil on canvas, 75 × 117.5 cm. Present whereabouts unknown

figs.66 and 67), winter landscapes (fig.63), panoramic landscapes (cat. nos.9 and 10 and figs.88, 89 and 94), beachscapes (cat. nos.5–7), woods (fig.15),[35] hunting pictures (cat. nos.11 and 12 and figs.102 and 103) and Italianate landscapes (cat. nos.13 and 14 and figs.11 and 16).[36] We also see the odd excursion into entirely different subject-matter, such as portraits (cat. no.4) or a barn interior (fig.17),[37] the latter reminiscent of the few barn interiors that Gerard ter Borch had painted a few years earlier (fig.18).[38]

It was around 1662–64 that this variety in Van de Velde's work reached its peak. One of the most remarkable pictures from these years is a genre scene of a *Woman drinking from a glass*, dated 1662, formerly in the Gemäldegalerie, Dresden, but untraced since the Second World War (fig.19).[39] It is unique in Van de Velde's oeuvre, and a prime example of the artist's uncanny ability to assimilate influences without producing a mere pastiche. The painting seems inconceivable without the example of Gabriel Metsu (1629–1667), who from c.1655 was living in Amsterdam;[40] his *Woman at a mirror* (fig.20), datable to the early 1660s,[41] provides a telling comparison. Yet Van de Velde's painting is a compelling picture in its own right, and would easily hold its own in the company of similar pictures by Metsu or Ter Borch. It is so unusual for the artist that, had it not been reliably signed,[42] one would not necessarily have attributed it to Van de Velde. One can only hope that one day it will resurface.

Woman drinking from a glass stands in stark contrast to the excursion back into Potter territory in his *Travellers asking a peasant for directions*, painted the same year (fig.21),[43] while a year later Van de Velde returns to the panoramic landscape in his *River landscape in the late afternoon* (fig.23),[44] a superbly sensitive picture of a subject that clearly brought out the best in him (see cat. no.3), as is also evident from a beautiful if not very well preserved river scene of 1664 in the Louvre (fig.22).

FIG.17
Adriaen van de Velde, *The forge*. Signed and
dated, lower right: *A.v.Velde 1658*. Oil on
panel, 28 × 38 cm. Museum Boijmans Van
Beuningen, Rotterdam, inv. no.1889

FIG.18
Gerard ter Borch, *Horse stable*. Signed, on back
of the panel: *GTB*. Oil on panel, 45.4 × 53.5 cm.
J. Paul Getty Museum, Los Angeles,
inv. no.86.PB.631

FIG.19
Adriaen van de Velde, *Woman drinking from
a glass*. Signed and dated, upper right:
A.v.Velde / 1662. Oil on panel, 21.5 × 19 cm.
Present whereabouts unknown (formerly
Gemäldegalerie Alte Meister, Staatliche
Kunstsammlungen, Dresden)

FIG.20
Gabriel Metsu, *Woman at a mirror*. Oil on panel,
23.7 × 19.5 cm. Petit Palais, Musée des Beaux-
Arts de la Ville de Paris, Paris, inv. no.P-DUT
00914

FIG.21
Adriaen van de Velde, *Travellers asking a
peasant for directions*. Signed and dated, lower
middle: *A.v. / Velde.f. / 1662*. Oil on canvas,
48 × 56.5 cm. Museumslandschaft Hessen
Kassel, Gemäldegalerie Alte Meister,
inv. no.GK 375

FIG.22
Adriaen van de Velde, *Cattle on a river bank*.
Signed and dated, lower right: *A.v.Velde 1664*.
Oil on canvas, 50 × 71 cm. Musée du Louvre,
Paris, inv. no.1918

FIG.23
Adriaen van de Velde, *River landscape in the
late afternoon*. Signed and dated, lower centre:
A.v.Velde. / 1663. Oil on panel, 31 × 43.8 cm.
Private collection

FIG.24
Adriaen van de Velde, *Allegory (Innocence between the Virtues and the Vices)*. Signed and dated, lower right: *A.Velde.f / 1663*. Oil on canvas, 77 × 170 cm. The Pushkin State Museum of Fine Arts, Moscow, inv. no.3249

It was in 1663–64 that Van de Velde also painted a number of religious pictures. The most unusual is his *Allegory (Innocence between the Virtues and the Vices)* of 1663 (fig.24).[45] As has been noted above, he married a Catholic woman and converted to Catholicism, while the couple's children were all baptized in clandestine Catholic churches in Amsterdam. On 2nd February 1670 their son Adriaen was baptized in the Catholic church Geloof, Hoop en Liefde (Faith, Hope and Love; located between the Spui and the Roskamsteeg), while in 1671 Van de Velde acted as a witness to the baptism of a daughter of his brother Willem there.[46] There is, in other words, a connection between the Van de Velde family and this place of worship. It is therefore perhaps not too farfetched to speculate that some seven years earlier Van de Velde was commissioned to paint for this church an allegory in which the Virtues that lent the church its name play such a prominent role, although the painting's relatively modest size and its intellectually slightly more demanding iconography perhaps point to it having been painted to decorate a rectory rather than the church itself.[47] Sadly the painting's provenance cannot be traced back further than the late eighteenth century,[48] so that we lack a more precise clue to its original destination.

Nothing in this painting suggests that it is the work of a landscape painter. The same is true for the cycle of Passion paintings that Van de Velde produced in 1664 for the Augustinian clandestine church 't Hart (figs.25 and 26).[49] In this case we are precisely informed about the original commission. Church records tell us that in 1664 Sybilla Fonteyn, a lay sister, donated a series of five paintings depicting the mysteries of the Passion to this church on the Oudezijds Voorburgwal in Amsterdam, whose interior has survived virtually intact and is now a museum ('Ons' Lieve Heer op Solder'; Our Lord in the attic). They had been commissioned from Van de Velde, who received

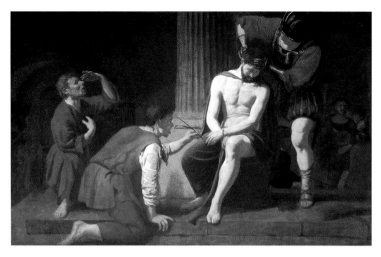

FIG.25
Adriaen van de Velde, *The Crowning with Thorns.*
Oil on canvas, 88 × 138 cm. Augustinian Order,
on loan to Museum Ons' Lieve Heer op Solder,
Amsterdam

FIG.26
Adriaen van de Velde, *The Lamentation.*
Oil on canvas, 88 × 138 cm. Augustinian Order,
on loan to Museum Ons' Lieve Heer op Solder,
Amsterdam

50 guilders apiece for them. The paintings are no longer in their original location, but would most probably have hung above the panelling, beneath the galleries; anyone who visits Ons' Lieve Heer op Solder today can easily imagine how these horizontal paintings would have fitted there.[50]

While the *Allegory* is a relatively attractive and inventive work with a carefully worked out, balanced composition, monumental biblical subjects involving large-scale figures were clearly not Van de Velde's forte, and the cycle's infelicitous mix of Caravaggesque (fig.25) and Flemish Baroque (fig.26) elements leaves the viewer ill at ease. One may even wonder whether assistants were involved in painting the series.[51] It is difficult to reconcile the magnificent study for the figure of St John discussed under cat. no.21 with the figure we encounter on the left in the painting of *The Lamentation* (fig.26); there he has not only turned into a different person – probably Joseph of Arimathea – but bears little resemblance to the magisterial figure seen in the drawing.

The most ambitious historical subject painted by Van de Velde is his *Migration of Jacob* of 1663 in the Wallace Collection (fig.27).[52] At a width of 180 cm, it is a monumental painting for an artist who almost always painted pictures on a relatively small scale. It is clear that here Van de Velde was again on home territory; the subject gave him every opportunity to excel as a landscape, figure and, above all, animal painter, the biblical story explaining how "Jacob rose up, and set his sons and his wives upon camels; And he carried away all his cattle, and all his goods which he had gotten, the cattle of his getting, which he had gotten in Padanaram, for to go to Isaac his father in the land of Canaan" (Genesis 31:17–18). Although the composition is possibly a little too crowded for comfort, in its details the picture is of phenomenal quality, and, as is always the case with Van de Velde, those details were meticulously prepared, as his study for the young man sitting on top of the camel demonstrates (fig.28).[53] We do not know what prompted Van de Velde to paint this large picture. It is conceivable that it was painted purely to demonstrate his talents. As such it may well have been acquired as a trophy for the celebrated cabinet of paintings of the comtesse de Verrue

FIG. 27
Adriaen van de Velde, *The Migration of Jacob*.
Signed and dated, centre left: *A Velde.f / 1663*.
Oil on canvas, 133.5 × 180 cm. The Wallace
Collection, London, inv. no.P80

FIG. 28
Adriaen van de Velde, *Study of a seated boy*.
Black chalk on paper prepared with grey wash,
26.2 × 18 cm. Harvard Art Museums, Cambridge
MA, inv. no.1980.75

(1670–1736), and, when her collection was sold in 1737, Van de Velde's
painting was the fourth most expensive picture in the sale.[54] This illustrious
French provenance no doubt played a role in the decision by the 4th
Marquess of Hertford (1800–1870) to acquire the work when it came up for
sale in 1845. The bequest to the British nation of the Wallace Collection in
1897 stipulated that no object should ever leave the collection, so this great
work is not in this exhibition. Van de Velde painted an equally ambitious
history painting, on a similar scale if entirely different in conception, in 1667
(see cat. no.19).

The same principle of choosing a historical subject that suited a landscape
painter is at play in Van de Velde's depictions of the subject of *Mercury, Argus
and Io*, also painted in 1663 (fig.105 on p.88),[55] although it is on a much
smaller scale and obviously depicts a classical subject. Again the story is as
much about the human figures as it is about animals, while the landscape
setting is inevitable. One imagines that Van de Velde must occasionally
have felt that he should elevate his art by painting biblical or mythological
subjects, as in the hierarchy of genres landscapes were considerably lower
down than historical subjects. It is a painting that the artist saw fit to
replicate – twice, once in 1664 and again in 1665 – which may indicate that
he had some success with it.[56] All three versions are autograph, but such
repetitions are exceptional in Van de Velde's oeuvre. In almost all cases when
one comes across a second version of a composition, alarm bells should start
ringing, as this often indicates that we are dealing with the work of a pupil
or follower.

The last group of pictures dating from 1662–64 that should be mentioned
here concerns a number of pastoral and Italianate paintings that in many
ways laid the foundations for Van de Velde's later output. We see in these
works how he slowly started to change his handling of light. The clarity of his
early works made way for stronger contrasts between light and dark. So while
in a picture such as his *Herders in a wood* in Moscow (fig.29) he still places the
figures and animals on an oval-shaped spotlit area, a stage-like device much
favoured by the artist in his early works (see cat. no.2), the overall contrast
between light and dark has intensified considerably.[57] The same is true for
two splendid small pastoral pictures – very much twins – in Cleveland and
London, both dated 1663 (figs.30 and 31),[58] as well as for the large pastoral
landscape of 1664 in the Fitzwilliam Museum, Cambridge (see cat. no.15).
Paradoxically, this more dramatic lighting goes hand in hand with an ever-
increasing emphasis on the idyllic nature of a scene. It is here that Van de
Velde's 'Dutch Arcadia' is born, with herders in peaceful surroundings,
whiling away the hours in harmony with their flock, occasionally with an
amorous element thrown into the background, evoking a dreamy and ideal
world in which there is little to suggest anything might ever go wrong (see cat.
nos.13, 15–16 and 30, and fig.172). The artifice in these pictures is of a wholly
different nature from that seen in Van de Velde's earlier pictures, which often
show more or less or indeed entirely plausible scenes whose artifice exists
in their carefully constructed compositions but not in the depicted subjects.
In his later work Van de Velde often extends the artifice to the subject itself,

which is also reflected in what one might call the theatrical lighting of his
scenes, which can be highly complex, with figures or animals half in sunlight
and half in the shadows, or occasionally with the protagonists entirely
shrouded in darkness, as is the case in fig.31 above. It is not surprising,
perhaps, that such scenes increasingly unfold against an Italianate backdrop,
as if the artist is making doubly sure that his Dutch viewers are immersed in a
world that can no longer be compared to what they might find if they were to
go for a stroll outside the city walls.

This is not to say that the conversion to such Arcadian subjects was
complete. As this exhibition shows, there are numerous later pictures that
do not belong in this category, such as Van de Velde's views of the Haagse
Bos (see cat. no.17 and fig.113), winter landscapes such as those in London
and Dresden (cat. nos.25 and 26) and hunting pictures such as *A hawking
party setting out* in the Royal Collection (cat. no.28) and *The hunting party* in
the Rijksmuseum (cat. no.29). But it is fair to say that the pastoral picture
became the staple of Van de Velde's later output. Quite why this was so is
difficult to say. Dutch artists of the period not only specialized in one genre,
but tended to specialize within that genre. It was perhaps the only way to
stand out among the crowd in a highly competitive market for paintings,
and Van de Velde may have been spurred on by the example of contemporary
landscape painters such as Philips Wouwerman (1619–1668), Adam Pynacker
(?1620–1673), Nicolaes Berchem (1621/22–1683) and Karel Dujardin, who
all created specialized types of pictures that were highly recognizable as
their own. Of these artists, Van de Velde is closest in spirit to Dujardin, both
in the conception of his compositions and in specific details, as can be
seen when a picture by Van de Velde in Leipzig (fig.32)[59] is compared with a
painting by Dujardin of a similar subject in the Rijksmuseum, Amsterdam
(fig.33).[60] Van de Velde seems to have known the latter picture, as is suggested
by the woman carrying a jug patiently waiting for the horseman to quench

FIG.32
Adriaen van de Velde, *Three horsemen before an inn*. Signed, lower right: *Velde* (?). Oil on panel, 37.7 × 44 cm. Museum der bildenden Künste, Leipzig, inv. no.358

FIG.33
Karel Dujardin, *Mounted trumpeter taking a drink*. Signed, lower right: *K.DU.IARDIN*. Oil on canvas, 44 × 35 cm. Rijksmuseum, Amsterdam, inv. no.SK-A-193

FIG.34
Details from figs.32 and 33

his thirst (fig.34). In the Leipzig picture we also see how the treatment of the sky has changed, with dark billowing clouds in bluish-purple tones featuring prominently. In Van de Velde's later work, such skies become more frequent,[61] as can be seen, for example, in his *Landscape with horses and other livestock* of 1669 in the Lugt Collection, Paris (cat. no.27).

If it was Van de Velde's strategy to specialize in pastoral subjects in the hope that this would benefit him financially, then there is reason to doubt it had the desired effect. Houbraken reports how Jan Griffier (c.1652–1718), while he was a pupil of the landscape artist Roelant Roghman (1627–1692), would go around Amsterdam visiting the studios of Van de Velde, Johannes Lingelbach (1622–1674), Jacob van Ruisdael (1628/29–1682) and Rembrandt (1606–1669),[62] which would suggest that Van de Velde was considered as successful as these artists. Yet, as Frensemeier has convincingly argued, there is every indication that the Van de Velde family was struggling.[63] The artists' biographer Johan van Gool (1685–1763) was probably correct in surmising that the household's financial circumstances left something to be desired because Van de Velde's wife ran a shop selling linen to supplement the family's income.[64] That she was indeed running such a shop is documented, while archival evidence also tells us that Van de Velde took out several substantial loans that he failed to repay, so that even after his death debts were still outstanding.[65] This is hardly what one would expect from a successful artist, but from c.1650 the demand for easel paintings in the Northern Netherlands was in decline,[66] so that artistic success would not necessarily lead to financial gain. As is discussed under cat. nos.57 and 58, at the end of his life Van de Velde took on jobs designing border illustrations for maps, the kind of work that an artist would take on to make ends meet, while he also appears to have produced more and more drawings for the

FIG.35
Adriaen van de Velde, *The Ferry*. Signed and
dated, lower left: *A.v.Velde f. / 1669*(?). Oil on
canvas, 112.8 × 166.2 cm. Staatliches Museum,
Schwerin, inv. no.G112

open market, which equally points to a lack of prosperity in his final years
(see cat. no.46). The fact that a good number of his etchings are dated 1670
also suggests that towards the end of his life the artist was looking for other
sources of income.

Even if Van de Velde's later compositions are always carefully considered
and beautifully balanced, and occasionally even sublime, the many variations
on the theme of amorous herders and their flock in idyllic surroundings
can sometimes come across as rather repetitive. The average quality of the
works remains high, but the works rarely match the freshness of approach
of his earlier work. One could describe this development as 'classicizing';
the protagonists are often distributed in the composition as one would
expect them to be in a grand history painting, with classical poses and
antique ruins to match (fig.35).[67] Van de Velde shows he can be on top of his
game in a beautiful pastoral picture such as *Shepherd and shepherdess with
cattle by a stream* of 1668 in the Royal Collection (cat. no.16), an ambitious
picture on account of its size alone, which is surpassed in grandeur only
by his *Landscape with cattle and figures* of 1664 in the Fitzwilliam Museum,
Cambridge (cat. no.15), while Van de Velde's *Hut* of 1671 (cat. no.30), which

FIG.36
Adriaen van de Velde, *A young woman as Pomona*.
Chalk, 42.4 × 29.5 cm. Crocker Art Museum,
Sacramento, inv. no.1871.186

FIG.37
Adriaen van de Velde, *Female nude*. Black and
white chalk, 33 × 20 cm. Present whereabouts
unknown

in the nineteenth century was among his most famous pictures, remains one of the most eloquent examples of the delicacy and refinement for which he is rightly renowned; it is a picture in which he married the originality of his early work with the idyllic ideal of his later paintings, a most felicitous finale to his brilliant but short career. The artist was buried in the Nieuwe Kerk in Amsterdam on 21st January 1672.[68]

Working methods

In the entries in this catalogue there is ample evidence of Van de Velde's meticulous working methods (see especially cat. nos.11–14, 30–39). Few artists seemed to have been quite so obsessive in the care they took to prepare compositions, groupings within those compositions, and individual motifs. Under cat. nos.19 and 20 it is described how Van de Velde made studies after the nude in preparation for his painting of *The Annunciation*. As is remarked there, he probably made not only a study of the nude model (cat. no.20), but also a study of the same model clothed, more or less as she would eventually appear in the painting. In that case no such study has survived, but a spectacular example is preserved at the Crocker Art Museum, Sacramento (fig.36), on a sheet that is even larger than the very sizeable study of *John the Evangelist Mourning* catalogued under cat. no.21.[69] In the Sacramento drawing the female model is shown as the clothed figure of Pomona, but she first appeared in the nude in a study whose whereabouts are unknown (fig.37).[70] The composition in which she would eventually play a role was prepared in a study now in the British Museum, London (fig.38), which formed the basis for the painting now in the Kunsthistorisches Museum, Vienna (fig.39). Taken together they form one of the best examples of the assiduous working methods of the artist. They also show that, however carefully Van de Velde prepared his compositions, his creative mind would never stop. In this particular example he decided that Pomona's lower legs should be uncovered again in the final composition, effectively creating a hybrid of the two drawn studies he had made for this figure.

The example demonstrates the extremely thorough manner in which Van de Velde reworked and synthesized his inventions, and these four works would have been very much at home in the selection for this exhibition, were it not for the obvious problem that the whereabouts of one of the drawings are unknown and, more importantly, the rather compromised condition of the painting in Vienna. This brings us to an aspect of Van de Velde's paintings that cannot go unmentioned. While he was obsessively concerned with the preparation of his compositions, he seems not to have taken the same care in the preparation of his paints. On close examination it is immediately clear that many passages in the painting in Vienna that were originally green have turned blue, a problem that plagues many of Van de Velde's paintings, although mostly those dating from after c.1662, when he seems increasingly to have turned to pigment mixtures that were less resilient. It tends to be particularly noticeable in the thinly applied highlights on feathery sprigs of foliage. In the worst affected paintings the colour has

FIG.38
Adriaen van de Velde, *Vertumnus and Pomona*.
Pen and brown ink, with grey and pink wash,
15.8 × 18.6 cm. British Museum, London,
inv. no.1895,0915.1033

FIG.39
Adriaen van de Velde, *Vertumnus and Pomona*.
Signed and dated, lower right: *A.v.Velde f. 1670*.
Oil on canvas, 76.5 × 103 cm. Kunsthistorisches
Museum, Vienna, inv. no.GG_6446

not only changed from green to blue, but the paint surface has a 'blanched'
effect, as can be seen, for example, in Van de Velde's *Resting herdsman with
animals* in Karlsruhe, a detail of which is illustrated here (fig.40). The most
likely cause of change is the disappearance of yellow pigments in the paint,
most probably yellow lake, whose colouring components originated from
organic dyestuffs that were mixed into a white or colourless substrate.
Although these yellow lakes have beautiful translucent colours when freshly
made, on exposure to light they fade at an alarming rate and may totally
disappear, especially where the paint is thinly applied (fig.40 shows how the
green has been much better preserved at the edge of the painting, where
the frame has protected the paint from the damaging effect of light). One of
the ways to avoid green turning blue would have been to use more complex

FIG.40
Detail of Adriaen van de Velde, *Resting herdsman
with animals*. Oil on canvas, mounted on wood,
31.5 × 40.8 cm. Staatliche Kunsthalle, Karlsruhe,
inv. no.292 (illustrated in full on p.156, fig.154)

pigment mixtures, for example not only yellow lake but also some yellow earth pigments (ochres), which do not fade. Van de Velde's problem seems to have been that he used very simple mixtures, probably ultramarine blue and yellow lake. The resulting effect is not unlike that found in old tapestries in which the trees and foliage have over time turned blue, again because yellow lake dyes had been used. As the lake pigments fade they leave only the blue component of the original pigment mixture. It seems likely that the fading would have taken place quite early on. The effect is sometimes partly disguised by discoloured varnish and only fully revealed when a picture is cleaned, which is why the conservation treatment of works by Van de Velde that have many green passages can be a hazardous undertaking; the picture may, after all, be less enjoyable after than before treatment. Over the centuries, over-enthusiastic cleaning procedures may also have removed any final yellow glazes that Van de Velde might have applied to his paintings, which would certainly make matters worse.[71]

This problem has had definite consequences for the selection of paintings in this exhibition. Greens that have turned blue can seriously distort the colour harmonies in a painting, and certain works are so badly affected that they could not be selected for the show. One such painting is Van de Velde's *Koekamp in The Hague* in the Gemäldegalerie in Berlin (fig.113 on p.95), even if it is unquestionably one of Van de Velde's masterpieces. As is explained under cat. no.17, the painting reproduces rather well and is often illustrated in handbooks devoted to seventeenth-century Dutch painting because of its superb composition and glorious depiction of sunlight, but its compromised condition makes it difficult to enjoy the picture in equal measure in the flesh. An exception was made for Van de Velde's *Landscape with cattle and figures* of 1664 in the Fitzwilliam Museum, Cambridge (cat. no.15), in which much of the background foliage of trees and bushes has turned a pale blue; it was nevertheless decided to include it on account of the sheer ambition of this large painting, a prime example of Van de Velde's fondness for Arcadian subjects. Although the problem is certainly noticeable, it does not severely compromise the enjoyment of the picture. The painting of a *Resting herdsman with animals* in Karlsruhe, illustrated in full on p.156 below and a detail of which is shown in fig.40, would have been an obvious choice for inclusion in the exhibition on account of its relation to the sheet with *Two studies of a resting shepherd* in the Rijksmuseum (cat. no.39), but because of its poor condition that idea had to be abandoned, especially because, conversely, the Rijksmuseum drawing is in fact in pristine condition, so that neither work would have gained from the juxtaposition.

Pupils and followers

There is more to this problem of condition than may appear at first sight.
Artists in Van de Velde's orbit (it is not unequivocally clear in all cases
whether we are dealing with pupils or followers) seem to have avoided using
this particular unstable paint mixture. There are quite a few variants of or
copies after Van de Velde compositions that are very unlikely to be by Van
de Velde or are indeed signed by another artist. What is curious is that they
never display the problem described above. The difference is so marked
that this 'blue problem', to give it a short name, almost functions as an
unintended 'signature' of Van de Velde's. A painting such as *The Koekamp
in The Hague* at the Konstmuseum, Göteborg (fig.118 on p.99) is suspicious
on that count alone; a painting with so many trees in which the greens seem
not to have deteriorated to any significant degree would be truly exceptional
within Van de Velde's oeuvre. There are also stylistic reasons to believe that
the painting is by a pupil or follower, in this case Jacob Koninck the Younger
(c.1648–1724; see discussion under cat. no.17).[72]

We do not know for certain that Jacob Koninck the Younger trained with
Van de Velde, but Koninck's early work is entirely in Van de Velde's manner,
while Houbraken claims that he was indeed a pupil.[73] Houbraken also
mentions Dirck van Bergen (c.1645–1690) as a pupil.[74] Van Bergen's paintings
are indeed so much inspired by Van de Velde that it is probably safe to
believe that he was. He had an uncanny ability to turn Van de Velde's scenes
and motifs into their exact opposite: while Van de Velde's compositions are
invariably carefully thought out and look entirely natural, Van Bergen's works
look like a hotchpotch of Van de Velde motifs, thrown into a composition
with little consideration for harmony and balance. He also has a tendency
to show especially the animals in contorted poses, usually a cow twisting its
neck at an impossible angle (fig.42). What is interesting about Van Bergen,
however, is that he must have had access to Van de Velde's drawings, which
is another indication that he is likely to have been a pupil. So while we do not
know of a painting in which Van de Velde used his study of a seated woman in
the Amsterdam Museum (fig.41), we do find her in a closely related pose in a
landscape by Van Bergen at Ham House, Richmond (fig.42).[75]

A third artist who should be mentioned here is Pieter van der Leeuw (1647–1679). Active in Dordrecht, he was almost certainly not a pupil but a follower of Van de Velde. He not only copied individual motifs of Van de Velde's but also closely followed his compositions. His manner can be deceptively similar to Van de Velde's, although his technique is not nearly as refined, while his figures can be rather clumsy. Whenever one comes across a known composition by Van de Velde (or a slight variation on a known composition) that lacks the master's refined style and, moreover, does not display what above has been described as the 'blue problem', one should be on high alert, as Van de Velde very rarely repeated a composition. Even if the work is signed, there is reason to be cautious. Van de Velde's signature is not too difficult to forge: the work illustrated in fig.43 bore what at first sight looked like a Van de Velde signature, but when it was cleaned it was revealed to have been fully signed and dated by Pieter van der Leeuw.[76] Van der Leeuw is hardly known today at all. It is interesting that in the eighteenth and nineteenth centuries connoisseurs seemed to have had a better understanding of his output. In an auction catalogue of 1718 it is remarked that a painting was "*na A. vande Velde, door P. van de Leeuw ongemeen gecopieert*" (after Adriaen van de Velde, meticulously copied by Pieter van der Leeuw),[77] while a century later, in 1815, the auctioneers recognized a painting signed with Van de Velde's name for what it was, remarking that "*Leeuw ne peignait jamais sans avoir un Vandevelde sous les yeux; et plus d'une fois il a tellement approché de se modèles, qu'on est excusable de ne pas reconnaître*" (Van der Leeuw never painted without having a Van de Velde before him; and more than once he comes so close to his examples, that one can be excused for not recognizing his hand).[78] Théophile Thoré was clearly also aware of Van der Leeuw's practice: "*Il y a de ses habiles pastiches qui ont passé et passent encore pour des originaux d'Adriaan van de Velde*" (There are clever pastiches that have passed and still pass for originals by Adriaen van de Velde).[79]

There is only one documented pupil of Van de Velde, a certain Jan Innevelt, who according to a contract drawn up between Van de Velde and Innevelt's parents was to train with Van de Velde from 4th October 1666 to 4th October 1671.[80] He must have stayed on as Van de Velde's pupil until at least 19th October 1669, when he acted as a witness to the drawing up of a will by Van de Velde and his wife in the presence of a notary in their house on the Schapemarkt in Amsterdam.[81] No works by Innevelt are today known.

Collaboration

When considering artists in Van de Velde's circle, an aesthetically far more rewarding subject is his collaboration with other artists. This exhibition emphatically concentrates on Van de Velde's autonomous works, although mention is made throughout the catalogue entries of the fact that he painted the figures and animals in other painters' work (see cat. nos.1, 5, 9–11 and 28). It is an aspect of Van de Velde's output that could be illustrated in numerous examples, but this would fall outside the scope of both this exhibition and this introduction. Suffice to say that, as is explained especially under cat.

no.28, Van de Velde was so good at integrating his figures and animals into
other artists' landscapes or cityscapes that his services were in great demand.
His highly characteristic figures (see also cat. no.1) and animals are almost
palpable in their three-dimensional presence. It is difficult to describe this
aspect, but perhaps the word 'sculptural' comes closest to conveying this
sense that they seem to exist in the round, as opposed to, for example, the
figures that an artist such as Johannes Lingelbach added to his colleagues'
landscapes, which, although perfectly competent, tend to be too lanky,
their gangly presence often not entirely convincing in relation to their
surroundings. This exhibition illustrates through many examples Van de
Velde's persistent study of the human figure, so it is hardly surprising that
he knew how to make his staffage look so convincing. The fact that major
landscape and cityscape painters such as Jacob van Ruisdael, Meindert
Hobbema, Jan Wijnants (see fig.92 on p.74), Jan van der Heyden, Jan Hackaert
(see fig.146 on p.138), Philips Koninck and Frederick de Moucheron all
entrusted their pictures to Van de Velde to enliven them with judiciously
inserted figures and animals is testimony to how much his contribution was
appreciated.[82] To what degree the fact that Van de Velde had contributed the
staffage to these paintings added to their value is difficult to say. Early auction
catalogues almost never fail to mention the fact, and one gets the impression
that at least in the eighteenth century it was considered to add to a work's
interest. In 1713, the well-known collector Valerius Röver (1686–1739), who
owned Jan van der Heyden's *View of Oudezijds Voorburgwal with the Oude
Kerk in Amsterdam* now in the Mauritshuis, The Hague (fig.44), specifically
mentioned in his account book that the "*Beeldjes*" (figures) in his painting
had been added by Adriaen van de Velde.[83]

It is a happy coincidence that a painting by Van der Heyden with figures by Van de Velde in Dulwich Picture Gallery, one of the venues of this exhibition, shows how Van de Velde reused the figure of the seated woman in his famous painting of *The Hut* (cat. no.30). In the lower left corner of Van der Heyden's *Two churches and a town wall* (fig.45) we find a miniature version of this figure, which we also know from Van de Velde's preparatory studies (cat. nos.32 and 34).[84] In the Dulwich installation of the show Van der Heyden's picture is shown in the presence of Van de Velde's *Hut* and those related studies, so that after almost three and a half centuries the three shepherdesses will be able to nod to their miniature version across the room.

Legacy

We have seen how Van de Velde's talents were cherished by his colleagues. Later audiences agreed. His work was soon recognized as belonging to the very best that the seventeenth century had to offer, his name being mentioned by Houbraken in 1719 in the same breath as Potter and Berchem in a passage lamenting the fact that artists of their calibre could no longer be found in his own day.[85] Van de Velde's reputation was on the rise. It has already been mentioned that as early as 1737 his *Migration of Jacob* (fig.27), now in the Wallace Collection, London, was among the four most expensive pictures in the sale of the celebrated collection assembled by the comtesse de Verrue. A brief glance at the provenances listed in this catalogue provides ample evidence that his paintings were highly sought after, with the most important among them, many of which are in this exhibition, commanding very high prices at auction. There is no evidence that Van de Velde ever paid off his debts with paintings, as some artists did, but, had he done so, his creditors would eventually have done very well out of them. We can read

FIG.47
Johannes Hulswit, *Landscape with trees along a stream*. Chalk, brush and ink, 20.6 × 24.2 cm. Rijksmuseum, Amsterdam, inv. no. RP-T-1888-A-1498.

FIG.48
Pieter Gerardus van Os, *Landscape with horseman, herders and cattle*. Oil on panel, 37 × 48 cm. Present whereabouts unknown

in the entry for the *Portrait of a family in a landscape* (cat. no.22) how this painting sold in 1824 for the phenomenal sum of 10,000 guilders, which may well have helped the painting become one of the must-see pictures once it went on public display in the Museum Van der Hoop, although its reputation was also helped by the fact that Van de Velde was thought to have portrayed himself and his family in the painting. But it is significant in itself that the idea that one would be looking at the artist himself would have been part of its appeal – such, apparently, was Van de Velde's fame.

In the entry for Van de Velde's *Colf players on the ice* in the National Gallery, London (cat. no.25), we can read how the artist's fame reached far and wide, with eighteenth-century engravings after his work reaching the studio of Francesco Guardi (see figs.136–39 on p.128), while we know that in the nineteenth century Eugène Boudin was very keen on Van de Velde's beachscapes (see figs.78 and 79 on p.66). It is beyond the scope of this introduction to provide a detailed account of Van de Velde's reputation, but a short, mostly visual excursion may be appropriate as a conclusion. In several entries in this catalogue that discuss Van de Velde's more finished drawings, we learn how a small coterie of brokers and dealers who were also artists were in one way or another involved in their sale (see, for example, cat. nos.44, 47 and 49). One of them was Gerrit Jan Michaëlis (1775–1857), who in addition to being an artist and dealer was also the curator and superintendent of Teylers Museum, Haarlem, and in that capacity in 1833 bought for the Museum Van de Velde's *Landscape with livestock crossing a river* (cat. no.49) for the extraordinary sum of 1,730 guilders. He clearly was a true admirer of Van de Velde's drawings, or so his own red-chalk drawing of a *Standing young woman* (fig.46) suggests, which is unthinkable without Van de Velde's example. Another name we encounter is the dealer-cum-artist Johannes Hulswit (1796–1844), whose *Landscape with trees along a stream* (fig.47) is also heavily influenced by the work of Van de Velde, down to such details as the handling of the foliage. A few years earlier, Pieter Gerardus van Os (1776–1839) had painted his *Landscape with horseman, herders and cattle* (fig.48), which is a veritable catalogue of Van de Velde motifs, including that of a young man asleep with his legs to one side.[86]

All this was happening around the same time that the London dealer John Smith published his nine-volume *Catalogue raisonné of the works of the most eminent Dutch, Flemish, and French painters* (1828–42), mentioned at the beginning of this introduction, in which Van de Velde's paintings were first catalogued. At that time Van de Velde's place in the canon of seventeenth-century Dutch art was self-evident, but eventually his reputation suffered a little. For those who championed Dutch art as evidence of a nation taking pride in its own land he was perhaps not Dutch enough, especially in his Arcadian scenes in Italianate settings, while for those who in the twentieth century revived the interest in Italianate landscape painting he was perhaps too Dutch to be welcomed into the fold. It is hoped that this exhibition demonstrates that Houbraken, Smith and Michaëlis, and with them a host of artists, collectors and connoisseurs over a period of some two and a half centuries, had the right idea all along.

1 As early as 1718 Arnold Houbraken must have reflected more than just his personal opinion when he described the preceding century as something of a Golden Age of Dutch art; see Houbraken 1718–21, II, pp.130–33.

2 The first eight volumes were simultaneously published in English as *A catalogue raisonné of the works of the most eminent Dutch painters of the seventeenth century based on the work of John Smith* (1907–27).

3 See Frensemeier 2001. Marietta Frensemeier's book represents an essential first step towards an overview of Van de Velde's paintings. She was the first to survey his career and work and her important contribution is therefore acknowledged throughout these pages.

4 Robinson 1979 and Robinson 1993; Van de Velde's Italianate drawings were recently surveyed and catalogued in Van den Eerenbeemd 2006.

5 Martin 1936, II, p.336.

6 Bartsch 1803–21, I, pp.209–28.

7 Hollstein 1949–2010, XXXII (1988), pp.213–39.

8 For an excellent overview of the Van de Velde family, see Daalder 2016, pp.35–47.

9 Ibid., pp.84–86.

10 Frensemeier 2001, pp.189–94, docs.2–27.

11 In a document dated 26th November 1671: "*Verklaring ten verzoeke van Adriaen van de Velde waaruit blyket: dat hy katholiek was …*'; ibid., p.194, doc.26.

12 Ibid., p.194, doc.28.

13 Daalder 2016, pp.155–56.

14 "*… vond zig van der jeugt af aan door een overgeerfde natuurdrift tot de Teeken- en Schilderkonst gedreven, en noch in 't Kinderschool zynde, wist zig steelswys van zyn Broeder Willems teekenpennen penceelen en verwen te bedienen, beteekende en bekladde met verf al wat hy vinden konde, tot de bedplank van zyn slaapstee, waar op hy … een Melkboertje met koleuren geschilderd had, zoo verwonderlyk naar die Jaren, en buiten onderwys, dat het noch lang na dien tyd daarom bewaard wierd. Dit heeft my zyn Dochter de Huisvrouw van den Makelaar Sodyn t'Amsterdam zelf verhaalt*"; Houbraken 1718–21, III, p.90.

15 The burial date of Willem van de Velde the Elder was also communicated to Houbraken by Adriaen's daughter Judith, who showed him the burial note in her possession; see Houbraken 1718–21, I, pp.355–56.

16 See, for example, Bode 1917, pp.224–26; Stechow 1966, p.31; and Slive 1995, p.212, who all point to the influence of Potter.

17 See Frensemeier 2001, pp.8–9, and Eisele 2000, nos.9 and 24.

18 In the will of his father drawn up in that year; see exh. cat. Amsterdam, Boston and Philadelphia 1987–88, p.523; Frensemeier 2001, p.9; and Eisele 2000, p.4.

19 The only fact that can be brought into play here is that at Potter's death in 1654 his address was given as Schapemarkt, Amsterdam (today Muntplein), in a distinctive row of five houses that were known as the 'English Houses' because they were owned and rented out by the English Church in Amsterdam. Adriaen van de Velde lived in the very same row of houses from at least 1669, when he is first recorded there. This could be coincidence, but, if Van de Velde had indeed been a pupil of Potter, he would already have been familiar with these houses and their owner. It is anyhow curious that two of the most celebrated painters of cattle and pastures in seventeenth-century Holland lived at more or less the same address. The 'English Houses', which were torn down in the nineteenth century, stood next to the Regulierstoren, which still exists but is today known as the Munttoren. For Potter's Amsterdam address, see exh. cat. The Hague 1994–95, pp.16–17; for that of Van de Velde, see Frensemeier 2001, pp.13 and 16; p.193, doc.21; p.195, doc.33; p.196, docs.39 and 40.

20 Not in Smith 1834; Hofstede de Groot 1912, no.234; Frensemeier 2001, no.42.

21 For the Potter, see exh. cat. The Hague 1994–95, no.8A (when it was still privately owned).

22 Not in Smith 1834; Hofstede de Groot 1912, no.201; Frensemeier 2001, no.41.

23 Not in Smith 1834; Hofstede de Groot 1912, no.215; Frensemeier 2001, no.39.

24 Stechow 1966, p.31.

25 Not in Smith 1834; Hofstede de Groot 1912, no.180; Frensemeier 2001, no.49.

26 See Dibbits, Verslype and Wallert 2008. For Van de Velde's *St Jerome*, which is not listed in Smith 1834, see Hofstede de Groot 1912, no.19, and Frensemeier 2001, no.11.

27 See Blankert 1968a, published in English in Blankert 2004, pp.21–30.

28 Especially when we take Van de Velde's preparatory drawing in the British Museum (inv. no.1836,0811.528) into account, where we see that the woman in Van de Velde's composition originally held a spinning rod, as in Van Laer's etching; see Hind 1931, no.15. For Van Laer's etching, see Hollstein 1949–2010, X, no.4; for Van de Velde's, ibid., XXXII, no.17. The same motif appears again in Van de Velde's 1653 etching of *A spinning woman and two men near a tent* (ibid., no.23). A comparison between Van de Velde's 1653 etching of *Three huntsmen with dogs* (ibid., no.24) and Van Laer's etching of *A man leading his horse* (ibid., X, no.9) is equally telling.

29 See exh. cat. Boston and Saint Louis 1980–81, no.147. We know Van de Velde must have studied Dujardin's etchings because he made a copy in red chalk of Dujardin's etching of a donkey (Hollstein 1949–2010, VI, no.2); Van de Velde's copy is in the Metropolitan Museum of Art (inv. no. 2002.426). The donkey also appears in Dujardin's painting of a *Mule driver at an inn* in the Rijksmuseum, Amsterdam (inv. no.SK-A-194; Kilian 2005, no.48). Van de Velde seems to have been keen on Dujardin's donkeys; in his drawing of a *Peasant man and woman by a fountain*, dated 1659, in the British Museum, London (inv. no.1895,0915.1324; Hind 1931, no.13), he copied the donkey in Dujardin's *A game of morra*, dated 1652, in the Wallraf-Richartz-Museum, Cologne (inv. no.2542; Kilian 2005, no.16); see Frensemeier, p.24, note 134.

30 See exh. cat. Dordrecht and Leeuwarden 1988–89, pp.29–35.

31 Inv. no. RCIN 400941; Smith 1834, no.109; Hofstede de Groot 1912, no.51; White 1982, no.202; White 2015, no.202.

32 Inv. no. 792; Kilian 2005, no.42.

33 Inv. no. 1095; Kilian 2005, no.80.

34 Inv. no. KMS3608; not in Smith 1834; Hofstede de Groot 1912, no.191; Frensemeier 2001, no.52.

35 Not in Smith 1834; Hofstede de Groot 1912, no.207; Frensemeier 2001, no.143.

36 Fig.16, not mentioned in Smith 1834, is Hofstede de Groot 1912, no.351; Frensemeier 2001, no.75. It was last recorded in New York in 1913; Emerson McMillin sale, American Art Association, New York, 20th–23rd January 1913, lot 197.

37 Not in Smith 1834; Hofstede de Groot 1912, no.25; Frensemeier 2001, no.20.

38 See exh. cat. Washington and Detroit 2004–05, nos.25 and 26.

39 Hofstede de Groot 1912, no.26; Frensemeier 2001, no.22.

40 See Waiboer 2005, p.90.

41 Waiboer 2012, no.A122, however, dates it to 1664–66, i.e. after Van de Velde painted the picture formerly in Dresden.

42 The signature and date cannot be discerned in the black-and-white photograph of the painting but careful tracings are reproduced in Woermann 1887, p.528, no.1656. They bear all the hallmarks of a perfectly authentic signature and date. I would like to thank Guido Jansen for discussing the painting with me and alerting me to the signatures reproduced in Woermann 1887.

43 Smith 1834, no.131; Hofstede de Groot 1912, no.33; Frensemeier 2001, no.29.

44 Smith 1834, no.83; Hofstede de Groot 1912, no.347; Frensemeier 2001, no.153.

45 Not in Smith 1834 or Hofstede de Groot 1912; Frensemeier 2001, no.16; Senenko 2009, p.379.

46 Frensemeier 2001, p.193, docs.22 and 23.

47 I would like to thank Xander van Eck for sharing with me his thoughts on the painting's possible original function.

48 Pierre-Joseph Lafontaine sale, Paris, 22nd February 1798 and following days, lot 32.

49 Not in Smith; Hofstede de Groot 1912, nos.11, 14–16 and 18; Frensemeier 2001, nos.5–9.

50 See Van Eck 2008, pp.178–81.

51 Frensemeier 2001, pp.105–09, esp. p.109,

52 Smith 1834, no.2; Hofstede de Groot 1912, no.2; Ingamells 1992, pp.380–82; Frensemeier 2001, no.2.

53 Robinson 1979a, no.D-2.

54 Jeanne Baptiste d'Albert de Luynes, comtesse de Verrue sale, Paris, 29th April and following days, lot 45 (3,000 livres). A painting by Nicolaes Berchem (lot 28) brought more (3,600 livres), while in the earlier part of the sale, held on 27th March 1737, lot 85, containing two large paintings by Claude Lorrain, sold for 8,007 livres.

55 Hofstede de Groot 1912, no.21; exh. cat. Zurich 1987, no.102; Frensemeier 2001, no.13.

56 The 1665 version is in the Petit Palais, Paris, inv. no. P-DUT 00932; see Smith 1834, no.50; Smith 1842, no.13; Hofstede de Groot 1912, no.20; Frensemeier 2001, no.13a. The version of 1664 was formerly in the J. Paul Getty Museum, Los Angeles, who deaccessioned the painting in 2007 (sale Sotheby's, New York, 25th January 2007, lot 9), after which it was at Jack Kilgore & Co., in whose New York premises the present writer saw it in October 2007. It is Frensemeier 2001, no.13b, which is not recorded in either Smith 1834 or Hofstede de Groot 1912.

57 Smith 1834, no.80; Smith 1842, no.16; Hofstede de Groot 1912, no.110; Frensemeier 2001, no.86; Senenko 2009, p.377.

58 Neither are in Smith 1834, while Hofstede de Groot 1912 lists only the picture in the Wallace Collection (no.218); Frensemeier 2001, nos.3 and 4. Frensemeier sees both pictures as referring to the Parable of the Weeds (Matthew 13:24–30); see ibid., p.64.

59 Not in Smith 1834; Hofstede de Groot 1912, no.34; Frensemeier 2001, no.31; Nicolaisen 2012, no.333.

60 Kilian 2005, no.25.

61 Frensemeier 2001, pp.69–70.

62 Houbraken 1718–21, III, p.358.

63 Frensemeier 2001, pp.13–16.

64 Van Gool 1750–51, p.20.

65 Frensemeier 2001, pp.14–16.

66 As discussed under cat. nos.53–54.

67 Smith 1834, no.128; Hofstede de Groot 1912, no.8; Frensemeier 2001, no.12.

68 Ibid., p.194, doc.28.

69 The fact that the signature at the bottom of this drawing is cut off indicates that the original sheet was even larger. The drawing is catalogued in exh. cat. Sacramento and Poughkeepsie 2010–11, no.27.

70 See Robinson 1979a, no.D-14.

71 See Saunders and Kirby 1994. I would like to thank Hayley Tomlinson, conservator at the National Gallery, London, for discussing with me this problem in Van de Velde's paintings when she was undertaking conservation treatment of Van de Velde's *Peasants with cattle fording a stream* (National Gallery, London, inv. no.NG868). I would also like to thank David Scrase, who as Keeper of the Fitzwilliam Museum, Cambridge, kindly shared with me the exemplary technical report that Joyce Plesters wrote in 1969 upon the completion of the conservation treatment carried out by Herbert Lank of the Museum's *Landscape with cattle and figures* (cat. no.15); the report is in the files kept for the painting at the Museum. It is surely testimony to the great care with which this picture was conserved that after 47 years the painting still looks in extremely good shape.

72 Jacob Koninck was the son of Jacob Koninck the Elder (1614/15–after 1690), who was the brother of the better-known landscape painter Philips Koninck (1619–1688); see Groenendijk 2008, p.470.

73 Houbraken 1718–21, III, p.286.

74 Ibid., III, pp.91–92.

75 Ham House has the dubious honour of holding the largest collection of Van Bergen's paintings anywhere; for the house and its collections, see Rowell 2013.

76 The work was offered as attributed to Adriaen van de Velde at Christie's, London, 3rd July 2013, lot 148, as inscribed and dated: *A v Velde 1663*. During cleaning this signature disappeared, while that of Pieter van der Leeuw appeared at lower left (*P. V. de Leeuw 1679*). It was subsequently offered at as a work by Pieter van der Leeuw at Christie's, South Kensington, London, 29th April 2014, lot 119, albeit that, confusingly, the artist was wrongly identified as the Pieter van der Leeuw who was active in Rome and Genoa c.1682, also known as Pietro di Leone, who is yet another artist; see Groenendijk 2008, p.484.

77 Lambert van Hairen sale, Dordrecht, 13th October 1718, lot 21.

78 A.L.C.H.T. de L'Espinasse de Langeac, comte d'Arlet sale, 4th January 1815 and following days, lot 76.

79 See Thoré-Bürger 1858–60, II, p.261. For Pieter van der Leeuw, see Veth 1890, pp.26–28. A fourth artist identified by Houbraken as a pupil of Van de Velde is Johannes van der Bent; see Houbraken 1718–21, III, p.288. Van der Bent's highly eclectic works show the influence of Berchem, Dujardin, Wouwerman and, indeed, Van de Velde.

80 See Frensemeier 2001, p.12, and p.192, doc.17.

81 Ibid., p.193, doc.21.

82 There is also archival evidence for Van de Velde's connection with some of these artists; we know that in 1664 he and a number of colleagues, among them Jacob van Ruisdael and Jan van der Heyden, were called upon to advise on the valuation of a number of paintings (see Frensemeier 2001, p.190, doc.10), while his acquaintance with Jan Hackaert is also documented (see ibid., p.191, doc.16).

83 See Moes 1913, p.19, no.44, cited in exh. cat. The Hague and Washington 2008–09, no.24.

84 See exh. cat. Greenwich and Amsterdam 2006–07, p.56 and p.62, note 94.

85 Houbraken, II, p.132: "*Wie* [*is 'er op gestaan*] *in 't schilderen van tam Vee naa de Dood van Berchem, Potter, A. van den Velde, en vander Does? … Die hun gelyk is of hen overtreft?*" (Who has appeared painting cattle after the death of Berchem, Potter and A. van de Velde, and Van der Does? … Who is their equal or surpasses them?).

86 Both Michaëlis's drawing and Van Os's painting are discussed in Te Rijdt 1990, p.232.

1

WILLEM VAN DE VELDE THE YOUNGER
AND ADRIAEN VAN DE VELDE

The shore at Scheveningen

Oil on canvas, 44.5 × 56.8 cm
The National Gallery, London, inv. no. NG 873

FIG. 49
Detail of cat. no. 1

It stands to reason that, although young Adriaen chose to paint landscapes rather than seascapes, the budding artist would have played some role in the studio of his father, the celebrated seascape painter Willem van de Velde the Elder. He probably collaborated both with his father and with his slightly older brother Willem van de Velde the Younger, who did follow in his father's footsteps to become a seascape painter. It is quite possible that on occasion the two brothers contributed to the same picture in their father's studio. It is thought that workshop pictures from his studio were signed with the initials 'WVV' (in angular letters),[1] and that Willem the Elder himself may have had only limited input into such works. It has proved difficult to identify who was responsible for what in such studio pictures. There is a handful of works for which we have to entertain the possibility that they are collaborative paintings by the two younger Van de Veldes (see below), but there are very few pictures about which there can be no doubt at all that they were painted by both. One of them is the work under discussion here. It is not, in fact, signed at all, and thus was probably not considered a 'WVV' studio picture but a collaborative work in its own right.

This was recognized as early as 1817, when our painting was auctioned and described as "A view of the beach at Scheveningen. Several small sailing boats on the beach and in the choppy sea, the beach and the sky attractively painted by Willem; his brother Adriaen has enriched this piece with a post-wagon drawn by two horses, while strolling men and women and other figures, who have a dog fetch something from the sea [fig. 49], embellish this in every part beautiful picture, exquisitely painted by both masters".[2] It has rightly been observed that such early references should be taken seriously, as they may well reflect much earlier indications of its authorship.[3] But we need not rely only on such notices, because the visual evidence is compelling. This is despite the fact that it can seem difficult to distinguish between the figures painted by Willem the Younger and Adriaen, especially when they are on a relatively small scale. Both artists display total ease in suggesting an entire figure with merely a few flicks of paint. After looking again and again at their paintings, however, one observes that Adriaen's figures tend to be more slender, and their clothes hang in such a way that one can still discern the body beneath. Willem's, on the other hand, tend to look as if they are wearing too many layers of clothing. It might be said that people at sea would wear more layers than the more leisurely figures usually portrayed by Adriaen, but the distinction goes beyond such a factual explanation, and must reflect Adriaen's far more developed understanding of the human form, which is hardly surprising when we consider that he repeatedly studied the human figure (see cat. nos. 37–42). There were, moreover, few artists who seemingly so effortlessly managed to integrate figures into a landscape, even if that landscape was by another painter. It explains why fellow painters frequently employed Adriaen to furnish their pictures with figures. There can be no doubt that the staffage in this picture was added by Adriaen; they bear all the hallmarks of his style, as is best illustrated with the detail mentioned in the quotation above (fig. 49).

We can even adduce something that could count as proof, as the horse-drawn carriage in the painting is virtually identical to those found in two

FIG.50
Willem van de Velde the Younger and Adriaen
van de Velde, *The embarkation of Charles II at
Scheveningen*, c.1661. Signed, lower centre,
on sack: *W.V.V.* Oil on canvas, 48.3 × 57.2 cm.
The Wallace Collection, London, inv. no.P194

FIG.51
Willem van de Velde the Younger and Adriaen
van de Velde, *The beach at Scheveningen*.
Signed and dated, lower right: *W.V.Velde 1659*.
Oil on canvas, 76.3 × 104.6 cm. Sale, London,
Sotheby's, 3rd December 1997, lot 12

signed pictures by Adriaen van de Velde, both of which are in this exhibition
(cat. nos.5 and 8). It can also be found in a not very well preserved painting
signed *WVV* in Indianapolis (fig.56) to which Adriaen added the figures.
He also must have added the staffage in a painting by Jan Wijnants in the
Rijksmuseum, or so the inclusion of this very detail seems to suggest. Details
of all five are reproduced here to illustrate the point (fig.52 and facing). One
would suspect that Van de Velde made a drawing of the motif viewed from
this precise angle, and used it on more than one occasion when adding a
horse-drawn carriage to a scene.[4]

Very similar to the present picture but nearly twice as large is a painting
signed *W.V.Velde 1659* that was on the market in 1997 (formerly Henle
collection; fig.51). It shows almost the same spot and it is fairly certain
that, despite its bearing only Willem's signature, the staffage in the picture
was added by his younger brother. A picture signed *W.V.V.* in the Wallace
Collection, London (fig.50), also seems to be such a collaborative work,
although here Adriaen's input may have been restricted to the figures on foot,
on horseback and in a wagon venturing into the sea. A picture depicting the
Dutch yacht *Mary* and other vessels off Amsterdam (fig.53) is in fact signed by
both artists, although, ironically, it is exceedingly difficult to tell just how the

FIG.52
Details of cat. nos.5 and 8; of fig.56; and of Jan
Wijnants, with figures by Adriaen van de Velde,
Hilly landscape with a rider on a country road,
1660s. Signed, lower right: *JW*. Oil on canvas,
23.5 × 29.5 cm. Rijksmuseum, Amsterdam,
inv. no.SK-A-491

FIG.53
Willem van de Velde the Younger and Adriaen van de Velde, *The Dutch yacht Mary and other vessels off Amsterdam*. Signed and dated by both artists on the ensign of the yacht on the extreme right: *A V V 1661* and *W.V. Velde*. Oil on canvas, 96.5 × 156.2 cm. Sale London, Sotheby's, 4th July 2007, lot 28

FIG.54
Adriaen van de Velde (and Willem van de Velde the Younger?), *View from the dunes to the sea*. Signed, lower right: *A.V.V.* Oil on panel, 28 × 38 cm. Formerly Anton Jurgens collection (1930s); present whereabouts unknown

FIG.55
Willem van de Velde the Younger (and Adriaen van de Velde?), *View from the dunes to the sea*, late 1650s. Signed, lower left: *W v Velde*. Oil on panel, 24.3 × 29.8 cm. Museum Boijmans Van Beuningen, Rotterdam, inv. no.2533

FIG.56
Willem van de Velde the Younger and Adriaen van de Velde, *Dunes at Scheveningen*, late 1650s. Signed, lower left: *W.V.V.* Oil on panel, 24.3 × 32.5 cm. Indianapolis Museum of Art, inv. no.40.253

two brothers divided their labour on this particular work, as many of the figures seem to be very much in Willem's style.

Mention should also be made here of three pictures (figs.54, 55 and 56) that show similar views from the dunes towards the sea. In each we see the masts of the small sailing boats on the beach peek out above the dunes, although the boats themselves cannot be seen. Each work is signed differently: the most striking of the three, whose current whereabouts are unknown (fig.54), is signed *A.V.V.*; that in Rotterdam (fig.55) is signed *W v Velde*; and the one from Indianapolis is signed *W.V.V.* (fig.56). And yet they are very likely to have been painted by the brothers Willem and Adriaen in collaboration, quite possibly in the studio of Willem van de Velde the Elder. It also seems probable they should be dated to well before 1660, the most likely date for the collaborative painting in the National Gallery. Fig.54 is perhaps the most intriguing one. As was observed in a review of Wolfgang Stechow's 1966 survey of Dutch landscape painting, in its conception and observation of a brisk coastal breeze, akin to those of a nineteenth-century work, it initially seems a striking picture and one that would appeal to a modern sensibility for *plein-air* painting, but its composition is in fact

FIG.57
Jacob van Ruisdael, *View from the dunes to the sea*, c.1655. Signed, lower right: *JvRuisdael*. Oil on canvas, 26 × 35.2 cm. Kunsthaus, Zurich, Stiftung Prof. Dr. L. Ruzicka, inv. no.R. 31

rather incoherent.[5] It is signed only with the initials *A.V.V.* This in itself is problematic as Adriaen van de Velde only used this monogram in a few etchings, and never signed his paintings with it, while inscriptions reading *AVV* found on his drawings are probably always by a later hand. Described in many publications as a highly original painting by Adriaen,[6] fig.54 instead seems to be a collaborative work. It quite possibly dates from before the 1658 beachscape in Kassel (see cat. no.5). The pictures in Rotterdam and Indianapolis are in much the same vein and must be similar in date.[7] The fact that these pictures take their cue from a painting by Jacob van Ruisdael from the mid-1650s (fig.57) reinforces an early dating.[8] Their incoherence soon made way for much tighter compositions in later collaborations between the two brothers, as the painting in the National Gallery and fig.51 attest. B.C.

PROVENANCE

Jurriaans sale, Amsterdam, 28th August 1817, lot 68*, bought by or bought in through Jeronimo de Vries (fl. 1,975); Gerrit Schimmelpenninck sale, Amsterdam, 12th July 1819, lot 124, bought by Albertus Brondgeest (fl. 1,794); in the collection of the comte de Pourtalès, Paris, and among the pictures bought from that collection in 1826 by John Smith and Thomas Emmerson and sold to Robert Peel for £800; purchased with the Peel collection, 1871

EXHIBITION

Rotterdam and Berlin 1996–97, no.77

REFERENCES

Smith 1835, no.119; Waagen 1838, II, pp.24–25, no.4; Jameson 1844, pp.368–69, no.59; Waagen 1854, I, p.412, no.4; London 1854, I, p.54; Hofstede de Groot 1912, no.363; Hofstede de Groot 1923, nos.13 and 15; Stechow 1966, p.108; Haak 1984, p.477; Robinson 1990, II, p.857, no.206; MacLaren 1991, p.452, no.873; Daalder 2016, p.88

NOTES

1 The problem of 'WVV' studio pictures is discussed in Robinson 1990, passim, whose proposals regarding the identification of Adriaen van de Velde's hand in pictures in this category – not all equally convincing and virtually impossible to find in his mammoth publication – are very usefully summed up in Daalder 2016, p.88.

2 "*Een Gezigt op het strand bij Scheveningen. Verscheidene pinken op het strand en in de woelende zee, zoo ook het strand en de lucht zijn door Willem fraai geschilderd; zijn broeder Adriaan heeft dit stukje verrijkt met een' postwagen met twee paarden bespannen, verders wandelende heeren, vrouwen en andere beeldjes, welke een' hond iets in zee laten opzoeken, versieren dit in alle deelen zeer fraaije schilderij, hetgeen door beide Meesters voortreffelijk geschilderd is*"; see Jurriaans sale, Amsterdam, 28th August 1817, lot 68*.

3 Exh. cat. Rotterdam and Berlin 1996–97, no.77.

4 He may well have made a counterproof of such a drawing, as this detail crops up again, albeit in reverse, in a painting by Jan Wijnants in which Van de Velde added the staffage; see sale Christie's, London, 3rd December 1997, lot 20; Eisele 2000, no.287. The fact that the same carriage appears in the beachscapes in Kassel (our cat. no.5) and The Hague (our cat. no.8) was noted in exh. cat. Amsterdam, Boston and Philadelphia 1987–88, p.494.

5 The picture's last recorded owner was Antonius Johannes Jurgens (1867–1945), whose firm the Margarine Unie merged in 1930 with Lever Brothers to form Unilever. He acquired the painting in 1928. If he did not sell the painting at some point, it is unclear what happened to it after his death (I would like to thank Erik Jurgens for making enquiries in his extended family). The picture has a distinguished provenance going back to the late eighteenth century; see Priem 1997, p.212, no.40. The observation about its incoherent composition is found in Blankert 1967–68, p.104.

6 See Michel 1888, p.276; Zoege von Manteuffel 1927, p.70; Martin 1936, II, p.338; and Stechow 1966, pp.108–09.

7 On the basis of the costumes of the elegant couple in the foreground, Stechow 1966, p.109, believed that the painting in Rotterdam (fig.55) should be dated to the late 1660s, but both the costumes (which are almost identical to the ones worn by the elegant couple in the 1658 painting in Kassel; see our cat. no.5) and the style and composition of the painting point to a much earlier date in the later 1650s.

8 For the Ruisdael painting, see Stechow 1966, p.105; exh. cat. The Hague and Cambridge 1981–82, no.26; Slive 2001, no.634; and exh. cat. Los Angeles, Philadelphia and London 2005–06, no.26.

2

A farm with a dead tree, 1658

Oil on canvas, 54.2 × 62.5 cm
Signed and dated, lower left: *A.V.Velde.f. / 1658*
The National Gallery, London, inv. no.NG867

FIG.58
Paulus Potter, *Driving the cattle to pasture in
the morning*. Signed and dated, lower right:
Paulus. Potter. f. 1647. Oil on panel, 38.5 × 50 cm.
Residenzgalerie Salzburg, inv. no.548

A farm with a dead tree must count as one of Van de Velde's masterpieces.
For an artist who was just twenty-two years old – the painting is signed and
dated 1658 – the painting's execution and beautifully balanced composition
is nothing short of astounding. Van de Velde's delicate painterly touch
and the crystalline clarity he managed to create are testimony to the
tremendous powers that he already possessed in this early phase of his
career. Gustav Waagen, the nineteenth-century art historian and director of
the Gemäldegalerie, Berlin, saw the painting in the 1830s, when it was still
in the collection of Sir Robert Peel (1788–1850), who twice served as Prime
Minister of the United Kingdom. Waagen remarked on the fact that the "warm
afternoon light diffuses over the whole a mild splendour", going on to describe
it as a "beautiful picture of the best time of the master for, independent of the
delicacy of the drawing, in which he excels all others in this branch, the minute
execution does not, as in many of his later pictures, degenerate into faintness;
the composition is very pleasing, the harmony remarkably bright and clear.
The impression of rural tranquillity, which is peculiar to such pictures of
Adrian Van de Velde, is found here in a very high degree."[1]

For all its "splendour", it cannot be denied that the picture still relies on
the example of Paulus Potter, but it departs from his example in significant
ways. To be sure, the influence of Potter seen in *Meadow with cattle* in Berlin
(see fig.5 on p.16), painted in the same year, is also apparent in the present
painting, although the simplicity of the Berlin picture has made way for
a far more elaborate composition that includes a number of groupings –
the farmer carrying a bucket talking to the milkmaid in the centre; a group
of resting and standing cows to the right; and a few farm animals slightly
further forward to the left. They are bound together by the fact that they have
all found a place on an oval-shaped spotlit area of the ground, a device much
favoured by the artist in this early phase of his career. In later years, Van de
Velde would increasingly reach more daring solutions when it came to the
disposition of light and shadow, but in this picture he very effectively chose
to show a scene as if it were a stage set.

There are a number of pictures that can be usefully compared to the
National Gallery painting. The most telling comparison is with a 1647
painting by Potter in Salzburg (fig.58).[2] Although Potter's painting provides a
much more close-up view, and Van de Velde moved the view towards the low
horizon to the right, the general composition is very similar. Van de Velde
took care to make the bull's horns stand out against the bright sky, much as
Potter had done a decade earlier. Potter's tree showing its first buds in spring
has been replaced by the dead tree that lends the picture its name, boldly
placed at the centre of the composition. Other motifs reminiscent of Potter
include the woman milking a cow talking to a farmer, much as she does in
Potter's *Farm near The Hague* of 1647 (fig.59) in a private collection and *Cows*

FIG.59
Paulus Potter, *Farm near The Hague*. Signed
and dated, lower left: *Paulus. Potter. f. 1647*.
Oil on panel, 39.7 × 50.2 cm. Private collection

FIG.60
Paulus Potter, *Cows reflected in the water*. Signed
and dated, centre right: *Paulus. Potter / f. 1648.*
Oil on panel, 43.4 × 61.3 cm. Mauritshuis,
The Hague, inv. no.137

FIG.61
Paulus Potter, *Two pigs in a sty*. Signed and
dated, upper left: *Paulus Potter f. 1649.* Oil on
canvas, 32.4 × 45.1 cm. Museum of Fine Arts,
Houston, inv. no.2009.556

FIG.62
Detail of cat. no.2 and detail of Adriaen van de
Velde, *Country scene with peasants and animals*.
Signed and dated, lower left: *A.V.Velde. f. 1664.*
Pen and brown ink and brown wash, with red
wash, 16.2 × 25.2 cm. British Museum, London,
inv. no.1895,0915.1328

reflected in the water of 1648 in The Hague (fig.60),[3] while one of the pigs is
very similar to that depicted by Potter in two paintings (one of them fig.61).[4]
Although not a study for this painting, a drawing by Van de Velde dated 1664
in the British Museum shows pigs in exactly the same pose (fig.62); both
painting and drawing are probably based on the same drawn study of pigs
by Van de Velde, even if the idea for them ultimately derives from Potter.[5]
The view towards the horizon with distant fields where animals graze is
also a distinctly Potteresque ingredient.

These comparisons make one realise just how familiar Van de Velde
must have been with Potter's work, yet the National Gallery painting also
demonstrates how Van de Velde departed from his model. Whereas Potter's
painterly touch can be very descriptive, with each tiny stroke applied very
deliberately and precisely, Van de Velde has a far more fluent painterly style.
Although there is a Potteresque attention to detail, he never loses himself in
the minutiae of the scene, which helps to give his paintings a softness of tone
and facture often lacking in the work of the elder master.

The painting also throws up an interesting aspect of Van de Velde's
working methods. As is explained elsewhere in this catalogue, the artist
often made elaborate drawn studies before putting brush to canvas. No
specific studies for this painting survive, but one can infer that one probably
existed. A painting in Philadelphia (fig.63) shows the very same farm not only
in a different season and in entirely different surroundings, but also with
the building in reverse. One would expect that at some point Van de Velde
made a chalk drawing of such a farm, of which he would then have made a
counterproof by wetting it, putting another sheet on top, and running the
two sheets through a printing press. It is an economical method of creating
an alternative version of a study. The Philadelphia painting has been dated
much later, to c.1668–69, but, as is explained under cat. nos.25 and 26, it is
far more likely to be an earlier work, which agrees with the artist employing
a study that must have existed as early as 1658.

There are at least two variations of the National Gallery painting. As has
been discussed in the Introduction, repetitions are rare in the artist's oeuvre.
When they occur, they are often variations or copies by a different hand.
What is certain in this case is that the version in a private collection (fig.64),
although signed and dated, is not nearly as sophisticated a picture as the

FIG.63
Adriaen van de Velde, *Winter landscape,* early 1660s. Oil on panel, 30.6 × 37 cm. Philadelphia Museum of Art, inv. no.603

FIG.64
Adriaen van de Velde, *A country house.* Signed and dated: *A.v.Velde.f / 1658.* Oil on canvas, 48.2 × 58.4 cm. Private collection

National Gallery's *Farm with a dead tree*, whose well-defined forms and exquisitely refined painterly touch it cannot match.[6]

It is interesting to note that two of the artist's most beautiful pictures, this one and another in this exhibition, Van de Velde's famous *Hut* in the Rijksmuseum (cat. no.30), were together in the early nineteenth century, when they formed part of the sizeable collection of Josephus Augustinus Brentano (1753–1821), a Dutch merchant of Italian descent who lived in Amsterdam. B.C.

PROVENANCE

Johan Christoph Werther sale, Amsterdam, 25th–26th April 1792, lot 162, bought by Josephus Augustinus Brentano (fl. 20); Claude Joseph Clos sale, Paris, 18th–19th November 1812, lot 41, bought by Jean-Louis Laneuville (4,735 francs); Emmerich Joseph, duc de Dalberg sale, London, 13th–14th June 1817, lot 45, bought in (£299 5s); anonymous [Varroc and Lafontaine] sale, Paris, 28th May 1821 and following days, lot 95, bought in (9,010 francs); Pierre-Joseph Lafontaine sale, London, 27th July 1821, lot 75, bought in (350 gns); Pierre-Joseph Lafontaine sale, London, 22nd–23rd March 1822, lot 89, bought by Robert Peel (£378); purchased by the National Gallery with the Peel collection, 1871

REFERENCES

Smith 1834, no.90; Waagen 1838, II, pp.16–17; Michel 1888, p.271; Hofstede de Groot 1912, no.95; Bode 1917, p.233; MacLaren 1991, p.441, no.867; Frensemeier 2001, no.67

NOTES

1 Waagen 1838, II, pp.16–17.
2 See exh. cat. The Hague 1994–95, no.12.
3 Ibid., nos.9 and 14.
4 Ibid., no.17 (fig.61), and Hofstede de Groot 1912, no.169.
5 Van de Velde also included the sitting pig in Jan Wijnants's *Landscape with a farm* in the Musée du Louvre, Paris (inv. no.1968), to which he added the staffage.
6 For the picture in the collection of the Duke of Westminster, see Jameson 1844, pp.274–75, no.129; Waagen 1854, II, p.168; Hofstede de Groot 1912, no.82; and Frensemeier 2001, no.68. I would like to thank Viola Pemberton-Pigott, who showed me this picture when she had it in her studio for conservation in 2011. A second variation (Hofstede de Groot 1912, no.88; Frensemeier 2001, nos.68a and 68b), very similar in composition to the Duke of Westminster's painting (the main difference being that in the centre foreground a sheep and a ram have been added), was engraved in 1770–71 as plate 26 of

the *Recueil d'estampes gravées d'après les tableaux du cabinet de Monseigneur le Duc de Choiseul*; see Etienne-François, duc de Choiseul sale, Paris, 6th April 1772, lot 73, bought by Louis-François-Jacques Boileau (2,000 livres), and Louis-François de Bourbon, prince de Conti sale, Paris, 8th April–6th June 1777, lot 416, bought by Jean-Baptiste-Pierre Lebrun (2,450 livres). This picture is possibly identical to that recorded in the nineteenth century as with R.P. Nichols, London (see Waagen 1857, p.240), and to a painting offered for sale at Christie's, London, 21st July 1989, lot 156 (when said to be signed and dated 1668), and subsequently at Glerum, The Hague, 25th November 1991, lot 171. The latter auction house also offered still another version, not recorded in the literature, on 10th November 1994, lot 36 (signed and dated: *A.V.Velde f. / 1659*; oil on canvas, 54 × 62.5 cm), which closely follows the composition of the National Gallery painting.

3

View of an estuary, 1658

Oil on panel, 24.3 × 32.6 cm
Signed and dated, lower right: *A.V. Velde 1658*
Museum der bildenden Künste, Leipzig, inv. no.1068

FIG.65
Salomon van Ruysdael, *River landscape*, c.1632.
Signed and dated (last two digits illegible),
lower left on the floating barrel: *SVR. / 16..* Oil on
panel, 65.6 × 94.4 cm. Alte Pinakothek, Munich,
inv. no.161

FIG.66
Adriaen van de Velde, *Panoramic river
landscape*, late 1650s. Oil on canvas, 41 × 66 cm.
Gemäldegalerie, Staatliche Museen zu Berlin,
inv. no.922B

When in 1857 Gustav Waagen described this painting as one of the treasures in the possession of the London collector John Henderson (1797–1878),[1] he rightly observed that "This little picture is a striking proof that very high art can be compressed within a very small space",[2] while in 1900, by which time the picture formed part of the collection of the German industrialist and art collector Alfred Thieme (1830–1906),[3] it prompted Wilhelm Bode to write one of his most evocative paragraphs on the artist: "... the truth and delicacy in the depiction of the hot summer morning is unsurpassable, the white haze that lies over the mirror-like water in the distance that hardly allows one to become aware of the horizon, the passive stillness of the animals, the limp sails of the boat – everything exudes a warm, Sunday stillness in nature; only a few white clouds rising above the water leave a sense that a stormy evening may follow this delightful day. The picture is completely filled with light and vapour, and yet the local colour is refined, and the drawing most delicate."[4]

The painting demonstrates that at the age of twenty-two Van de Velde had completely mastered the art of aerial perspective. More importantly, he had fully understood how to turn a landscape into art. In the hands of a lesser artist the same motif could so easily have become a numbing exercise in careful description, but Van de Velde managed to unify all parts of the scene into a harmonious whole, with every form and every colour in the composition in perfect tune with its surroundings – from the lowered sail set off against the background of the receding bank, beautifully reflected in the still river, and the tiny glimpse of a sail on the horizon, faintly mirrored in the water, to the counterpoint of the goat and horse silhouetted against the bright horizon. This is not a depiction of an observed Dutch landscape, but a very careful artificial construct that is meant to evoke a mixture of serenity, warmth and melancholy. It is, one could say, a beautiful lie.

Such artifice is also seen in the strict choreography of the animals on the river bank. There is a satisfying symmetry in the opposing directions of the two recumbent sheep, while the side view of the horse and the much smaller goat facing in opposite directions is gratifying precisely because it is not

quite symmetrical, their difference in size allowing the overall arrangement of forms on the right of the composition to balance those on the left.

All Van de Velde's river scenes date from a short period early in his career, and almost all are of distinctively Dutch landscapes.[5] The most relevant comparison is with a much larger painting in Berlin (fig.66).[6] Although there are clear differences – the painting in Berlin is oblong and shows the riverbanks parallel to the picture plane – it is equally successful in rendering the very same qualities and, like the present picture, must count as one of Van de Velde's masterpieces, even if its heavy craquelure slightly detracts from its enjoyment when seen in the flesh. It is not dated but must have been executed in the late 1650s. Another example is a small panel of 1661 in London (fig.67), which if restored would almost certainly regain its former glory.[7]

An important precedent for such compositions was set by artists such as Jan van Goyen and, especially, Salomon van Ruysdael, who as early as the 1630s painted river scenes with a receding river bank, although they are usually on a larger scale (fig.65). Ruysdael clearly considered the composition so successful that he repeated it time and again, with the unfortunate effect that the motif became rather formulaic, and he rarely used elements in the foreground of the composition as a repoussoir to help push back the horizon and create the impression of a vast space, something Van de Velde managed to do in this picture to great effect. Van de Velde's supreme command of aerial perspective also sets his pictures apart from those by Ruysdael, which tend to be harsher in this respect. In light of the fact that such river scenes clearly brought out the best in Van de Velde, it is perhaps surprising that after the early 1660s he never returned to the subject. B.C.

PROVENANCE

By 1857 in the collection of John Henderson, London; his sale, London, Christie's, 16th–18th February 1882, lot 385; collection of Wilhelm Gumprecht, Berlin; in 1895 acquired from this collection by Alfred Thieme, Leipzig; bought by the Museum in 1916 as part of the Thieme collection

EXHIBITIONS

Leipzig 1914, no.133; Leipzig 1916, no.81

REFERENCES

Waagen 1857, p.212; Bode 1900, p.141; Thieme 1900, pp.43 and 75, no.81; Hofstede de Groot 1912, no.350; exh. cat. Leipzig 1916, p.25; Stechow 1966, pp.60–61; exh. cat. Leipzig 1995, p.199; Frensemeier 2001, no.150; Nicolaisen 2012, no.335

NOTES

1 Henderson bequeathed a number of his antiquities to the University of Oxford, while other works in his wide-ranging collection went to the British Museum. He also bequeathed a number of Old Master paintings to the National Gallery, London.
2 Waagen 1857, p.212.
3 His son was the art historian Ulrich Thieme (1865–1922), best known as the original editor, together with Felix Becker (1864–1928), of the *Allgemeines Lexikon der bildenden Künstler von der Antike bis zur Gegenwart*, which eventually ran to 37 volumes, published between 1907 and 1950.
4 Thieme 1900, p.43.
5 The exception is the mountainous river landscape of 1656 in the Musée des Beaux-Arts, Strasbourg, inv. no.MBA 424: Hofstede de Groot 1912, no.345; Frensemeier 2001, no.149.

6 Hofstede de Groot 1912, no.348; Frensemeier 2001, no.152.
7 Hofstede de Groot 1912, no.81; Frensemeier 2001, no.76. Mention should be made here of an early small river landscape, which in the nineteenth century was in the collection of the duc d'Arenberg but whose present whereabouts is unknown (Thoré-Bürger 1859, no.64; Hofstede de Groot 1912, no.349; Frensemeier 2001, no.151); of *Cattle on the bank of a river* of 1664 in the Musée du Louvre, Paris, illustrated as fig.22 on p.22 (Hofstede de Groot 1912, no.120; Frensemeier 2001, no.155; Foucart 2009, p.282); and of the panoramic *River landscape* of the early 1660s illustrated as fig.88 on p.72 (Hofstede de Groot 1912, no.47; Frensemeier 2001, no.80). In the last two the emphasis is respectively on the cattle and on the panoramic view, so that they hardly qualify as pure river landscapes.

4

Portrait of a man on horseback,
1658

Oil on canvas, 33 × 25.5 cm
Signed and dated, lower centre: *A.V.Velde. f. 1658*
Private collection

FIG.68
Rembrandt van Rijn, *Frederick Rihel on horseback*.
Faint remains of signature and date, lower left:
R..brandt 1663(?). Oil on canvas, 294.5 × 241 cm.
The National Gallery, London, inv. no.NG6300

Equestrian portraits depicting prominent citizens rather than members of the nobility are rare in seventeenth-century Dutch painting, and most date from the latter half of the century.[1] Examples include Rembrandt's large *Frederick Rihel on horseback* of 1663 (fig.68) and Paulus Potter's even larger *Dirck Tulp on horseback* of 1653 (fig.69). It was always thought that in the latter half of the century it was Thomas de Keyser who pioneered such portraits on a smaller scale, as seen in pictures dating from 1660 and 1661 (fig.70 and 71), but, with the rediscovery of the painting under discussion here, which is dated 1658, we have to allow for another contender.[2]

Until recently we only knew of Van de Velde's equestrian portrait from written sources. It was last seen in public in 1877 at an exhibition at the Royal Academy in London. No photograph of it was known until, in 2012, the fully signed and dated painting was first published with a black-and-white illustration.[3] In this exhibition the work is publicly shown for the first time in almost 140 years and illustrated in full colour.[4] What makes Van de Velde's early work so attractive is that he depicts such a great variety of subjects. Although it is known that he painted the odd portrait, it was with the reappearance of this equestrian portrait, undoubtedly a commissioned painting, that the artist's early ambitions as a portrait painter became clear.[5]

One cannot deny that in turning to this type of portrait Van de Velde was slightly overambitious. While every detail of the painting is exquisitely finished – in that respect we are looking at a twenty-two-year-old artist who was already approaching the top of his game – the painting also displays a certain awkwardness. It demonstrates a masterly control over the composition but is somewhat compromised by the fact that the man is rather too large compared to the horse, probably the result of Van de Velde having little experience with the genre of portraiture, let alone equestrian portraiture, although this fault is found in a good number of equestrian portraits of the period. The horse itself, however, is almost perfect anatomically and especially in the entirely convincing depiction of the sheen of its coat. Moreover, the overall dark colouring of the horse is beautifully offset by the colours of its rider, who is immaculately dressed in a variety of white, yellow, red and gold tones, his saddle in much the same colours, while it was a clever idea of the artist to contrast the horse's stately pace with the speed of the hound just behind it. And, should we be in doubt as to who painted this picture, the view of meadows with grazing cows in the distance recalls the fields extending to the horizon that we see in Van de Velde's early landscapes.

In 1834 the London art dealer John Smith was much enamoured of the picture, even if he underestimated Van de Velde's age: "This beautiful and exquisitely-finished picture is dated 1658; so that, if the artist's historiographers be correct, he was only nineteen years of age when he painted it; yet nothing in art can be more sweetly pencilled, or more perfect in drawing and colour",[6] while twenty-three years later Gustav Waagen,

FIG.69
Paulus Potter, *Dirck Tulp on horseback*. Signed
and dated, on the tree: *Paulus Potter f. / 1653*.
Oil on canvas, 310 × 274 cm. Collectie Six, Amsterdam

FIG.70

Thomas de Keyser, *Pieter Schout Muilman on horseback*. Signed and dated, on the saddle: *TDK F. 1660*. Copper, 86.1 × 69.6 cm. Rijksmuseum, Amsterdam, inv. no.SK-A-697

FIG.71

Thomas de Keyser, *Two men on horseback*. Signed and dated, on the saddle of the rider on the right: *TDK F. 1661*. Oil on canvas, 98 × 92.5 cm. Gemäldegalerie Alte Meister, Staatliche Kunstsammlungen, Dresden, inv. no.1543

director of the Gemäldegalerie, Berlin, described the painting as "Very delicately conceived, and of masterly though miniature-like execution in a very harmonious tone".[7] Smith also maintained that the painting represented Frederik Hendrik, Prince of Orange, but the sitter does not resemble the prince, who had anyhow died more than a decade before Van de Velde painted the portrait. The sitter's dress – his buff leather coat, or *kolder*,[8] his pistol and bandolier (from which hangs his sword, which was always worn on the left and is thus not visible in the picture) – probably has military connotations, rather than referring to the aristocratic pursuits of riding and the hunt, despite the hunting dog bounding across the field in the background. There seems little doubt that the richly embroidered gun holster displays a coat of arms, its shield supported by two griffins and surmounted by an ornate helmet. This shield may well hold the key to the identification of the sitter, but it is difficult to tell precisely what it shows, so that for the time being the distinguished sitter has to remain anonymous.[9] B.C.

PROVENANCE

Corneille-Louis Reynders sale, Brussels, 6th August 1821 and following days, lot 100, bought by the London dealer Christianus Johannes Nieuwenhuys or 'Vandenhouten' (fl. 1,000); collection of Baron von Mecklenburg, Paris; sold by him in 1824 to the London dealer John Smith (5,000 francs); sold by him on 28th April 1825 to Abraham Robarts, London; private collection

EXHIBITION

London 1877, no.51

REFERENCES

Smith 1834, no.103; Waagen 1857, p.162; Hofstede de Groot 1912, no.28; Duparc 2012; Sebag Montefiore and Armstrong-Totten 2013, p.57

NOTES

1 See exh. cat. Leeuwarden, Den Bosch and Assen 1979–80.
2 It so happens that the landscape background of fig.70, which is in every way the closest parallel to our picture, has in the past been attributed to Adriaen van de Velde; see Schneider 1927, cited in Duparc 2012, p. 344. There is no reason to follow this suggestion.
3 See Duparc 2012.
4 It is not in Frensemeier 2001.
5 An even earlier portrait by Van de Velde is his rather clumsy *Portrait of a family in a landscape*, dated 1655; see Frensemeier 2001, no.18. It was last recorded in 1999 as with the dealer Hoogsteder & Hoogsteder, The Hague. The only other portrait by the artist is our cat. no.22. Cornelis Hofstede de Groot mentions two further paintings that may be equestrian portraits, although they may just as well refer to paintings that are not portraits but landscapes that

prominently feature a man on horseback; see P.F. de Noter sale, Ghent, 27th December 1842, lot 73, and Hélène Herry sale, Antwerp, 18th September 1848, lot 100, quoted in Hofstede de Groot 1912 under nos.28a and 28b ("Portrait of a Horseman" and "A Gentleman on Horseback").
6 Smith 1834, p.204.
7 Waagen 1857, p.162.
8 See Sint Nicolaas and Stevens 2006.
9 A poor rectangular copy of our picture was sold at Christie's, London (South Kensington), 1st October 2013, lot 422, as an anonymous work. It is unclear whether we need to attach any importance to the fact that the frame of this copy bears a label with the name August Querfurt, a German painter of battle and hunting scenes as well as equestrian portraits who from 1743 was active in Vienna and whose work is much indebted to that of Philips Wouwerman; see exh. cat. Kassel and The Hague 2009–10, p.51.

5

The beach at Scheveningen, 1658

Oil on canvas, 52.6 × 73.8 cm
Signed and dated, lower left: *A.V.Velde. f. / 1658*
Museumslandschaft Hessen Kassel,
Gemäldegalerie Alte Meister,inv. no.GK 374

6

Carriage on the beach at Scheveningen, 1660

Oil on panel, 37 × 49 cm
Signed, lower right: *A.V.Velde. f. 1660*
Musée du Louvre, Paris, inv. no.1915

7

Figures on the coast at Scheveningen, 1660

Oil on canvas, 38.2 × 50 cm
Signed and dated, lower right: *A.V.Velde. f. / 1660*
The Royal Collection / HM Queen Elizabeth II,
inv. no.RCIN 404802

8

View of a beach, 1663 or 1665

Oil on panel, 42 × 54 cm
Signed and dated, lower left: *Av velde f / 166[3 or 5?]*
Mauritshuis, The Hague, inv. no.198

AMSTERDAM ONLY

There is no documentary evidence that Van de Velde ever visited The Hague and the fishing village west of that city, Scheveningen, but some of his paintings indicate that at some point early in his career Van de Velde must have spent time in the city and its environs; he painted the so-called Koekamp (see cat. no.17), a deer park in The Hague that still exists, and also a number of pictures of the beach at Scheveningen, which are discussed here together with his other beachscapes.

In his *Handbook of Painting. The German, Flemish, and Dutch Schools* of 1860, Gustav Waagen wrote in glowing terms about Van de Velde's coast scenes, leaving little doubt as to the artist's supreme position among his peers: "At the age of nineteen he was already in this department one of the greatest masters that ever lived; the picture dated 1658, in the Cassel Gallery, No.593, displaying a tender feeling for nature, a mastery of drawing, and a delicacy of chiaroscuro and harmony which are truly astonishing".[1] Indeed, there is no question that the beachscapes under discussion here, especially that in Kassel, are among the most memorable works of the Dutch Golden Age.

Van de Velde was certainly neither the first nor the only Dutch artist to depict a beach. It is fair to say, however, that with him this sub-genre within seventeenth-century Dutch landscape painting came into its own. In the first decades of the century beaches invariably appeared as the almost incidental background in pictures that chronicled a special event, such as an embarkation or landing, or the stranding of a whale. In the 1630s the beach became a far more conspicuous element in genre-like depictions of sea-related activities on the coast. It was then that the compositional scheme for these pictures was established, especially the device of showing the coastline receding diagonally into space. In the most advanced stage of this development the beach became a subject in its own right, and Van de Velde's beachscapes not only squarely belong in the last category, but are also the finest examples in existence.

A foretaste of Van de Velde's paintings can be found in Jan van Goyen's *Selling fish on the beach at Scheveningen* of 1632 in Leipzig (fig.72), Simon de Vlieger's *Beach at Scheveningen* of 1633 in Greenwich (fig.73) and, a little closer in date, Van Goyen's *Beach with fishing boats* of the early 1650s in New York (fig.74). The same was thought to be true of a painting by Hendrick van Anthonissen in Cambridge of c.1641 (fig.75), but during recent conservation treatment it was revealed that this painting, whose composition seemed particularly relevant to Van de Velde's painting in Kassel,[2] in fact belonged to the category of beachscapes illustrating an exceptional event, as it was then that the stranded whale, which at some point had been painted out, was discovered.

The painting in Cambridge serves to illustrate the leap made by Van de Velde, who saw no need to include any specific event as a vehicle for his beachscapes, although a remnant of this tradition is found in the inclusion of what looks like the carriage belonging to a dignitary in the beachscape from the Louvre (cat. no.6), while in the painting from The Hague (cat. no.8) more genre-like elements resurface, recalling the works of Van Goyen and De Vlieger. What sets Van de Velde's beachscapes apart is not only the

5

PROVENANCE

Acquired before 1749 by Landgraf Wilhelm VIII
von Hessen-Kassel

EXHIBITIONS

The Hague 1948, no.267; Schaffhausen 1949,
no.177; Paris 1950–51, no.89; Cologne 1954, no.27;
Brussels 1971, no.108

REFERENCES

Causid 1783, no.100; Smith 1834, no.130; Waagen
1860, II, p.411; Parthey 1863–64, II, p.704, no.2;
Michel 1888, pp.275–76; Hofstede de Groot 1912,
no.355; Zoege von Manteuffel 1927, p.68; Stechow
1966, pp.107–08; Herzog 1969, no.13; Bol 1973,
p.245; Adler *et al.* 1981, pp.84 and 86–87; exh. cat.
Los Angeles and Boston 1981–82, p.100; Haak 1984,
pp.471–72; Slive 1995, p.212; Schnackenburg 1996,
I, p.302; Frensemeier 2001, no.163

6

PROVENANCE

Johan van Schuylenburg sale, The Hague, 20th September 1735, lot 77, bought by "Clock" (fl. 155); Jeronimus Tonneman sale, Amsterdam, 21st October 1754 and following days, lot 23, bought by Gerrit Braamcamp (fl. 260); his sale, Amsterdam, 31st July 1771 and following days, lot 238, bought by Pieter Fouquet (fl. 1,000); in the collection of Etienne-François, duc de Choiseul-Stainville, Paris, by whom given in 1775 together with 17 other pictures to Louis-François de Bourbon, prince de Conti, Paris; his sale, Paris, 8th April 1777, lot 413, bought by "Feuiller" or "Fueillet" (5,072 livres); Louis-François Trouard sale, Paris, 22nd–27th February 1779, lot 114, bought by Joseph Hyacinthe François de Paule de Rigaud, comte de Vaudreuil (3,800 livres); his sale, Paris, 24th–25th November 1784, lot 66, bought by Alexandre Joseph Paillet for Louis XVI (6,801 livres), and exhibited at the opening to the public of the Louvre in 1793[3]

REFERENCES

Bastide 1766, p.98; Smith 1834, no.13; Nagler 1835–52, XX, p.29; Waagen 1860, II, p.411; Michel 1888, p.276; Hofstede de Groot 1912, no.360; Bille 1961, I, pp.34 and 87, and II, pp.58–58a and p.125, no.238; Stechow 1966, p.108; exh. cat. Los Angeles and Boston 1981–82, p.100; Edwards 1996, pp.61 and 338; Frensemeier 2001, no.164; Dubreuil 2001, p.135, no.92; Bailey 2002, p.291, note 55; Foucart 2009, p.281

7

PROVENANCE

Inherited by Mary D'Arcy, Countess of Holderness (daughter of Francis Doublet of Groeneveldt); her sale, London, 6th March 1802, lot 70, bought by George Stainforth for his father-in-law, Sir Francis Baring (£162 15s); acquired by George IV in 1814 with the Baring collection

EXHIBITIONS

London 1946–47, no.367; London 1962, no.46; exLondon 1971–72, no.46; London 1975–76, no.37; London 1988–89, no.53; Edinburgh, London and Barnard Castle 2010–12, no.14

REFERENCES

Smith 1834, no.79; Waagen 1838, II, p.365; Jameson 1844, p.57, no.152; Waagen 1854, II, p.15; Waagen 1860, p.411; Hofstede de Groot 1912, no.357; Stechow 1966, p.108; Bol 1973, p.245; exh. cat. Los Angeles and Boston 1981–82, p.100; White 1982, no.203; Frensemeier 2001, no.165; White 2015, no.203

8

PROVENANCE

Coenraad van Heemskerck sale, The Hague, 7th October 1765, lot 38 (16.50 fl.); Govert van Slingelandt sale, The Hague, 18th May 1768, lot 36, but the entire Slingelandt collection sold before the sale to Willem V; Prince Willem V, The Hague, 1768–95; from 1795 to 1815 at the Musée du Louvre, Paris; returned to the Royal Picture Gallery, 1815; Royal Picture Gallery 'Mauritshuis', 1821[4]

EXHIBITIONS

Rotterdam 1945–46, no.47; Dordrecht 1964, no.79; The Hague and London 1970–71, no.106; Paris 1986, no.49; Amsterdam, Boston and Philadelphia 1987–88, no.103; Madrid 1994, no.68

REFERENCES

Terwesten 1770, p.716; Smith 1834, no.149; Thoré-Bürger 1858–60, I, pp.265–66; Gower 1875, p.36; Michel 1888, p.276; Michel 1892, p.104; Hofstede de Groot 1892, p.230; Hofstede de Groot 1912, no.356; Zoege von Manteuffel 1927, p.69; Preston 1937, p.51; Martin 1950, no.129; Frerichs 1966; Stechow 1966, pp.107–08; Bol 1973, pp.245–46; Drossaers and Lunsingh Scheurleur 1974–76, III, p.234, no.165; Brenninkmeyer-de Rooij 1976, p.173; Duparc 1980, pp.108–09; Hoetink 1985, pp.302–03, no.92; Broos 1987, no.61; Buvelot 2004, p.316

ABOVE: FIG.72
Jan van Goyen, *Selling fish on the beach at Scheveningen*. Signed and dated, bottom right: *VG 1632*. Oil on panel, 29.5 × 43 cm. Museum der bildenden Künste, Leipzig, inv. no.1010

FIG.73
Simon de Vlieger, *The beach at Scheveningen*. Signed and dated *S. de Vlieger / 1633*. Oil on panel, 68.6 × 106.7 cm. National Maritime Museum, Greenwich, inv. no.BHC0774

BELOW: FIG.74
Jan van Goyen, *Beach with fishing boats*. Signed and dated on boat in foreground: *vG 165[3?]*. Oil on panel, 27.9 × 43.2 cm. The Metropolitan Museum of Art, New York, inv. no.2005.331.2

FIG.75
Hendrick van Anthonissen, *View of Scheveningen sands*. c.1641. Indistinctly signed and dated, lower left on plank leaning against boat. Oil on panel, 56.8 × 102.8 cm. The Fitzwilliam Museum, University of Cambridge, inv. no.43

freshness of his approach but also his tendency to employ intense colour values. Wolfgang Stechow memorably described this quality in a passage in his survey of Dutch landscape painting of 1966 that is worth quoting in full: "Adriaen van de Velde is not interested in tonality, neither of the van Goyen nor of the van de Cappelle variety. His day on the beach is the one which so many people miss on Dutch beaches: the day when all forms stand out in unadulterated colours, bathed in a fresh, clean light which softens their contours without blurring them. In the painting in Kassel, the effect of the complete permeation of the picture surface with a glorious sunlight, which a thin film of clouds deprives only of its harshest glare, is entirely the master's own."[5]

The most original of the four beachscapes under discussion here is that in Kassel (cat. no. 5), which is also the earliest. It is astonishing that at the age of twenty-two Van de Velde had already produced what is his absolute masterpiece, and it is on seeing a work such as this that one is quite ready to believe his earliest biographer Arnold Houbraken, who in his compendium of artists' lives of 1718–21 suggested that Adriaen was something of a *Wunderkind*.[6] It is also one of the reasons why historians such as Stechow were so keen to compare Van de Velde to Mozart, a comparison that was also informed by the fact that both artists died in their thirty-sixth year.[7] One only needs to think of the work of an artist such as Moses ter Borch, Gerard ter

FIG.76
Jacques-Philippe Le Bas after Adriaen van de
Velde, *Petite Marine*. Engraving and etching,
27.7 × 35.6 cm. Amsterdam Museum,
inv. no.A 11538

FIG.77
Details of cat. no.5 and of fig.76 in reverse

Borch the Elder's exceptionally gifted son, to realise that in the seventeenth
century artists could reach a level of maturity at a remarkably early age.

In the Kassel painting we look from a slightly elevated viewpoint along
a coastline from which the sea has retreated, allowing the expanse of the
sandy beach to take centre stage, with some pools of water reminding us that
not long before the sea had been encroaching on the land. Small groups of
people are scattered around, while a figure with his hands behind his back
stands near the waterline contemplating the horizon, his bare feet in the
wet sand. He must count as one of the most glorious figures in seventeenth-
century Dutch painting. At first sight he seems to have no other purpose
than to survey the sea, but it is through him that viewers are made aware of
the peacefulness of the scene, a peace that comes with a hint of melancholy.
Some seventeenth-century Dutch artists – Gerard ter Borch springs to mind
– understood the power of a figure seen from behind, making the beholder
engage with the scene by imagining that person's state of mind, a trick that
provides the perfect antidote to the anecdotal, and Van de Velde here shows
himself in supreme command of the device. It is equally ingenious of the
artist to have placed this figure relatively close to the viewer and to the edge
of the composition; as we visualize what this man is looking at we become
aware of the extent of the sea in front of him. Without him, the edge of the
painting would have abruptly closed off the scene on the right, but through
his presence the panorama in effect extends far beyond the picture plane.

The same figure crops up again in a beachscape, now untraced, first
recorded in the 1775 sale of the collection of the celebrated connoisseur
Pierre-Jean Mariette (1694–1774). The auction catalogue mentions that
"*on en connait l'Estampe, gravée par M. le Bas, sous le titre de petite Marine*"
(fig.76).[8] We see virtually the same person standing on the shore. As is often
the case with reproductive prints, he is shown in reverse, but this means
that in the lost painting he featured in the same direction as in the Kassel
beachscape. In *Petite Marine* he is standing in the dunes by the beach,
turning his head towards a man reclining in the sand beside him. Even his
shadow faithfully follows that in the painting in Kassel (fig.77). It provides yet
another example of the artist reusing a motif in a different context, as can be
seen in other works in this exhibition (see cat. nos.1, 11, 15, 28 and 30).

Contemporary sources confirm that the beach was not just a place where
fishermen went about their business, although it was clearly their domain;
it was also a place of pleasure and repose, especially in the summer months,

when townspeople would go there to take the fresh air. In 1668 the poet Jacob van der Does described the pleasures of Scheveningen beach in a long poem in praise of a newly constructed road connecting The Hague to Scheveningen: "In the evening, when the sun dives into the sea / and closes her all-seeing eye on our world, / one can search here for a little cooling and through the water/ trot, so that the sea splashes around the nose and ears".[9] One of the most attractive qualities of the painting in Kassel is perhaps that one would be hard pressed to identify what the painting is about other than the recreation on offer at the beach. It is this lack of a specific subject that in the nineteenth century must have appealed to an artist such as Eugène Boudin, who copied Van de Velde's beachscape at the Louvre (cat. no.6; fig.78). The Impressionists' rediscovery of the beach as a motif may well have been informed by the work of their seventeenth-century colleagues, and Boudin made a speciality of the subject. One may even wonder whether he was also familiar with the painting in Kassel, as various beachscapes by him seem to suggest (fig.79).

Van de Velde's scattering of various figures in a wide view along the shoreline gives way to much tighter groupings in his later beachscapes. Especially in the Louvre painting (cat. no.6), which shows the beach at Scheveningen this time looking north, the focus is on the carriage drawn by six horses and followed by a train of footmen dressed in blue livery who are accompanied by several dogs. We observe this procession coming towards us, much like the fisherman with his fishing net walking across the scene in the foreground. No doubt a person of some importance is visiting the beach, and for a long time it was believed that the picture recorded a visit by Prince William of Orange, later King William III; now it is recognized that this cannot be proven. Evidently lower down the social spectrum are the elegant couple in conversation and, a little further on, the fisherman and his child. Although less assured than the Kassel picture, this is still a masterly composition that displays a wonderful cadence of forms against the background sloping from right to left, while the choreography of the figures is close to perfection.

As befits a masterpiece, the Louvre painting's provenance reads like a roll-call of the great and the good of the eighteenth century, when it was owned by such illustrious Dutch collectors as Johan van Schuylenburgh, Jeronimus Tonneman and Gerrit Braamcamp, then finding its way into various French aristocratic collections, including those of the duc de Choiseul, the prince de Conti and the comte de Vaudreuil, at whose sale it was bought by the famous art dealer Alexandre Joseph Paillet for Louis XVI. In addition to the Louvre beachscape, Jeronimus Tonneman (1687–1750) was fortunate enough also to own Van de Velde's *Koekamp* now in the Gemäldegalerie, Berlin, discussed under cat. no.17, as well as the watercolour of *The Ferry* (cat. no.47).

Neither the painting in the Royal Collection (cat. no. 7) nor that in the Mauritshuis (cat. no. 8) show any clues as to the locality, but the chances are that they also depict the beach at Scheveningen or, more precisely, the shore, as the viewer is now standing slightly further inland at some distance from

FIG.82
Details of cat. no.7 and of Jan van der Heyden,
with figures by Adriaen van de Velde,
An architectural fantasy, c.1665–70. Signed
on a block of stone in the right foreground:
I.vd.Heijde. Oil on panel, 51.8 × 64.5 cm.
The National Gallery, London, inv. no.NG 992

FIG.80
Details of cat. no.7 and fig.76

FIG.81
Details of cat. no.7 and fig.76

the sea, especially in the Royal Collection picture, where we see the green
vegetation so characteristic of the dunes. In this painting we again encounter
the standing man shown with a reclining figure (fig.80), albeit that this time
he has crossed his arms in front of him while the configuration of the two
figures has been slightly adjusted. We also see the same dog as in the print
(fig.81), a dog that we find in practically the same pose in numerous paintings
by Van de Velde, as well as in those of Jan van der Heyden and Jan Wijnants to
which Van de Velde contributed the staffage. The peg-legged beggar making
way for the wagonload of townspeople also crops up elsewhere (fig.82).

Both the Royal Collection and Mauritshuis pictures differ from those in
Kassel and Paris in that the horizontal composition unfolds parallel to the
picture plane. In the Royal Collection picture the entire social spectrum is
represented, from beggars to fishermen and well-to-do townspeople taking
the air. In the Mauritshuis picture we move closer to the scene, so that most
figures are larger. Towards the mid-1660s Van de Velde tended to emphasize
the figures and move them closer to the picture plane. The date is difficult
to decipher and can be read as either 1663 or 1665: both are plausible. In
the later 1660s Van de Velde tended to place the horizon in his landscapes

higher, which led to less panoramic views. The fact that the horizon in
the Mauritshuis painting is still rather low, leaving room for the sky with
billowing clouds to take up more than three quarters of the picture plane,
perhaps points to 1663 as the most probable date. That large sky overarches
a scene of resting fishermen, the long horizon interrupted only by a man
making his dog jump, a young boy carrying another, and a carriage being
driven towards the sea. Young and old sit in front of a tent and are gloriously
idle, the dog as indolent as its owners. Here is a Dutch idyll that makes use of
perfectly plausible motifs, but in the hands of Van de Velde the picture has
become far more than the sum of its parts.

Van de Velde painted at least two more beachscapes. In Buenos Aires
is a little-known, almost square and tiny picture (fig.83) that must date
from around the same time as the beachscape in the Royal Collection,[10]
while another in the Los Angeles County Museum of Art (fig.84) was made
towards the end of Van de Velde's life. Like other late works by the artist,
it is far more brooding in character and anticipates Jacob van Ruisdael's
dramatic beachscapes of the 1670s (fig.85). It is a far cry from Van de Velde's
joyous early depictions of the beach in which a 'Sunday atmosphere' reigns
supreme.[11] B.C.

FIG.84
Adriaen van de Velde, *The beach at Scheveningen*.
Signed and dated, lower left, on boat: *A.v.velde f/
1670*. Oil on canvas, 39.4 × 50.2 cm. Los Angeles
County Museum of Art, inv. no.M.2009.106.14

FIG.85
Jacob van Ruisdael, *The shore at Egmond aan
Zee*, c.1675. Signed, lower right: *JvRuisdael*.
Oil on canvas, 53.7 × 66.2 cm. The National Gallery,
London, inv. no.NG 1390

NOTES

1 Waagen 1860, II, p.411. Waagen believed that
   Van de Velde was born in 1639, which would
   indeed have made him nineteen when he
   painted the Kassel picture; in 1658 he was in
   fact twenty-two years old.
2 See Bol 1973, p.245.
3 For this provenance, see Foucart 2009, p.281,
   who corrects errors in those given in Hofstede
   de Groot 1912 and Bille 1961.
4 Duparc 1980, p.108, Broos 1987, p.365, and
   Buvelot 2004, p.316, mistakenly mention
   Jeronimus Tonneman as the painting's earliest
   known owner, but the beachscape in his
   collection was not the Mauritshuis painting
   but the beachscape now in the Louvre; see the
   provenance under cat. no.6.
5 Stechow 1966, p.108.
6 Houbraken 1718–21, III, p.90.
7 See our cat. no.9, especially footnote 2.
8 Pierre-Jean Mariette sale, Paris, 15th November
   1775–30th January 1776, lot 11, bought by
   Robert Quesney (260 livres): "*Autre Tableau par
   le même, portant 13 pouces sur 10 pouces de haut,
   représentant une Vue de la mer au bout du Village*
   *de Skerwing, avec une partie des Dunes; sur le
   devant, plusieurs jolies Figures bien dispersées le
   rendent agréable: on en connaît l'Estampe, gravée
   par M. le Bas, sous le titre de petite Marine*". The
   picture was subsequently recorded almost
   twenty years later in the Alexandre-Louis
   Hersant Destouches sale, Paris, 21st March
   1794 and following days, lot 148, bought by
   Louis-François-Jacques Boileau (300 livres):
   "*Un port de mer, avec terrains sablonneux; il est
   orné de différens groupes de figures, dont deux
   matelots sur le devant, l'un couché & l'autre
   debout, regardant une grande étendue de mer,
   enrichie de plusieurs chaloupes*"; "*sur toile, H. 9
   pou., larg. 13 pou.*". The picture is Hofstede de
   Groot 1912, no.361, who was not aware that the
   painting was once in the collection of Pierre-
   Jean Mariette. In the RKD-Netherlands Institute
   for Art History, The Hague, is a tiny black-
   and-white photograph of a painting showing
   the composition in reverse of the print. It is
   a modern print of what looks to be a very old
   negative. It is inscribed in pencil on the reverse:
   Soprintendenza Venezia. The photograph is so
   small and of such poor quality that it is difficult
   to determine the picture's status, but it may
   record Van de Velde's original painting. There
   are no further indications as to where it might
   be today.
9 Van der Does 1668, p.107: "*Hier kan men
   'savonts, als de Son in Zee gaet duycken, / En haer
   al-siende oogh voor onse Wereldt luycken, / Een
   koeltjen aen het Strandt gaen soecken, en door 't
   nat / Heen draven, dat de Zee om neus, en ooren
   spat*". The translation is a slightly adapted
   version of that given in Furnée 2011, pp.35–36.
10 Hofstede de Groot 1912, no.362; it is first
   recorded in the Alexandre-Louis Hersant
   Destouches sale, Paris, 21st March 1794 and
   following days, lot 140, bought by Guillaume-
   Jean Constantin (482 livres), the same sale
   which also included as lot 148 the untraced
   beachscape known from the print illustrated
   in fig.76; see note 8 above.
11 "*Sonntagsstimmung*" was the word used by
   Wilhelm von Bode to describe Van de Velde's
   works; see Bode 1906, p.15.

9

Panoramic summer landscape with a horseman and a post wagon, 1661

Oil on canvas, 37.8 × 49 cm
Signed and dated, lower right: *A.V.Velde / 1661*
Private collection

FIG.86
Pierre Chenu after Adriaen van de Velde,
La moisson ou l'été. Engraving and etching,
41.7 × 49.3 cm. National Library of Poland,
Warsaw, inv. no.G.34981/WAF.762

FIG.87
Salomon van Ruysdael, *A panoramic landscape
with travellers on a path, the city of Amersfoort
beyond*. Signed and dated, lower centre:
SVRuysdael 1634. Oil on canvas, 102 × 136 cm.
Private collection

Anyone discussing seventeenth-century Dutch landscape painting owes much to the art historian Wolfgang Stechow, who was the first to map the subject in a comprehensive survey published in 1966, a publication that remains indispensable. It is especially appropriate to refer to him for the painting under discussion here, which Stechow knew well because just after the Second World War it was loaned from the Mayer collection for an exhibition at the Allen Memorial Art Museum, the university museum that is part of Oberlin College, Ohio, where the German émigré art historian served as professor from 1940 to 1963.

On the occasion of this exhibition the museum devoted an entire issue of the *Bulletin of the Allen Memorial Art Museum* to the Mayer collection, in which Stechow, a keen violinist and pianist, memorably described the painting as "a landscape of such serene beauty and golden softness that its comparison with a Mozart melody will not, the writer hopes, be dismissed as farfetched", reinforcing the comparison by drawing attention to the fact that both artists had died in their thirty-sixth year.[1] Stechow returned to the theme in his 1966 survey mentioned above, remarking on the painting's "serene translucency which evokes the memory of great chamber music".[2]

A rural tranquillity pervades this panoramic view, in which a man on horseback is given directions, a woman is travelling with two children, while a shepherd tends to his flock and in the distance a post wagon is making its way up the hill. Except for the man on horseback, the staffage – on a small scale, as is characteristic of Van de Velde's early landscapes – is largely in shadow, as is the distant view of a small village and its church tower, which contrasts with the sunlight illuminating the cornfield, which is 'populated' by four wheat sheaves, almost as if the artist felt the need for the landscape to have a set of characters of its own. The hazy tones in the far distance alert the viewer to the fact that we have before us a vast expanse, spanned by a blue sky with fleeting clouds, contributing to the sensation of a late summer afternoon.[3]

In this painting Van de Velde adopted what Stechow dubbed the "one wing" composition pattern as it had been developed some thirty years earlier by Salomon van Ruysdael, in which a large tree to the side introduces the spectator to the panoramic view, with the viewer standing, as it were, in the landscape on the level of the foreground, the terrain sloping down towards the middle distance (fig.87).[4] Van de Velde employed this pattern to great effect, enhancing it by making the clouds on the right answer the tree on the left diagonally into the receding space, while the shape of the crowns of the trees on the left follow the contours of the hills behind, as if they are pieces in a jigsaw puzzle. The achievement is all the more remarkable because the painting is on a relatively small scale.

The picture belongs to a group of panoramic views the artist painted in the early 1660s, one of which is cat. no.10, while others include two pictures whose whereabouts are unknown (figs.88 and 94), a painting in the Museum Bredius, The Hague (fig.89) and a beautiful picture in the Residenzgalerie Salzburg (fig.90).[5] There is also an obvious connection to the watercolour discussed under cat. no.48 below. It is noteworthy that the painting under

FIG.88
Adriaen van de Velde, *River landscape*,
early 1660s. Oil on canvas, 44 × 56 cm.
Present whereabouts unknown

FIG.89
Adriaen van de Velde, *Summer landscape,* c.1661.
Oil on panel, 28 × 38 cm. Museum Bredius,
The Hague, inv. no.205-1946

FIG.90
Adriaen van de Velde, *River landscape*.
Signed and dated, lower right: *A.V.Velde 1663*.
Oil on canvas laid down on wood, 33 × 44.5 cm.
Residenzgalerie Salzburg, inv. no.554

FIG.91
Jacob van Ruisdael, *View of cornfields with a
distant town*, c.1670. Signed, lower left: *JvR[...]
dael*. Oil on canvas, 51.4 × 64.8 cm. Los Angeles
County Museum of Art, inv. no.M.2009.106.12

discussion here inspired the slightly older Jacob van Ruisdael, whom Van de Velde must have known personally because he frequently contributed the staffage in his landscapes: Ruisdael's *View of cornfields with a distant town* (fig.91), painted almost ten years later, seems to take its cue from Van de Velde's work, including the motif of a hilly cornfield in brilliant sunlight.[6]

As is often the case with a major work, the painting's provenance is no less illustrious than the work itself. Its earliest known owner is recorded in an eighteenth-century print by Pierre Chenu (fig.86), whose caption tells us it was then in the renowned collection of Heinrich Graf von Brühl in Dresden. In 1769 it was acquired as part of the Brühl collection by Empress Catherine II of Russia and transported to St Petersburg, where it remained until the 1920s. By this time the picture belonged to the Russian state, which in the late 1920s decided to raise funds by selling off works of art from the Imperial collections, including this landscape, which was offered for sale at Rudolph Lepke's auction house in Berlin in 1929. Not long afterwards the painting must have entered the collection of Adolf Mayer, while in the 1950s it belonged to J.C.H. Heldring (1887–1962) in the Netherlands, whose important collection included major works such as Pieter Saenredam's *Interior of St Bavo, Haarlem* now in the J. Paul Getty Museum, Los Angeles.[7]

B.C.

PROVENANCE

Possibly identical to the "*Koore acker*" (Cornfield) by Adriaen van de Velde mentioned in the inventory of the estate of the painter Jan van der Heyden (1637–1712), Amsterdam, which painting was inherited by his daughter, Sara van der Heyden;[8] Heinrich Graf von Brühl, Dresden (when engraved; see fig.86); acquired in 1769 as part of the Brühl collection by Empress Catherine II of Russia, St Petersburg; Pavlovsk Palace Museum, St Petersburg (inv. no.259); sale, Rudolph Lepke's Kunst-Auctions-Haus, Berlin, 4th June 1929 (*Kunstwerke aus den Beständen Leningrader Museen und Schlösser*, II), lot 88; advertised on p.xiv of the September 1929 issue of *The Burlington Magazine* as with Van Diemen & Co., Berlin, Amsterdam and New York; in 1936 recorded as in the collection of Adolf Mayer, The Hague; recorded as with his heirs in 1948; in 1955 recorded as in the collection of J.C.H. Heldring, Oosterbeek; his sale, London, Sotheby's, 27th March 1963, lot 23, bought by Agnew's, London, on behalf of an English private collector (£6,200); thence by descent, until sold in 2006, through Agnew's, London; private collection

EXHIBITIONS

The Hague 1936–37, no.199; Providence 1938, no.56; Detroit 1939, no.40; Oberlin 1948, no.15; Arnhem 1958, no.33; Oslo 1959, no.80; Utrecht 1960, no.22.

REFERENCES

Smith 1834, no.140; Hofstede de Groot 1912, no.67; Charinowa-Zaynowska 1923, p.94; Gerson 1952, p.50 and fig.146; Hannema 1955, no.32a and pl.26a; Van Gelder 1959, fig.78; Stechow 1966, pp.32 and 39; Frensemeier 2001, no.77

NOTES

1 See exh. cat. Oberlin 1948, p.8. Stechow was not, in fact, the first to compare the two; Charles Blanc had already made a point of linking the two exceptionally gifted artists whose lives were prematurely cut off in Blanc 1861, II, 'Adrien van de Velde', pp.13–14.
2 Stechow 1966, p.40.
3 The motif of a man on horseback seen from behind is also frequently found in contemporary works by Philips Wouwerman, for example in his *Dune landscape with horse and wagon and horsemen* of 1660 in the Museum Boijmans Van

Beuningen, Rotterdam, inv. no.2537(OK).
4 Stechow 1966, p.40. As Stechow rightly remarks, Van de Velde's take on the 'one wing' pattern is not strictly 'Dutch' in character, the scenery being too hilly for that, but then the same is true for many of Ruisdael's pictures of cornfields, which one would still instinctively describe as 'Dutch' landscapes.
5 For the Bredius painting, see Blankert 1991, no.171. For the picture in the Residenzgalerie, see Juffinger 2010, I, pp.258–59, and II, p.534.
6 See Slive 2001, no.97.
7 Inv. no.85.PB.225; J.C.H. Heldring sale, London, Sotheby's, 27th March 1963, lot 17.
8 This must remain conjectural because the inventory does not provide any details other than that it was valued at 40 guilders. The *Panoramic summer landscape* is, however, the only work in Van de Velde's extant oeuvre in which a cornfield plays such a prominent role. It is of course possible that the inventory refers to a now lost work. The same inventory also lists a "*Koreacker*" by Jacob van Ruisdael, which may well have been one of the works discussed below. For the inventory of the estate of Van der Heyden, see Bredius 1912, pp.135–36.

10

Hilly landscape with a high road

Oil on panel, 28 × 39 cm
Signed, lower centre: *A.V.Velde f.*
Rijksmuseum, Amsterdam, inv. no.SK-A-444

AMSTERDAM ONLY

It has often been claimed that Van de Velde was a pupil of the landscape painter Jan Wijnants, mainly because Arnold Houbraken reported this in his compendium of artists' lives of 1718–21. The biographer indicated that he had received information on Van de Velde from the artist's daughter.[1] There would thus seem to be good reason to believe him, but he is highly unlikely to be correct, mainly because Wijnants was only four, possibly five, years older than Van de Velde. There is, moreover, precious little in the style of Van de Velde's earliest landscapes to suggest that he was trained by Wijnants. Wijnants's style was anyhow not yet fully developed in the period in which Van de Velde would have received his training. However, in the 1660s Van de Velde frequently contributed the staffage to Wijnants's landscapes (fig.92), and there is no denying that some of Van de Velde's landscapes from the 1660s are indebted to Wijnants, but this must have resulted from their collaboration rather than from any teacher–pupil relationship. If Van de Velde's daughter was indeed Houbraken's source on this subject, she may have conflated accounts of her father's apprenticeship with those relating to his frequent collaboration with Wijnants.

A prime example of Wijnants's influence is the small but sparkling picture under discussion here. The similarities with Wijnants are obvious when we compare it to a similarly crystalline painting by that artist in Zurich, in which Van de Velde contributed the staffage (fig.92).[2] There is evidently scope for confusion in these matters, for in the late nineteenth century Cornelis Hofstede de Groot attributed the Rijksmuseum painting to Wijnants, clearly unaware that it is signed by Van de Velde.[3] And although this type of empty landscape finds its most harmonious expression in the 1660s in the works of Wijnants and Van de Velde, its origins go back to works by slightly older artists such as Jacob van Ruisdael and Philips Wouwerman, who in the 1650s painted similar landscapes in which people play an insignificant role (fig.93).

FIG.92
Jan Wijnants, *Dune landscape with herdsmen and tavern*. Signed, lower right: *JWynants / 1660*. Copper, 67 × 95.5 cm. Kunsthaus Zürich, Betty and David Koetser Foundation

FIG.93
Philips Wouwerman, *View near Haarlem*, 1650s.
Signed, lower left: *PHLSW*. Oil on canvas,
76 × 67 cm. State Hermitage Museum,
St Petersburg, inv. no.853

FIG.94
Adriaen van de Velde, *Dune landscape*, early
1660s. Signed, lower right: *A.v.Velde.* Oil on
canvas, 49 × 63 cm. Present whereabouts
unknown

It is not clear exactly when *Hilly landscape with a high road* was painted. It was long thought to be dated 1663, but when it was cleaned in 1979 no such date was found. The similarities with the painting in Zurich, which is dated 1660, suggest that this picture must date from the early 1660s, as do similarly panoramic landscapes with small staffage by the artists such as a *River landscape* whose present whereabouts are unknown (fig.88) and the *Summer landscape* in the Museum Bredius, The Hague (fig.89), to which can be added another superb picture that is only known from a black-and-white photograph (fig.94). B.C.

PROVENANCE

Sold in 1836 by the art dealer J.A.A. de Lelie (fl. 1,600); by 1850 in the collection of Jan Rombouts, Dordrecht; by descent to Leendert Dupper, Dordrecht, by whom bequeathed to the Rijksmuseum in 1870

EXHIBITIONS

Eindhoven 1948, no.68; Dordrecht 1949–50, no.48; Bolsward 1950, no.57

REFERENCES

Hofstede de Groot 1899, p.169 (as by Jan Wijnants); Hofstede de Groot 1912, no.176 (as possibly only the figures by Adriaen van de Velde); Stechow 1966, p.31 (as by Adriaen van de Velde); Frensemeier 2001, no.81

NOTES

1 Houbraken 1718–21, III, p.90.
2 Waddingham and Klemm 1988, no.29.
3 Hofstede de Groot 1899, p.169.

11

Departure for the hunt, 1662

Oil on canvas, 47 × 61 cm
Signed and dated, lower left: *A.v.Velde f / 1662*
The Schroder Collection

12

Departure for the hunt, 1662

Black chalk, pen in black, grey and brown ink,
grey wash, 24.2 × 35.7 cm
Signed and dated, lower left: *adriaen vande / velde f 1662*
Petit Palais, Musee des Beaux-Arts de la Ville de Paris,
inv. no.D-DUT 1023

FIG.95
Adriaen van de Velde, *Halt on the way*. Signed
and dated, lower left: *A.V.Velde fe 166(6?)*. Oil
on canvas, 89 × 111 cm. The State Hermitage
Museum, St Petersburg, inv. no.6827

When the painting of *Departure for the hunt* was last seen in public, at an exhibition at the Royal Academy of Arts, London, in the winter of 1952–53, Horst Gerson, the reviewer of the show in *The Burlington Magazine*, remarked: "The well-to-do English collector of the eighteenth century loved to possess a good Adriaen van de Velde with his Wouwermans and Aert van der Neer. The brilliant colours and the refined technique of these artists appealed to the cultivated taste of the upper class. '*Le Rendez-vous de Chasse*' (373) and the coast-scene (406) by Adriaen van de Velde are rich examples of this aspect of Dutch art, worth exhibiting again and again."[1] It nevertheless took more than sixty years for *Departure for the hunt* to make another public appearance; here it is shown with a closely related finished drawing (cat. no.12).

The colours in the painting are indeed exceptionally brilliant, even for Van de Velde, who liked to provide his pictures with the occasional colour accent, but in this case he has gone to town, which makes it all the more satisfying that the picture is here reproduced in colour for the first time. Gerson's observation about the eighteenth-century collector is also apt, although in singling out the English collector he shows he was perhaps unaware of the French provenance of *Departure for the hunt*, but the principle he describes was as true in France as it was in England. While it is true that a picture by Adriaen van de Velde was high on the list of eighteenth-century collectors, the appeal of this painting lay as much in its author as in the subject of the aristocratic pursuit of the hunt. Its eighteenth-century owner, Pierre Louis Paul Randon de Boisset (1708–1776), had no fewer than five paintings by Van de Velde, of which three depicted the hunt; his other two hunting pictures are discussed below.

Departure for the hunt includes an unusually large number of people and animals; in all there are sixteen figures, eight horses and 23 dogs, although only the elegantly dressed couple, the man on horseback blowing his hunting horn and the young groom holding the grey horse by its bridle catch the full light and our immediate attention. In the background there are wonderfully observed details such as the dog-handler on the far right whose dog seems to be walking the man rather than vice versa. The beggars to the left are in a deep shadow cast by the wall surmounted by a statue of Hercules, a detail suggesting the riches that lie beyond, no doubt the grand country estate where the elegant couple resides. The painting thus contrasts two extremes of the social spectrum.

It is indicative of Van de Velde's economic use of drawn studies that, except for its hind legs, the grey horse matches the one seen in the artist's *Halt on the way*, probably painted in 1666, in St Petersburg (fig.95), which also depicts a meeting of patrician and humble characters.[2] The bay horse behind is also virtually identical, so that one suspects that a study for the horses existed, which would have indicated the exact shadows giving volume to the animals: note how the shadow cast by the grey horse's left ear is identical in both paintings (fig.96).[3]

In 1660 those who held important governmental functions had successfully challenged the aristocracy's exclusive right to pursue the hunt,[4] which must account for the increasing popularity of hunting pictures. Philips

11

PROVENANCE

Pierre Louis Paul Randon de Boisset sale, Paris, 27th February–25th March 1777, lot 138, bought by "Millon Dailly" (4,999 livres 19); Louis-Antoine-Auguste, duc de Rohan-Chabot sale, Paris, 10th–15th December 1787, lot 34, bought by "Hamon" or "Aumont" (3,981 livres); Prince Galitschin sale, Paris, 28th February 1825, lot 45, bought by "Poignon" (1,600 francs); Thimothée Francillon sale, Paris, 14th April 1828, lot 128, bought by Bon-Thomas Henry (11,540 francs); by 1830 in the collection of Baron J.G. Verstolk van Soelen, with whose collection sold in 1846 through the London art dealer John Chaplin to a consortium of Samuel Jones Loyd, Humphrey Mildmay and Thomas Baring (the picture went to Baring); Thomas Baring, 1st Earl of Northbrook, by whom sold in 1885 to Baron Alfred de Rothschild, Halton; by inheritance to Almina, Countess of Carnarvon; her sale, London, Christie's, 22nd May 1925, lot 100, bought by A. Tooth & Sons (£840); Baron Bruno Schröder, no later than 1938; thence by descent

EXHIBITIONS

London 1938, no.241; London 1952–53, no.373

REFERENCES

Smith 1834, no.32; Waagen 1854, II, pp.185–86; Waagen 1860, pp.409–10; Blanc 1861, II, 'Adrien van de Velde', p.9; Hofstede de Groot 1912, no.169; Bode 1917, p.232; Gerson 1953, p.51; Robinson 1979a, under no.C-1; Frensemeier 2001, no.35

12

PROVENANCE

Pieter Testas the Younger sale, Amsterdam,
29th March 1757, lot 538, bought by Gerard
Hoet (fl. 41); J.W.B. Wuytiers sale, Utrecht, 17th
September 1792, lot 11, bought by "Philip"
(fl. 21.5); Jacob Roelofs sale, Amsterdam, 8th March
1824, Kunstboek E, lot 1; Jonkheer Pieter Hendrik
Goll van Franckenstein, Amsterdam (Lugt 2987;
not in the Goll van Franckenstein sale of 1833);
Frederik Karel Theodoor, baron d'Isendoorn à
Blois van Cannenburg, Vaassen (Lugt 1407); his
sale, Amsterdam, 19th August 1879, lot 171, bought
by Clément for Dutuit (fl. 490); Eugène and Auguste
Dutuit, Rouen (Lugt 709a); bequeathed by Auguste
Dutuit to the city of Paris, 1902

EXHIBITIONS

Zurich 1947, no.119; Paris 2004, no.81

REFERENCES

Lapauze 1907, no.1023; Lapauze 1910, p.139;
Lapauze, Gronkowski and Fauchier-Magnan 1925,
no.1078; Lugt 1927, no.78; exh. cat. Paris 1970a,
under no.124; Robinson 1979a, no.C-1; Plomp
2001, pp.225–26; Frensemeier 2001, under no.35;
Van den Eerenbeemd 2006, no.48

FIG.96
Details of cat. no.11 and fig.95

FIG.97
Jan Blom, *A park with a villa*. Remnants of a
signature and date, lower left: [...] *f 1654*. Oil on
canvas, 67.8 × 62.8 cm. Galleria Luigi Caretto,
Turin

FIG.98
Karel Dujardin, *Departure for the hunt*. Signed
and dated, on the pedestal right: *D W I* [or *L*] *10.
K. DV IARDIN f 16..* [last two digits illegible]. Oil
on canvas, 54.6 × 66.7 cm. IZIKO / ISANG The
South African National Art Gallery, Cape Town,
inv. no.14/14

Wouwerman catered for this market,[5] and Van de Velde must have looked
at his work, but it has rightly been pointed out as significant that when in
1667 Van de Velde and Jan Hackaert decided to reconcile their differences
in a dispute over the sale of some drawings and prints in the presence of a
notary, they called upon the painter Jan Blom to act as a witness,[6] and it was
Blom who in the 1650s painted a good number of park scenes with figures
engaging with hawks and hounds in preparation for (or returning from) the
hunt (fig.97). Blom's paintings are decidedly awkward and a far cry from Van
de Velde's more balanced and naturalistic interpretations of the subject,
but Blom's motifs seem to have inspired his fellow artists. A prime example
of this is a painting by Karel Dujardin in Cape Town (fig.98), which not only
relies on Blom's example but also suggests knowledge of Van de Velde's
composition; Dujardin's picture is in fact a curious mix of the two.[7] Dujardin

FIG.99
Adriaen van de Velde, *Departure for the hunt*.
Signed and dated, lower left: *a.v.velde f / 1664*.
Pen and brown ink and grey wash,
18.2 × 22.2 cm. Musées d'Angers,
inv. no.MTC 4983

FIG.100
Jacques Philippe Lebas after Adriaen van
de Velde, *Departure for the hunt*. Etching,
50.3 × 44.4 cm. Teylers Museum, Haarlem,
inv. no.KG 13329

was Van de Velde's senior by fourteen years, and, while we can often detect the influence of the older artist on the young Van de Velde, in this case Dujardin seems to have looked to his younger colleague for inspiration.

A detailed drawing by Van de Velde shows the same composition (cat. no.12). The function of such drawings is discussed in detail under cat. no.14, as there is some debate as to whether they served as *modelli* – detailed drawings made in preparation for a painting – or *ricordi*, which record a composition. Whatever the case, such a highly finished drawing could be sold by the artist as a work in its own right, albeit rather more affordable than its painted version. As Van de Velde never travelled to Italy, he must have copied motifs such as the Farnese *Hercules* and the Baroque church in the background from prints, or possibly from paintings or drawings by fellow artists.[8] In addition to this finished drawing, there is a sketch in Angers made two years later in which both the beggars and the elegant couple reappear in similar poses and comparable surroundings (fig.99).[9] This drawing was later copied by Jan Verkolje, which testifies to both the subject's and the artist's popularity.[10]

As indicated above, there were two more hunting pictures in Randon de Boisset's collection. One of them is known today only through the eighteenth-century print after it (fig.100),[11] while the other is known only through a compositional study at the British Museum, London (fig.101).[12] The latter picture was recorded in 1946 at the Central Collecting Point, Munich (CCP), and had been confiscated during the Second World War by the Einsatzstab Reichsleiter Rosenberg (ERR) and ordered by Hermann Göring to be removed from the Jeu de Paume, Paris. After the War, on 19th September 1946, it was returned to Paris to its rightful owner, Edouard Alphonse James de Rothschild, and today is still in the family collection. The picture, dated 1662, is published here for the first time (fig.102).[13]

Completing this group of hunting pictures of the early 1660s is a work belonging today to the Croome Heritage Trust (fig.103). Taking its cue

FIG.101
Adriaen van de Velde, *A hunting party in the grounds of a country house*. Signed, lower right: *a.v.velde*. Pen and brown ink and grey wash, 22.1 × 21.6 cm. British Museum, London, inv. no.Oo,11.243

FIG.102
Adriaen van de Velde, *A hunting party in the grounds of a country house*. Signed and dated, lower left: *A.V.Velde / 1662*. Oil on canvas, 51.2 × 42.5 cm. Private collection

FIG.103
Adriaen van de Velde, *Departure for the hunt*. Signed and dated: *A.V.Velde f 1661*. Oil on panel, 38.1 × 49.5 cm. The Croome Heritage Trust

from Wouwerman, this picture is perhaps the least successful of the group, as it follows too closely the older master's propensity for incoherent compositions. It does, however, have the distinction of having once belonged to François Boucher.[14]

Both the Croome Heritage Trust and Rothschild paintings are indebted to hunting pictures by Wouwerman, but Van de Velde evidently made this sub-genre his own, as seen in the main painting discussed here, and in his turn set an example followed not only by Dujardin but also by artists such as Jan Hackaert and Frederik de Moucheron, who took up the more peaceful and decorative aspects of Van de Velde's painting. Two more pictures by Van de Velde depicting the hunt are discussed in this catalogue under nos.28 and 29.
B.C.

NOTES

1 Gerson 1953, p.51.
2 Smith 1834, no.23; Smith 1842, no.5; Hofstede de Groot 1912, no.37; Frensemeier, no.28. See also exh. cat. Dijon 1993, no.35 (with earlier literature).
3 An exact replica of the horse behind (albeit as a grey) is found in a picture of a *Man on horseback asking for the way* whose present whereabouts are unknown; see Frensemeier 2001, no.27, illustrated p.244, fig.56.
4 See Frensemeier 2001, p.58, citing De Jongh 1986, p.262.
5 See, for example, Philips Wouwerman's *Departure for the hunt* in the Musée du Louvre, Paris, inv. no.1953; Foucart 2009, p.298.
6 Frensemeier 2001, p.57, and pp.191–92, doc.16.
7 See exh. cat. Salzburg and Vienna 1986, p.68. Fransen 1997, no.16, argues that, instead, Dujardin influenced Blom, but works with such themes by the latter predate those by Dujardin by at least ten years.
8 See exh. cat. Paris 2004, no.81.
9 Van den Eerenbeemd 2006, no.5. We encounter the seated beggar in a slightly different pose in Jan van der Heyden's *Imaginary town gate with triumphal arch* in the Harold Samuel Collection, Corporation of London, in which the figures were added by Van de Velde; see Sutton 1992, no.27.
10 Sale, Sotheby's, New York, 29th January 2014, lot 161, erroneously inscribed on its reverse: *Verkolje na Breenbergh*. Verkolje also made a variation of this copy, sold Amsterdam, Sotheby's, 8th November 2000, lot 73.
11 Smith 1834, no.26; Smith 1842, no.21; Hofstede de Groot 1912, no.156; Frensemeier 2001, no.208 (who, without providing reasons, catalogues this picture under wrongly attributed paintings). Its provenance is given here because it is easy to confuse it with the provenance of another hunting picture by Van de Velde (fig.102, for whose provenance see footnote 13): possibly Seger Tierens sale, The Hague, 23rd July 1743, lot 132 (fl. 250); possibly in 1752 in the collection of Willem Lormier, and his sale, 4th July 1763, lot 315 (fl. 595); Pierre

Louis Paul Randon de Boisset sale, Paris, 27th February–25th March 1777, lot 139, bought by Alexandre-Joseph Paillet (4,999 livres 19); Bouquet sale, Paris, 26th January 1797, lot 7, bought by Alexandre-Louis Roëttiers de Montaleau (5,001 francs); his sale, Paris, 19th–29th July 1802, lot 167, bought by Bon-Thomas Henry (6,600 francs); sale, Paris, 26th June 1809 and following days, lot 55; Joseph-Guillaume-Jean-Godefroy-Colomb Emler sale, Paris, 27th December 1809, lot 29, bought by Féréol Bonnemaison (7,300 or 7,360 francs); Alphonse-Claude-Charles-Bernardin, comte Perregaux sale, Paris, 8th December 1841, lot 38, bought by Samuel Mawson for Baron James de Rothschild (26,850 francs); his son Baron Edmond de Rothschild, Paris. Frensemeier 2001, no.208, mistakenly mentions a 1935 sale as the last time this painting was recorded, but, as the photograph at the RKD-Netherlands Institute for Art History, The Hague, of that work (David Citroen sale, London, Christie's, 29th November 1935, lot 24) shows, this was in fact a poor copy after Lebas's print. It is this confusion that must have led her to catalogue the work under wrongly attributed paintings.
12 Hind 1931, p.77, no.19; Robinson 1979a, no.B-17.
13 Smith 1834, no.27; Hofstede de Groot 1912, no.155; Frensemeier 2001, no.34. Confusingly, the picture was recorded at the Central Collecting Point as a work by Philips Wouwerman; see the CCP documentation for the painting at the German Bundesarchiv, made available online via the website of the Deutsches Historisches Museum (a work by Wouwerman). Provenance: probably Izaak Hoogenbergh sale, Amsterdam, 10th April 1743, lot 22 (fl. 380); possibly in 1752 in the collection of Willem Lormier, and his sale, 4th July 1763, lot 314 (fl. 825); Pierre Louis Paul Randon de Boisset sale, Paris, 27th February–25th March 1777, lot 140, bought by Charles-Louis de Beauchamp, comte de Merle (4799 livres 19); his sale, Paris, 1st–4th March 1784, lot 72, bought by François Basan for Ange-Joseph Aubert (7,500 livres);

collection of the Earl of Liverpool; exchanged with the late Earl of Liverpool by John Smith at the estimated value of 300 gns in part payment for a picture by Ruisdael; Baron J.G. Verstolk van Soelen, with whose collection sold in 1846 through the London art dealer John Chaplin to a consortium of Samuel Jones Loyd, Humphrey Mildmay and Thomas Baring (the picture went to Baring); Thomas Baring, 1st Earl of Northbrook, by whom sold in 1881 to Baron Alphonse de Rothschild, Paris; his son Edouard Alphonse James de Rothschild, Paris; confiscated during the Second World War; returned to Edouard Alphonse James de Rothschild, Paris, in 1946; thence by descent.
14 François Boucher sale, Paris, 18th February–9th March 1771, lot 1827, bought by the marquis de Saint-Céran (1079 livres 19): "*Un départ de chasse, composé d'une dame sur un cheval blanc, proche d'une chaumière; un homme qui lui parle, a son chapeau à la main; deux autres hommes sont assis à terre & jouent avec trois chiens; il y a proche d'eux un domestique habillé de rouge, qui tient un cheval par la bride, pendant que son maître accommode ses bottines; un peu plus loin deux chiens. Sur un second plan une femme & trois hommes à cheval, un domestique & un chien. Plusieurs arbres sur différens plans, & un beau ciel. Ce bon tableau est peint sur bois, par Adrien Vanden Velde. sur bois, 14 pouces de haut, sur 18 de large.*" Both the description and the dimensions match the Croome Heritage Trust picture, which is not listed in Smith 1834 and Hofstede de Groot 1912, but is catalogued in Frensemeier 2001, no.33, who was not, however, aware of the Boucher provenance. In 1952–53 the picture was exhibited at the Royal Academy, London, and, according to the exhibition catalogue (exh. cat. London 1952–53, no.478), it was bought by the Earl of Coventry in 1801. Indeed, in 1801 a "Landscape with Horses and Figures going out to the Chase" on panel by Adriaen van de Velde was in the John Purling sale, London, 16th–17th February 1801, lot 89, where it was bought by Charles Birch (£57 15s), presumably for the Earl of Coventry.

13

Pastoral scene, 1663

Oil on canvas, 48.5 × 62.5 cm
Signed and dated, lower right: *A.V.Velde. f. / 1663*
Museo Thyssen-Bornemisza, Madrid,
inv. no.417 (1978.56)

14

Pastoral scene at a waterfall, 1662

Point of brush, black and grey ink, 24.2 × 35.4 cm
Signed and dated, lower left: *A.V.Velde. f. / 1662*
Morgan Library & Museum, New York,
inv. no.I, 149

While most of Van de Velde's early works depict Dutch landscapes in which one can detect the influence of Paulus Potter, the artist soon also turned his attention to Italianate landscapes. An early instance is the *Horseman at a ford, asking the way of a herdswoman* of 1659 in the Royal Collection (see fig.11 on p.19),[1] which is clearly inspired by the example of his slightly older colleague Karel Dujardin. Because there is no record of Van de Velde ever having visited Italy, he must have taken his cue from Italianizing works by fellow artists or from prints or drawings depicting Italian landscapes. It is difficult to say why Van de Velde turned to such subjects, although one could point to the increasing presence of Italianizing painters in Amsterdam since the mid-1650s, including Nicolaes Berchem, one of the most successful artists in that genre, and one would suspect that in the 1660s there was a healthy demand for this type of painting. The picture in Madrid (cat. no.13) is a prime example of an Italianate work by Van de Velde. Painted in 1663, a few years later than the painting in the Royal Collection, it shows the archetypal pastoral subject of a herdsman and herdswoman resting in idyllic surroundings.

One conspicuous element in this picture seems to confirm that Van de Velde did not see this kind of landscape at first hand: the mountain in the background is rather bizarrely placed among gently sloping hills, which suggests that it sprang from the imagination rather than from first-hand experience. In his finished drawing of what at first may seem to be exactly the same composition (cat. no.14), this mountain has a far more plausible shape. In fact the mountain is only one of many differences between the painting and drawing. In the former Van de Velde has extended the entire composition vertically upwards and horizontally to the right, with the result that the horizon has been moved upwards, while the sky has been extended to allow the trees more space, so much so that the tree on the far right in the drawing has moved even further to the right to make space for another tree, not found in the drawing, and two men accompanied by three dogs, likewise not seen in the drawing. In the painting the Italianate building in the background has been moved a little closer to the viewer, its more prominent position emphasizing that this is a southern landscape. The overall effect is that, while in the drawing the pastoral idyll takes place in a relatively enclosed space, in the painting the same intimate gathering of resting herdsmen and animals is situated in a much more monumental setting.

This exercise in spotting the difference between painting and drawing serves a purpose. There is some discussion as to whether Van de Velde made such elaborate drawings in preparation for a painting, that is to say that they are *modelli*, or whether in such drawings he recorded finished paintings, known as *ricordi*.[2] In light of the many differences between drawing and painting, there seems little room for doubt that this particular drawing is indeed a *modello* on which the artist elaborated while painting what is in essence the same composition. Further to this argument, it is difficult to ignore the fact that the drawing is dated 1662, while the painting is clearly marked 1663. It would seem odd to document a painting in a drawing after it and then record the wrong date, which contradicts the very essence of what

13

PROVENANCE

Antony Sydervelt sale, Amsterdam, 23rd–24th April 1766, lot 9, bought by the Amsterdam dealer Jan Yver (fl. 1,810); probably J. Hoofman, Haarlem; probably inherited by his daughter Maria Hoofman, Haarlem, and bought in 1844 with the collection by the London dealer C.J. Nieuwenhuys; Robert Stayner Holford, London and Westonbirt, Gloucestershire; inherited by his son George (subsequently Sir George) Lindsay Holford, Dorchester House, London; his sale, London, Christie's, 17th–18th May 1928, lot 66, bought by the Amsterdam dealer D.A. Hoogendijk on behalf of Baron Heinrich Thyssen-Bornemisza (£650); inherited by his daughter, Baroness Adolphe Bentinck, by whom sold, London, Christie's, 25th March 1977, lot 61, bought by the London dealer Thomas Agnew (£12,000), from whom acquired by the Collection in 1978

EXHIBITIONS

London 1887, no.53; Munich 1930, no.335; Paris 1970b, no.41; Düsseldorf 1970–71, no.56; London 1978, no.26; Novosibirsk 1988, no.6

REFERENCES

Terwesten 1770, p.511, no.9; Smith 1834, no.4; Waagen 1854, II, p.201; Hofstede de Groot 1912, no.216; Benson 1927, II, no.146; Heinemann 1937, I, no.436 (mistakenly as by Nicolaes Berchem); Müllenmeister 1973–81, III, no.466; Robinson 1979a, under no.C-2; exh. cat. Paris, Antwerp, London and New York 1979–80, p.146; Borghero 1981, no.315a; Borghero 1986, no.315a; Gaskell 1990, no.106; Pita Andrade and Borobia Guerrero 1992, no.417; Frensemeier 2001, no.97

14

PROVENANCE

Jonkheer Johan Goll van Franckenstein the
Younger, Amsterdam (Lugt 2987); his sale,
Amsterdam, 1st July and following days, 1833,
Album T, lot 1, bought by Samuel Woodburn
(fl. 900); Samuel Woodburn, London; possibly his
sale, London, Christie's, 12th–14th June 1860,
lot 1537, bought by "Tiffin"; C.J. Nieuwenhuys,
Brussels and London (according to Charles Fairfax
Murray); Robert Stayner Holford, London and
Westonbirt, Gloucestershire (Lugt 2243); his sale,
London, Christie's, 11th–14th July 1893, lot 676,
bought by George Salting (£46); George Salting,
London; Charles Fairfax Murray, London and
Florence; from whom purchased in 1909 through
Galerie Alexandre Imbert, Rome, by Pierpont
Morgan (1837–1913), New York; his son, J.P.
Morgan, Jr. (1867–1943), New York

EXHIBITIONS

Ann Arbor 1964, no.65; Paris, Antwerp, London and
New York 1979–80, no.123

REFERENCES

Fairfax Murray 1905–12, I, no.149; Robinson 1979a,
no.C-2; Andrews 1985, under no.RSA 378; Gaskell
1990, p.450; Pita Andrade and Borobia Guerrero
1992, under no.417; Fusconi et al. 1992, fig.272;
Frensemeier, under no.97; Turner and Stampfle
2006, no.295; Van den Eerenbeemd 2006, no.37

FIG.104
Adriaen van de Velde, *Cows, goats and sheep*.
Signed and dated, lower left: *A.v.velde / 1662*.
Pen and ink and wash, 17.6 × 26.1 cm.
Musée du Louvre, Paris, inv. no.23066

FIG.105
Adriaen van de Velde, *Mercury, Argus and Io*.
Reported as being signed and dated *A.V.Velde f.*
1663 (today no longer visible). Oil on canvas,
71 × 91 cm. Liechtenstein, The Princely
Collections, Vaduz–Vienna, inv. no.689

a *ricordo* is meant to do. When Van de Velde signed such a drawing, this may merely indicate that he intended to sell it after it had served its purpose. It is surely also significant that in another drawing dated 1662 Van de Velde explored the same groupings of animals (fig.104); we see them rehearsed almost verbatim, albeit in different surroundings and in a slightly different configuration.[3]

Throughout this catalogue mention is made of instances where Van de Velde reused motifs for which he relied on drawn studies. It is therefore not surprising that there is still another work that features exactly the same group of a recumbent cow and sheep (fig.105). This time the artist depicted the mythological subject of Mercury, Argus and Io, one that was especially suitable for Van de Velde because the story cannot be told without the depiction of animals (see also his painting of *The Migration of Jacob* in the Wallace Collection, London, discussed in the Introduction on pp.24–26). The painting has come down to us in no fewer than three versions, and all are definitely by Van de Velde himself.[4] Illustrated here is the *Mercury, Argus and Io* in the Liechtenstein collection, which is believed to have once been dated 1663, the same year as the pastoral picture in Madrid; the other two versions are in a private collection (formerly J. Paul Getty Museum, Los Angeles) and in the Petit Palais, Paris, respectively dated 1664 and 1665.[5] It should be pointed out here that the recumbent cow also appears in our cat. nos.27, 30, 33, 35 and 52.

As can be seen from their provenance, our picture and drawing have lived apart for most of their lives but in the nineteenth century were briefly reunited in the collection of Robert Stayner Holford. They soon went their separate ways again and are once more reunited in this exhibition, which is probably only the third time they have met. B.C.

NOTES

1 Smith 1834, no.109; Hofstede de Groot 1912, no.51; White 1982, no.202; Frensemeier 2001, no.94.
2 Van den Eerenbeemd 2006, pp.13–15.
3 See Turner and Stampfle 2006, no.295, esp. notes 7 and 8, where attention is also drawn to the fact that the Morgan drawing's inscribed date of 1662 contradicts the idea that it would be a *ricordo* rather than a *modello*.
4 Repetitions are rare in the artist's oeuvre, and should usually alert one to the possibility that they were painted by a pupil or follower, as is explained in the Introduction on p.34.
5 Hofstede de Groot 1912, nos.20 and 21; Frensemeier 2001, nos.13, 13a and 13b. For the Liechtenstein painting, see exh. cat. Zurich 1987, no.102.

15

Landscape with cattle and figures, 1664

Oil on canvas, 125.7 × 167 cm
Signed and dated, lower right, on tree log:
A.V.Velde. / 1664
The Fitzwilliam Museum, University of Cambridge,
 inv. no.88

16

Shepherd and shepherdess with cattle by a stream, 1668

Oil on canvas, 64.3 × 78.2 cm
Signed and dated, centre left: *A.V.Velde f / 1668*
The Royal Collection / HM Queen Elizabeth II,
inv. no.RCIN 404137

FIG.106
Adriaen van de Velde, *Study of a standing
woman*. Red chalk, 25.6 × 15.2 cm. The
Pushkin State Museum of Fine Arts,
Moscow, inv. no.4739

While Van de Velde made some paintings of Italianate scenes in his early
years, mainly inspired by the example of Karel Dujardin, in the course of the
1660s he increasingly turned to such subjects, presumably because there was
a ready market for them. One of the most distinctive examples is the painting
of 1664 in the Fitzwilliam Museum, Cambridge (cat. no.15), which, at about
twice the size of most of Van de Velde's pastoral pictures, is also his most
ambitious painting of this type. In 1869 the Reverend William Bennett Pike,
fellow of Downing College, Cambridge, reported in the *Cambridge University
Gazette* that the painting had been bequeathed to the Fitzwilliam Museum:
"I can hardly speak in terms of sufficient admiration of the landscape by
Adrian Van de Velde given to the Museum by Mr. Vansittart. It is a first-rate
example of that rare and choice master, and takes rank among the very best
pictures in the gallery."[1] Today the painting still hangs in a prominent place
in the Museum's gallery devoted to Dutch paintings.

The work speaks of Van de Velde's self-confidence not just because
of its size, but also in its daring use of overlap between the various parts
of the composition. Such overlap occurs in his early works, but in those
Van de Velde usually kept the overall composition relatively simple to
avoid having to deal with the complexities of convincingly conveying a sense
of depth between the figures or figures and animals. In the Cambridge
picture he no longer shows any such restraint, while his clever use of light
ensures that the viewer does not get lost in what could so easily have been
a cluttered composition. As in his *Farm with a dead tree* of 1658 (cat. no.2),
the artist has placed the various figures and animals in an oval-shaped spotlit
area, as if we are witnessing a scene acted out on a stage, but in the earlier
picture the overall distribution of light is still fairly even, with all elements
casting similar shadows as a result of the sunlight coming from low on the
left. By contrast, in the later picture our attention is drawn to the brightly
illuminated man on horseback who turns to the equally well-lit herdswoman
sitting on the ground wearing a bright blue dress. It is only then that we
realise that the woman's appearance has also caught the attention of a young
man sitting next to her, who is rather obscured by being in shadow. So is the
cow behind him, which functions as a counterweight to the brightly lit cow
on the left. Goats, sheep and dogs, some in shadow, some catching the light,
are distributed throughout the scene, but the cow at left and goat at right,
in mirrored poses and bracketing the central scene, break down the 'fourth
wall' by looking straight at the spectator.

Much the same characteristics are found in the pastoral picture in
the Royal Collection (cat. no.16).[2] Although smaller than the painting in
Cambridge, it is still a sizeable work compared to most such scenes by the
artist. Painted four years later, it is also characterized by a strictly controlled
distribution of light and shadow to structure the composition. The scene's
warm Italian light complements the classicizing composure and grace of the
two protagonists, while the reflection of the herdswoman and cow drinking
from the shallow stream gives the composition stability. A goat appears in the
lower left corner, as it does in the painting in Cambridge and, for that matter,
in the same pose as in the latter in the pastoral picture in Madrid

15

PROVENANCE

Edward King; bequeathed to his widow, Susanna
King, 1807; bequeathed to her late husband's
niece, Anne Windsor, later Countess of Plymouth,
1820; bequeathed to her great-nephew, Augustus
Arthur VanSittart, 1850; by whom given to the
Museum, 1864

EXHIBITION

London 1879, no.155

REFERENCES

Smith 1834, no.1; Pike 1869, p.159; Hofstede de
Groot 1912, no.50; Gerson 1960, p.131; Robinson
1979a, no.B-6; Frensemeier 2001, no.92; Van den
Eerenbeemd 2006, nos.57 and 64

16

PROVENANCE

Collection of Gerrit Braamcamp, Amsterdam, 1766; his sale, Amsterdam, 31st July 1771 and following days, lot 236, bought by Jan van Diemen for Nicolaas Doekscheer (fl. 1,800); his sale, Amsterdam, 9th September 1789, lot 51,[3] bought by Cornelis Ploos van Amstel (fl. 3,000); Pieter de Smeth van Alphen sale, Amsterdam, 1st and 2nd August 1810, lot 105, bought by Pierre-Joseph Lafontaine (fl. 7,650); his sale, London, 12th June 1811, lot 60, bought by Francis Charles Seymour-Conway, 3rd Marquess of Hertford, for the Prince of Wales, later George IV (£1,890)

EXHIBITED

London 1946–47, no.380; London 1971–72, no.32; Edinburgh and London 2004–05, pp.162–63

REFERENCES

Bastide 1766, p.95; Smith 1834, no.5; Waagen 1838, II, p.366; Jameson 1844, p.58, no.156; Waagen 1854, II, p.16; Waagen 1860, p.410; Hofstede de Groot 1912, nos.211 and 270a; Bille 1961, II, pp.58–58a and pp.124–25, no.236; Van Eeghen 1971, p.175; White 1982, no.208; Frensemeier 2001, no.99; White 2015, no.208

FIG.107
Adriaen van de Velde, *Landscape with herders and man on horseback*. Signed and dated, lower right: *A.V.V. / 1664*. Black chalk on parchment, 16.4 × 14.4 cm. Sale, Amsterdam, Christie's, 14th November 1994, lot 69

FIG.108
Adriaen van de Velde, *Landscape with cattle and figures*, c.1664. Black chalk, grey wash, 19.4 × 30.9 cm. Sale, Weinmüller, Munich, 20th–21st May 1941, lot 897

FIG.109
Adriaen van de Velde, *Study of a seated woman*. Inscribed, lower right: *A v velde*. Red chalk, 29.2 × 17.9 cm. Amsterdam Museum, inv. no.TA 10342

(see cat. no.13). We also encounter the same herdswoman wearing exactly the same clothes as in the Cambridge painting. She is, moreover, accompanied by a dog whose pose is identical to that in the earlier work. Even if their coats are different, the animal must be based on the same study, although this has not survived. There is, however, a preparatory study in red chalk for the herdswoman in the Royal Collection picture (fig.106).[4]

One would expect a similar figure study to have existed for the seated woman in the painting in Cambridge, but no such drawing is known, although the model appears in several of Van de Velde's figure studies, including one in the Amsterdam Museum (fig.109) in which she makes the same gesture with her left hand as in the painting.[5] In the drawing Van de Velde has shown her left arm a second time in the lower left corner, viewed from a slightly different angle, which shows the hand almost as it does in the painting. He may well have drawn the model again, this time having positioned himself a good deal further to the right, which would have resulted in a figure study that he could have used for the painting.

There are two composition studies that are related to the painting in Cambridge. One is a drawing in chalk that shows the central group but in reverse (fig.107).[6] Apart from the tree, the painting follows this study in almost every detail, so that it is quite possible that Van de Velde made a counterproof of this drawing. The other is a quick sketch in chalk and wash in the same direction as the painting and with almost all the elements of the final composition in place (fig.108).[7] We also see the tree on the right, but the original tree is still accorded its slightly awkward position in the centre of the composition, from where it was wisely removed in the painting in Cambridge. Matters are complicated by the fact that there is another, much smaller, version of the painting, last recorded in 1912 in a private collection in Paris (fig.111).[8] Painted on panel, it measures only some 30 by 35 cm. and includes the pollarded willow in the centre. It may thus be that the drawings were made in preparation for the smaller painting, which follows the drawings more closely, and that Van de Velde decided against the inclusion of the willow in the larger version, in which he also added a recumbent cow next to the man on horseback and some sheep in the left background.

FIG.110
Details of cat. nos.30 and 15

FIG.111
Adriaen van de Velde, *Landscape with cattle and figures*, c.1664. Signed: *A. v. Velde*. Oil on panel, c.30 × 35 cm. Present whereabouts unknown

Some seven years later we encounter the man on horseback in the painting in Cambridge again in a very closely related if reversed version in Van de Velde's famous painting of *The Hut* in the Rijksmuseum, Amsterdam (see cat. no.30 and fig.110). Although there are slight differences in the pose of both horse and rider, there are sufficient similarities between the two to infer that Van de Velde made two very similar studies of the same man on horseback, of which he then made a counterproof. The main difference between the riders is that one sits sideways while the other straddles the horse. Nevertheless they rest their hands on the animal in much the same way, while especially the treatment of the shadows on the horse's coat, which beautifully convey the horse's anatomy, is nearly identical. Indeed, it would have sufficed to draw the alternative study without even reaching for a fresh sheet; as fig.109 shows, Van de Velde sometimes made alternative studies of a subject on the same sheet. A counterproof would then have made yet another application of the very same study possible. B.C.

NOTES

1 Pike 1869, p.159.
2 There is a copy in Jagdschloss Grunewald, Berlin; see Börsch-Supan 1964, no.19 (as by Dirck van Bergen). A poor copy of just the central group is in the Musée des Augustins, Toulouse; see Fiozzi 2004, p.104, no.34 (as attributed to Adriaen van de Velde).
3 At the time of the Doekscheer sale, Jurriaen Andriessen (1742–1819) made a drawing with copies after six seventeenth-century paintings in the Doekscheer collection, including this

painting by Van de Velde; see Van Eeghen 1971, p.175 and pp.178–79, figs.5 and 6.
4 This has not been noted before and is thus not listed in Robinson 1979a, nor is the connection made in the recent catalogue of the Dutch and Flemish drawings preserved in Moscow (Sadkov 2010, no.405).
5 See Broos and Schapelhouman 1993, no.145 (and no.146, the counterproof of this drawing). No painting has as yet been connected to this study; it has not been noticed before that the

herdswoman does make an appearance in a painting by Dirck van Bergen in Ham House, Richmond (see Introduction, fig.42 on p.33).
6 Van den Eerenbeemd 2006, no.64.
7 Ibid., no.57.
8 Hofstede de Groot 1912, no.55 (as in the collection of S. de Jonge, Paris); Frensemeier 2001, no.92a. In 1905 the painting was with the Paris dealer Charles Sedelmeyer (1837–1925), who illustrated the work in cat. Paris 1905, no.43.

17

Figures in a deer park

Oil on panel, 21.1 × 28.6 cm
The Museum of Fine Arts, Houston,
The Edward and Sally Speelman Collection

This exquisite picture is Van de Velde's smallest painting of a deer park
that is usually identified as the Koekamp, in the south-western end of the
Haagse Bos in The Hague, a spot that was popular with artists from all
over the country. It belongs to a series of paintings all depicting more or
less the same place. The most famous example is a painting of 1666 in the
Gemäldegalerie, Berlin (fig.113), but, despite its high reputation, it is not
included in this exhibition because it is in rather poor condition,[1] even if the
painting reproduces rather well and is often illustrated in handbooks devoted
to seventeenth-century Dutch painting because of its superb composition and
glorious depiction of sunlight.[2] The present *Figures in a deer park* is on a much
smaller scale, and it is therefore all the more remarkable that it is as powerful
an image as its larger sibling in Berlin. The atmosphere in this picture is more
brooding, the late afternoon sun only occasionally penetrating the dense
foliage of the trees, resulting in a beautiful play of light on individual leaves
high up in the trees and on the edges of the tree trunks below.

It seems not to have been noted before that the Berlin painting was once
in the important collection of Jeronimus Tonneman (1687–1750) and that
its subject was already identified as the Koekamp when his collection was
sold in 1754.[3] Not only should such early references be taken seriously, as
they often reflect knowledge that was handed down over generations (and
in 1754 we are within a century of the creation of the work), but we also
have the benefit of still being able to visit the Koekamp in The Hague today,
which in the seventeenth century was already a green belt protected by law.
Even though in the nineteenth century the site was re-landscaped in the
English style, it is still very recognizable as the location painted by Van de

FIG.112
Adriaen van de Velde, *The Koekamp in The Hague*,
mid-1660s. Signed, lower right: *A.V.Velde f.*
Ink, 28.5 × 45.6 cm. Amsterdam Museum,
inv. no.TA 10348

FIG.113
Adriaen van de Velde, *The Koekamp in The Hague*.
Signed and dated, lower left, on the fence:
A. V. Velde. f / 1666. Oil on canvas laid down on
panel, 63 × 78 cm. Gemäldegalerie, Staatliche
Museen zu Berlin, inv. no.922C

FIG.114
Joris van der Haagen, *View of the Koekamp outside The Hague*. Inscribed, lower left: *dit is inde koekam. buyts de haegh*. Signed and dated, lower centre: *JvHagen 1653*. Brush, 40 × 55.9 cm. Rijksprentenkabinet, Rijksmuseum, Amsterdam, inv. no.RP-T-1884-A-343

FIG.115
Paulus Potter, *Departure for the hunt*. Signed and dated, lower left: *Paulus Potter.f: 1652*. Oil on canvas, 60 × 76 cm. Gemäldegalerie, Staatliche Museen zu Berlin, inv. no.872A

Velde. For further proof we can turn to several drawings of the Koekamp by contemporaries that show closely related scenes. Illustrated here is a drawing of 1653 by Joris van der Haagen, which is identified as the Koekamp in an inscription by the artist himself (fig.114). A very free sketch by Van de Velde recording the exact spot depicted (and amplified) in the painting in Berlin has also survived (fig.112).[4] It may well have been the work of Van der Haagen that inspired Van de Velde to depict the Koekamp, as no other landscape artist so frequently depicted the Haagse Bos in both paintings and drawings, some of which date from at least a decade before Van de Velde turned to the subject,[5] although the example of Paulus Potter is possibly even more pertinent (fig.115).

As in the painting in Berlin, in our picture we are looking at a clearing in a fenced-off wooded area in which deer are roaming. An elegant couple accompanied by their page are taking a stroll. One deer is fleeing the scene while another between the trees observes the human intruders. Light plays on the dense foliage of the trees, catches the grass in the far background and bounces off some of the obliquely placed slats in the fences. Through the trees in the distance we can just about discern the red roofs of small buildings behind the enclosure, possibly a woodsman's cottage. They are much clearer in the Berlin version of the scene, but the fact that we are looking at precisely the same spot is evident from the identical arrangement of the fences, while we see the same trees lined up on the right, including the old tree leaning into the clearing at the end of this row and the fairly young Y-shaped tree next to it. The main difference is that in *Figures in a deer park* we are further away from the scene.

Van de Velde reused motifs in different paintings on many occasions, but one would not perhaps have expected this practice to extend to his depiction of trees. The gnarled tree further to the right must have been based on a

FIG.116
Adriaen van de Velde, *Peasants with cattle fording a stream*, late 1660s. Oil on canvas, 32.4 × 37.8 cm. The National Gallery, London, inv. no.NG868

FIG.117
Adriaen van de Velde, *Cattle and sheep resting under trees, a shepherdess asleep*. Signed and dated, lower right: *A.V.Velde.f.1668*. Oil on panel, 37.6 × 42.8 cm. The Royal Collection / HM Queen Elizabeth II, inv. no.RCIN 404815

FIG.118
Style of Adriaen van de Velde (Jacob Koninck the Younger?), *The Koekamp in The Hague*, 1660s. Oil on canvas, 92.5 × 124.5 cm. Gothenburg Museum of Art, inv. no.GKM 1044

FIG.119
Here attributed to Jacob Koninck the Younger, *Cattle in a wood*, 1660s. Apocryphally signed and dated, lower left: *AvVelde/f.1656*. Oil on canvas, 35.7 × 40.6 cm. Philadelphia Museum of Art, inv. no.Cat. 602

specimen recorded in a now lost drawing, as we find the same tree in at least two other paintings with entirely different compositions (figs.116 and 117).[6]

This brings us to what could be dubbed the 'Koekamp conundrum'. We find the same tree in two more paintings, one in Gothenburg and the other in Philadelphia (figs.118 and 119),[7] which are closely related to the Koekamp compositions discussed above but are unlikely to be by Van de Velde himself because of their lack of detail, uncertain execution and uncharacteristically brownish colouring. There are also technical reasons to believe they cannot be by Van de Velde. Most of the green passages in these two works seem to have survived intact, that is to say that they have not turned blue because of the fading of the yellow pigments, something that unfortunately plagues the greens in most authentic works by Van de Velde, almost functioning as an unintended signature. Closely related to these two paintings is a work in Rotterdam (fig.120), signed *J. Konin ....* There can be no doubt this is the Jacob Koninck mentioned by Arnold Houbraken in the third volume of his compendium of artists' lives (1721): "... Jacob Koning, a pupil of Adriaen van de Velde. Initially imitating the manner of his master, he painted

fine landscapes and animals."[8] The artist in question is Jacob Koninck the Younger.[9] The work in Rotterdam not only corroborates Houbraken's statement, but also throws up the possibility that this Jacob Koninck was responsible for the Göteborg and Philadelphia pictures, although it is tempting to see in the former the contribution of Van de Velde himself at least in the depiction of the figures, which are virtually indistinguishable from figures that are certainly authentic.[10]

To complete this round-up of paintings of the Koekamp, mention should be made of a painting depicting the site that was last listed in 1912 on the basis of descriptions of the work in early auction catalogues, as its whereabouts were even then unknown.[11] It is currently in a private collection and is published here for the first time (fig.121). It is a relatively large work, of rather better quality than those in Göteborg and Philadelphia, and shows the same spot from a very different angle. It bears what appears to be an autograph Van de Velde signature, so that we have to entertain the possibility that this is an authentic work by the artist. Sadly it is difficult to assess the painting because it is covered in an old, degraded varnish that has substantially darkened it. If the painting were to be cleaned, a better idea of its status could be formed.

As things stand, Van de Velde's certain depictions of the Koekamp are the relatively large painting in Berlin and the beautiful little work shown in this exhibition.[12] The most important characteristic of *Figures in a deer park*, however, is that, although it is identifiable as the Koekamp, it is far more than a topographical record, evoking a mood that transcends the particulars of the motif. It is, in other words, a prime example of the way Van de Velde managed to turn a landscape into art. B.C.

PROVENANCE

Mrs John Ashley, London; sale, London, Sotheby's, 31st May 1907, lot 51, bought by Sir Hugh P. Lane (£168); Edward Speelman

EXHIBITIONS

Zurich 1987, no.101; Washington 1998, no.58

REFERENCES

Hofstede de Groot 1912, no.172; Wheelock *et al.* 2000, no.17; Frensemeier 2001, no.148

NOTES

1 Smith 1834, no.138; Hofstede de Groot 1912, no.80; Frensemeier 2001, no.147. Its state of preservation is severely compromised by the fact that the yellow pigments in many green passages have almost completely faded, which means that they now appear as bluish green or even a fairly bright blue (see also the Introduction, p.32).

2 The painting is prominently illustrated in, for example, Haak 1984, p.471, and Slive 1995, p.211.

3 See Jeronimus Tonneman sale, Amsterdam, 21st October 1754 and following days, lot 22: "*Een kapitaal stuk van Adriaan van de Velde, zynde een zeer aangenaam gezigt in de Koekamp, zeer rykelyk gestoffeert, met Koeijen, Paarden, Schaapen, en Beelden, zo heerlyk en schoon, dat nooit beter by de Liefhebbers van hem gezien is, hoog 25, breed 30 duim*" (A capital piece by Adriaen van de Velde, being a very pleasant view of the Koekamp, very richly furnished with cows, horses, sheep and figures, so glorious and beautiful, that never was anything better by him seen by lovers of art, height 25, width 30 *duim*). The Amsterdam *duim* is 2.6 cm, so that the measurements of the Tonneman painting amount to 65 × 78 cm, which almost exactly matches the Berlin painting's measurements of 63 × 78 cm. The painting was bought for the enormous sum of fl. 1,500 by the Rotterdam collector Jan Bisschop (1680/81–1771), whose collection was bought en bloc in 1771 by Adrian Hope (1709–81) and his nephew John Hope (1737–84) of the mercantile and banking dynasty of Scottish descent residing in Amsterdam. The descendants of the latter are the earliest owners mentioned for the painting in the catalogue of the collection of the Gemäldegalerie, Berlin; see Bock 1996, p.123. For the acquisition en bloc of the Bisschop collection in 1771, see Van Wiersum 1910, esp. p.175, where Van de Velde's *Koekamp* is indeed listed.

4 Broos and Schapelhouman 1993, no.137.

5 For an excellent overview of paintings and drawings of the Haagse Bos and the Koekamp, see Dumas 1991, pp.177–87.

6 Smith 1834, nos.8, 82 and 112; Hofstede de Groot 1912, nos.69, 210 and 261; Frensemeier 2001, nos.95 and 93. See also MacLaren 1991, p.442, and White 1982, no.207, and White 2015, no.207. See also Frensemeier 2001, p.55.

7 For the unsigned Göteborg painting see Frensemeier 2001, no.145 (as by Van de Velde), and for the Philadelphia painting Scott 1994, p.68 (erroneously as by Jacob Koninck the Elder). I would like to thank Eva Nygårds of the Göteborgs Konstmuseum for sharing with me information from the files kept for the painting, and Malin Borin, conservator at the Göteborgs Konstmuseum, for sharing with me her thoughts on its condition.

8 Houbraken 1718–21, III, p.286: "*… Jacob Koning, een Discipel van Adr. vanden Velde. Dees in 't eerste de handelinge van zynen meester nabootsende, schilderde fraje Lantschappen en Beesjes ….*"

9 He was the son of Jacob Koninck the Elder (1614/15–after 1690), who was the brother of the better-known landscape painter Philips Koninck (1619–1688).

10 Matters are confused by the fact that the museums in Rotterdam and Philadelphia both incorrectly identify the artist responsible for these works as Jacob Koninck the Elder. The unsigned Göteborg painting was offered for sale as a work by Van de Velde by the art dealer Douwes in Amsterdam in 1934, but on that occasion judged by Horst Gerson to be by Jacob Koninck (although, again, mistakenly Jacob Koninck the Elder); see the Hofstede de Groot index cards at the RKD-Netherlands Institute for Art History, The Hague, box no.329, card no.1701415. The Göteborg painting may well be identical to a picture of much the same dimensions twice sold at auction in the eighteenth century in France as a work by Van de Velde: see the Alexandre-Joseph Paillet sale, Paris, 13th–14th November 1775, lot 5, bought by Louis-François de Bourbon, prince de Conti (2,700 livres): "*L'entrée du bois de La Haye; sous les arbres, au bord d'un chemin, se voit un grouppe de chasseurs; sur le second plan, plusieurs animaux répandus sur l'herbe enrichissent ce tableau dont le site est intéressant, & le feuillé des arbres d'une touche savante; ce morceau est connu & regardé comme un des plus capitaux de ce Maître, sur toile, Largeur 46 p., hauteur 32 & demi*"; and subsequently his sale, Paris, 8th April–6th June 1777, lot 417, bought by "*Martin Peintre rue St Jean en greve*" (900 livres): "*Le bois de la Haye dans lequel on voit plusieurs animaux, sur toile, 2 pieds 10 pouces de haut, sur 3 pieds 9 pouces de large*". Gabriel de Saint-Aubin (1724–1780) famously illustrated the latter sale catalogue with small sketches of the lots in a copy preserved at the Bibliothèque Nationale de France, Paris (Reserve 8-YD-5276), but the one for lot 417 is so sketchy that it cannot prove or disprove such an identification. It should also be pointed out here that if in the 1660s Jacob Koninck the Younger painted wooded landscapes in the style of Van de Velde, we have to entertain the possibility that it is he who is responsible for a drawing of a wooded landscape signed *J.Koning.1665* in the Frits Lugt Collection, Paris, where it is currently given to his father. Its style is reminiscent of that of Jan Lievens, something that is equally true for Van de Velde's drawing of the Koekamp (our fig.112); for the Lugt drawing, see exh. cat. Paris and Haarlem 1997–98, no.75, where similar sheets in the Museum Boijmans Van Beuningen, Rotterdam, and the Kupferstich-Kabinett, Dresden, are mentioned.

11 Hofstede de Groot 1912, no.338; not in Frensemeier 2001.

12 A poor copy by a follower of *Figures in a deer park* was sold at Christie's, New York, 30th September 2005, lot 12.

18

Haymakers resting in a field, c.1663

Oil on canvas, 31 × 37 cm
Private collection, United Kingdom

FIG.122
Philips Wouwerman, *Peasants in the fields, hay harvest*, c.1655–60. Signed, lower left: *PHILS W* (PHILS in monogram). Oil on panel, 41.3 × 35.9 cm. Dulwich Picture Gallery, London, inv. no.DPG182

This small picture once enjoyed tremendous fame. William Buchanan (1777–1864), one of the most successful early nineteenth-century British art dealers, briefly owned Van de Velde's *Haymakers resting in a field* in 1817, and rightly observed in his memoirs published in 1824 that "there are sometimes pictures in which a master surpasses himself". He assured the reader that his "opinion of this picture is supported by that of the best connoisseurs".[1] Ten years later, the London art dealer John Smith (1781–1855) agreed that "it is impossible to commend too highly this excellent production of art; whether the eye be directed to the composition, the expression, the drawing of the figures, the colouring, or execution, each will be found to possess a degree of perfection rarely attained",[2] while four years afterwards Gustav Waagen (1794–1868) wrote that "this picture, which is of the first class, is equally attractive for the genuine rural feeling, the beautiful drawing, the full tone, and the most delicate and exquisite finish".[3]

There can be no doubt that this is an exceptional work. Its subject-matter stands in stark contrast to the *Departure for the hunt* discussed under cat. no.11, with its portrayal of the landed gentry; here we see farm labourers, although the emphasis in this serene painting is on the moment they take a break from work. The group in the foreground is reminiscent of the gathering seen in the beachscape in The Hague (cat. no.8), the date of which is difficult to decipher, but it was probably painted in 1663. The picture under discussion here is one of the few undated pictures in the exhibition, but there are good reasons to believe that it too must date from that year. In addition to the resting people, it shares with the painting in The Hague a low horizon that allows a bright blue sky to set the tranquil mood, which points to the earlier 1660s. More specifically, the painting chimes well with Van de Velde's dated pictures for the year 1663, when he seems to have experimented with new subject-matter (see Introduction, pp.20–23); he had never painted this subject before, nor did he ever return to it.

It says a great deal about Van de Velde's artistic abilities that, on the one occasion that he turns to the subject of haymakers, he immediately rises far above the efforts of his colleagues. The theme was painted on several occasions by artists such as Philips Wouwerman and Johannes Lingelbach, but, however attractive or well painted their examples may be in detail, their compositions are somewhat incoherent, if not chaotic (figs.122 and 123). Van de Velde, by contrast, has arranged his group of people and the cart laden with hay in a tightly controlled pyramidal composition that provides the picture with a firm centre of gravity. He has also ingeniously placed the cart and horses at an oblique angle; had they been parallel to the picture plane, the effect would almost certainly have been that of a tableau being acted on a stage. Instead, we feel we can engage with the scene before us

FIG.123
Johannes Lingelbach, *Haymaking*, early 1660s. Signed, lower left: *J: Lingelbach*. Oil on panel, 41.3 × 53.4 cm. Museumslandschaft Hessen Kassel, Gemäldegalerie Alte Meister, inv. no.GK 364

FIG.124
Adriaen van de Velde, *Studies of a peasant woman and a boy*. Signed, lower left: *A.v.d.Velde f.*
Red chalk, over black chalk, 21.1 × 32.7 cm.
British Museum, London, inv. no.1875,0612.14

FIG.125
Adriaen van de Velde, *Studies of a peasant woman and a boy*. Counterproof of fig.124, 20.5 × 27.5 cm.
British Museum, London, inv. no.1990,1215.3

and can lose ourselves in observing how the various individuals enjoy this moment of repose, from the pensive man smoking his pipe and the boy quenching his thirst to the seated woman at the heart of the composition whose bright blue skirt finds its echo in the blue socks of the young boy taking a nap on the right.

The only real incident in the picture concerns the man with his back to the viewer flirting with a woman. It is perhaps not too far-fetched to think that his pose is based on a study of a young man in the British Museum, London (fig.124), even if it is not an exact match. The counterproof made of this drawing, also in the British Museum (fig.125), shows a very similar pose, and one wonders whether Van de Velde adapted the figure to incorporate him in this painting.[4] Alternatively, there may have been a now lost drawing of the same model but in a pose that exactly matches our figure in reverse; a counterproof of that drawing could then have served as Van de Velde's guide. Be that as it may, it is probable that most of the protagonists in this picture were prepared in figure studies, which were then skilfully combined into a scene in which an intricate play of overlapping figures creates a coherent composition.

Both the subjects and execution of some of Van de Velde's pictures display an elegance and refinement that belongs to a general trend in Dutch painting of the second half of the seventeenth century. We can observe this tendency in the landscapes of Philips Wouwerman, for example, or the genre painting by artists such as Gerard ter Borch and especially the so-called *fijnschilders*, but also in the late works of Jan Steen. It could be argued that Van de Velde's *Haymakers* equally gives a foretaste of what was to come; just as the artist's red-chalk drawings seem to anticipate the seductive beauty and elegance of drawings in the same medium by eighteenth-century artists such as François Boucher and Jean-Honoré Fragonard, it is probably not going too far to

consider our picture as the ancestor of the harvest scenes painted a century later in England by George Stubbs (fig.126). Even if there is no evidence that Stubbs knew of this example, it is difficult to imagine that he was not familiar with similar pictures of the Dutch school. Van de Velde's painting must have enjoyed a considerable reputation in the eighteenth century; in 1779 Aert Schouman copied the painting in watercolour,[5] while in 1795 it was engraved in France (fig.127).

The provenance of *Haymakers resting in a field* bears witness to the picture's fame in the nineteenth century, when it was considered a highly desirable work by a string of important collectors, fetching high sums when it changed hands.[6] It is easy to understand how the aristocratic subject-matter of a picture such as the *Departure for the hunt* (cat. no.11) appealed to certain collectors, but they were clearly equally enamoured of the refined manner in which Van de Velde treated this more humble subject. The two pictures in fact spent time in the same collection, as they were both bequeathed by Baron Alfred de Rothschild (1842–1918) to his daughter Almina, Countess of Carnarvon (1876–1969), the two paintings rubbing shoulders as neighbouring lots in the sale of her collection in 1925.[7] After more than ninety years, they meet again in this exhibition. B.C.

FIG.127
Jean Jacques de Boissieu after Adriaen van de
Velde, *Haymakers resting in a field*. Inscribed,
lower left: *DB.J.J. / slup: aqua forti 1795*;
lower right: *adrien Vanden Velde*. Etching
with drypoint, 29.5 × 37.6 cm. Bibliothèque
Municipale, Lyon, inv. no.F18BIO001494

PROVENANCE

Marin sale, Paris, 22nd March 1790 and following days, lot 58, bought by Joseph-Alexandre Lebrun (6499 livres 19); François-Antoine Robit sale, Paris, 6th December 1800 and following days, lot 85; François-Antoine Robit sale, Paris, 11th–18th May 1801, lot 162, bought by Jean-Louis Laneuville for Armand Séguin (9,900 francs); Charles-Jacques Chapelain de Séréville sale, Paris, 22nd–24th January 1812, lot 29, bought by Jean-Baptiste-Pierre Lebrun (10,010 francs); Charles-Maurice de Talleyrand-Périgord, prince de Bénévent sale, Paris, 9th July 1817, lot 40 (scheduled for sale, but all 46 pictures were purchased privately beforehand for 320,000 francs by William Buchanan and all but five brought to England; see Buchanan 1824, II, pp.305–08); purchased from Buchanan for 300 gns before 1819 by Alexander Baring, created Baron Ashburton in 1835, and by descent to Francis, 5th Baron Ashburton, whose collection was purchased en bloc by Agnew's and other London dealers in August 1907; Baron Alfred de Rothschild; by inheritance to Almina, Countess of Carnarvon; her sale, London, Christie's, 22nd May 1925, lot 101, bought by Tancred Borenius (£441); purchased by Viscountess Harcourt as a present for her son-in-law, Alexander Francis St Vincent Baring, 6th Lord Ashburton, probably in 1925; his sale, London, Christie's, 23rd April 1993, lot 19 (£276,500); Galerie Sankt Lucas, Vienna, winter 1993–94; private collection

EXHIBITIONS

London 1871, no.207; London 1890, no.115

REFERENCES

Buchanan 1824, II, pp.310, 313 and 341–42, no.40; Smith 1834, no.54; Waagen 1838, II, p.280; Waagen 1854, II, p.108; Blanc 1857–58, II, p.196; Blanc 1861, II, 'Adrien van de Velde', p.16; Hofstede de Groot 1912, no.118; Bode 1917, p.233; Gibson 2000, p.129; Frensemeier 2001, no.26

NOTES

1 Buchanan 1824, II, p.342.
2 Smith 1834, pp.191–92.
3 Waagen 1838, II, p.280.
4 The online collection database of the British Museum casts doubts on the attribution of the drawing to Van de Velde and, moreover, doubts the counterproof is of this particular drawing. There is no reason whatsoever to doubt the authenticity of the drawing, which is entirely characteristic and of superb quality, while an exercise in Photoshop in which the counterproof is reversed and overlaid on top of the drawing shows that they are an exact match, up to the tiniest details. Where there are minute differences between drawing and counterproof, they are clearly the result of the latter having been worked up in chalk in certain areas. See www.britishmuseum.org/research/collection_online/search.aspx, searching for the inventory numbers 1875,0612.14 and 1990,1215.3 (accessed 21st November 2015).
5 Aert Schouman after Adriaen van de Velde, *Haymakers resting in a field*. Signed and dated, on the reverse: *A.S. / 1779*. Watercolour, 23.3 × 29.7 cm. Royal Museums of Fine Arts, Brussels, inv. no.4060/3335.
6 The painting also has the distinction of being one of only a few works by Van de Velde that were illustrated in Charles Blanc's *Histoire des peintres de toutes les écoles: Ecole hollandaise* of 1861, in an engraving by François Auguste Trichon; see Blanc 1861, II, 'Adrien van de Velde', p.13.
7 Almina, Countess of Carnarvon sale, London, Christie's, 22nd May 1925, lots 100 and 101.

19

The Annunciation, 1667

Oil on canvas, 128 × 176 cm
Signed and dated, lower right: *A.V.Velde. f / 1667*
Rijksmuseum, Amsterdam, inv. no.SK-A-2688

AMSTERDAM ONLY

20

Kneeling female nude

Black chalk, highlights in white chalk,
on grey paper, 23.8 × 18 cm
Ashmolean Museum, University of Oxford,
inv. no.WA1863.291

21

St John the Evangelist Mourning

Black chalk, highlights in white chalk, on grey
prepared paper, 40.6 × 25.5 cm
Signed(?), lower left: *A.v.d. Velde / f* (black chalk)
Kupferstichkabinett, Staatliche Museen zu
Berlin, inv. no.KDZ 2393

Of all the paintings of Adriaen van de Velde, those least appreciated by the art-loving public have always been his religious scenes with large figures. Adriaen's first biographer, Arnold Houbraken, kept his own counsel, leaving his readers to form their own verdict: "And what he could accomplish with his brush, beyond the little cows, bullocks, sheep and landscape paintings, is displayed by the diverse paintings of the Passion in the Roman Catholic Church in Amsterdam in the Spinhuissteeg, and in the church opposite the Appelmarkt, where a half-life-sized Deposition can be seen".[1] That is all; the reader can decide for himself. The paintings of the Passion to which Houbraken refers are five paintings that Adriaen van de Velde produced in the 1660s for the clandestine church 't Hart.[2] Marietta Frensemeier describes them in her study of 2001 as a low point in the artist's oeuvre. In her view, they prove that making a history painting with large figures lay beyond Van de Velde's artistic powers. Honesty compels her to concede that the paintings are in appallingly bad condition and that it is also possible that they were in part painted by another hand, but her final verdict remains damning. Nineteenth-century authors were sometimes equally dismissive. In the relevant volume (1834) in John Smith's *Catalogue Raisonné of the Works of the Most Eminent Dutch, Flemish, and French painters*, the wildly enthusiastic exposition on the large Amsterdam group portrait (see cat. no.22) is followed by a curt entry on a *Christ in Gethsemane* (offered for sale in 2002),[3] which concludes: "This is an unsuccessful attempt at historical painting, and can only be viewed with regret by the amateur of the general works of this accomplished painter".[4] Of the narrative religious scenes with large figures, *The Annunciation* has generally enjoyed a milder critical reception, although it too has sometimes attracted scorn – but we shall come to that later.

The story of the Angel Gabriel descending to earth to tell Mary that she will soon be with child and give birth to the son of God is told in only one of the Gospels, Luke (1:26–38). Although Protestant Bible readers might have read this story any day of the week, it was rarely depicted in seventeenth-century paintings of the Northern Netherlands, probably because many Protestants saw the emphasis on Mary's role as the recipient of divine grace as veering too close to Papist hagiolatry. We can conclude that Van de Velde's painting was almost certainly made for a Catholic client.

The painting is an odd combination of virtuoso technique and a slightly clumsy *mise-en-scène*; it leaves the viewer with mixed feelings. The angel is the least successful of the two figures. There is nothing in the appearance of this celestial being to suggest that he has just flown down to earth at top speed to announce the birth of God's son. He delivers his tidings in a serene contrapposto with his left leg advanced. He makes a rather vague, languid gesture over his shoulder towards something indeterminate behind him. His attire appears to have been borrowed from the costumes collection of the local Chamber of Rhetoric, which also served as an amateur dramatic society. He wears a white shirt that leaves his right shoulder uncovered, with a blue satin tunic over it, from beneath which emerges a gold ochre satin robe. If we imagine the figure without his large swan's wings (which, like the satin, are certainly painted with masterly skill), he looks as if he would be more at home

FIG.128
Hendrick ter Brugghen, *The Annunciation*.
Signed and dated, lower right: *HTBrugghen 1629*.
Oil on canvas, 216.5 × 176.5 cm. Stedelijk
Museum de Hofstadt, Diest

FIG.129
Pieter de Grebber, *The Annunciation*.
Monogrammed and dated on the lectern:
PdG 1633. Oil on panel, 85 × 112.5 cm.
Present whereabouts unknown

in a pastoral scene or a bacchanal by Nicolas Poussin than in a Bible story. Comparison with an *Annunciation* by Hendrick ter Brugghen that was painted less than forty years earlier shows how such a figure might be depicted (fig.128).[5] Ter Brugghen's angel is surrounded by streaming draperies – as if he had grabbed the nearest large cloth to cover his heavenly nudity while hastening to depart – and has landed amid the loud rustle of wings. With a keen sense of drama he points upwards: his tidings come straight from Heaven. His face, seen in profile, is cast almost entirely in shadow, lending him an intangible, mysterious air. The Haarlem artist Pieter de Grebber also resolved the problem of the angel's apparel, in particular, far more elegantly than Van de Velde.[6] In De Grebber's 1633 painting (fig.129) the angel wears a gold-embroidered, dazzling black brocade dalmatic over a white alb, the vestments of a priest about to say mass. Compared to the angels depicted by his two predecessors, Van de Velde's Gabriel cuts a sorry figure. Moreover, while Van de Velde's angel is surrounded by clouds, to suggest that he has just descended from Heaven, his clouds look suspiciously like the brownish-grey smoke from a damp wood fire. To make matters worse, the angel casts a black shadow on the clouds. In other words, the heavenly light that the angel should radiate appears instead to emanate from a spotlight.

In contrast to this gawky angel, Van de Velde's Virgin Mary is highly original, a marvellous invention. In Ter Brugghen and De Grebber she submits to the divine will, eyes closed, hands pressed together or crossed before her breast in prayer. In Van de Velde she is active, self-possessed, as indeed is reflected in the text of the Gospel. The gesture she makes with her hands, although possibly reflecting a certain alarm, seems mainly to express surprise, and she is about to say "How shall this be, seeing I know not a Man?". She has no intention of taking the divine message on trust without challenging it: the angel will have to convince her. It is Mary who is in control in this scene; the angel is little more than an extra. She is dressed like a Madonna by Guido Reni or Sassoferrato, in pinkish-red and dark blue, with a light yellow veil over her head.

We can trace the development of some of the artist's small landscapes with figures almost from one stage to the next, on the basis of initial sketches, highly finished designs and figure studies. In the case of the religious paintings with large figures, however, we have almost no material of this kind. Just one figure study can confidently be linked to *The Annunciation*, a nude study for the Virgin Mary in the Ashmolean Museum, Oxford (cat. no.20). The positions of the arms, hands and upper torso coincide almost completely with those of the Virgin Mary in the painting. The pose of the legs seems to be in reverse image: perhaps Van de Velde used a counterproof of the drawing in Oxford for this section. In the drawing Mary's head is angled more upward and her gaze appears to be directed rather higher than eventually in the painting. This could suggest that Van de Velde initially intended to place the angel a little higher in the picture plane. It is safe to assume that the artist also produced a detailed study for a fully clothed Virgin Mary; no such drawing has been preserved, however. Still, we can gain an idea of what a monumental study of draperies for a large religious painting would have looked like by

19

PROVENANCE

Jacob Hoofman sale, Amsterdam, 19th October 1818 and following days, lot 54, bought by "L'Année" (fl. 42); Viscount Weymouth sale, London, 18th–22nd April 1828, lot 455, bought in (£157 10s); anonymous sale, London, 28th–29th May 1829, lot 85, bought by "Cap Peat" (£120 15s); anonymous sale, London, 11th April 1832, lot 64, bought in; anonymous sale, London, 9th May 1832, lot 128, bought in (£79 16s); Exeter Hall (Strand) sale, London, 27th–28th July 1832, lot 76, bought in (£79 16s); Exeter Hall (Strand) sale, London, 14th–15th March 1833, lot 152 (£52 10s); G. Robinson sale, London, 12th July 1834, lot 115, bought by

Edward W. Lake (£57 15s); his sale, London, 7th April 1848, lot 151, bought by J.S. Woodin (£40 19s); Robert Langton Douglas, London, from whom bought by the Rijksmuseum in 1913 for fl. 400; on loan to Museum Amstelkring, Amsterdam, 1954; transferred by the Rijksmuseum to the Dienst voor 's Rijks Verspreide Kunstvoorwerpen, 1959; returned to the Rijksmuseum, 1996

EXHIBITIONS

Amsterdam 1934, no.65; Rome 1956–57, no.306; Washington, Detroit and Amsterdam 1980–81, no.66; Rotterdam and Frankfurt 1999–2000, no.64

REFERENCES

Smith 1834, no.108; Van Eijnden and Van der Willigen 1816–40, III, p.423; Hofstede de Groot 1912, no.3; Plietzsch 1916, p.129; Martin 1936, I, pp.110–11; Heppner 1948, p.119; Slive 1956, p.8; De Wolf 1967, p.8; Blankert 1968b; Van Thiel 1976, p.557; Robinson 1979a, nos.D-8, D-9, D-10 and D-11; Robinson 1993, pp.58 and 62; Slive 1995, p.212; Van Eck 1999, p.81; Frensemeier 2001, no.10

PROVENANCE

Bequeathed by Francis Douce, 1834

REFERENCES

Parker 1938, pp.96–97, no.225; Robinson 1979a,
no.D-8; Robinson 1993, p.58; Frensemeier 2001,
under no.10

20

studying an impressive drawing in the Kupferstichkabinett in Berlin (cat.
no.21). Drawn in black chalk, with highlights here and there in white chalk,
on grey prepared paper, this drawing occupies a unique position in Van de
Velde's figure studies, not only because of its size – it is 40 cm in height –
but more especially because of its strong evocation of tragedy. The beardless
man uses the hem of his cloak to wipe away his tears: this cannot be anything
but a study for the figure of John the Evangelist, either in a scene of the
crucified Christ with Mary and John or in a Lamentation. The drawing
evidently served as an aid when the artist painted the figure on the far left
in his *Lamentation* (fig.130), one of the five Passion scenes mentioned above.
In the painting, however, John has mutated into an elderly bearded man
wearing a little cap, probably Joseph of Arimathea. The monumental cloak
that adorns John in the drawing, falling in heavy folds, metamorphosed into
an impenetrable jumble in the painting.

The art historian William W. Robinson believed that a *Standing male nude*
in red chalk was a study for the angel in the *Annunciation*. A direct connection

PROVENANCE

Unknown

REFERENCES

Zoege von Manteuffel 1927, p.55; Bock and
Rosenberg 1930, I, p.292; Robinson 1979a,
no.D-3; Frensemeier 2001, under no.9

21

can be ruled out, since there is not a single detail in the drawing that
corresponds to the painted angel. The only shared element is the somewhat
hesitant hand gesture, so at most it is conceivable that the drawing was a study
for an earlier version of the angel. Nonetheless, there is a striking similarity
between the facial features of the man in the drawing and the angel in the
painting: the artist evidently used the same model here as for the drawing
that eventually served as the preparatory sketch for the painted angel.[7]

FIG.130
Adriaen van de Velde, *Lamentation*, 1664.
Oil on canvas, 88 × 138 cm. Augustinian Order,
on loan to Museum Ons' Lieve Heer op Solder,
Amsterdam

The painting's provenance cannot be traced back any further than the early nineteenth century. We do not know who ordered the painting or for what location. Given its size, it too must have been destined to hang in one of the Roman Catholic clandestine or house churches in Amsterdam.

Scarcely a word was written about the painting in the nineteenth century. This was because after the Hoofman sale in 1818 it roamed from one auction house and private collection to the next in a journey that lasted almost a century. In 1834 Smith included the work in his *Catalogue Raisonné*, but without comment – suggesting that he never actually saw it. It was only after the painting had been purchased by the Rijksmuseum in 1913 that it entered the art-historical literature. It did not exactly receive a warm welcome. The harshest criticism came from Willem Martin (1876–1954): "A visitor to the Rijksmuseum who gazes upon the *Annunciation* by Adriaen van de Velde, which is painted entirely in the Bolognese style, will be astonished that this aristocrat among landscape painters could ever have wanted to make such a thing".[8] The verdict of Albert Heppner published in 1948 was a little kinder: "Anyone who becomes acquainted with the best of them [i.e. of the religious paintings with large figures], namely the 'Annunciation' (in the Rijksmuseum, Amsterdam), will undoubtedly be surprised by the nobility and taste with which it is painted. Were it not for a slight coldness of expression and colour, one would be put in mind of an Italian work. For the aim here has been to pursue the Italian ideal of beauty and grace, which inspired all those who had not fallen under the spell of the apostate Caravaggio. If Adriaen van de Velde had not painted a single other religious painting, he would have been thought capable of playing a significant role in this genre."[9] However, these kind remarks are unfortunately followed by another tirade against the five reviled Passion scenes, which appear to have permanently wrecked Van de Velde's reputation as a history painter. It was not until the end of the twentieth century, in the exhibitions *God, Saints and Heroes* (1980–81) and *Dutch Classicism in Seventeenth-century Painting* (1999–2000), that the painting once again received the recognition it deserved – that of a work that, while not entirely successful as a large history painting, is nonetheless in many respects an admirable venture into this field. M.S.

NOTES

1 "*En wat zyn penceel buiten het Koetjes, Osjes, Schaapjes en Lantschapschilderen vermocht, toonen de verscheiden Passystukken in de Roomsche Kerk tot Amsterdam in de Spinhuissteeg, en in de Kerk over de Appelmarkt, waar een afneming van 't Kruis half leven, groot te zien is*"; Houbraken, III, p.91.

2 Frensemeier 2001, pp.105–09 and nos.5–9; see also Van Eck 1999, pp.80–82, and Van Eck 2008, pp.178–81.

3 Not in Frensemeier 2001; sale Christie's, London, 10th July 2002, lot 51; Smith 1834, no.101.

4 Smith 1834, no.101.

5 Exh. cat. Washington, Detroit and Amsterdam 1980–81, no.13.

6 Ibid., no.47.

7 Robinson 1979a, no.D-11; exh. cat. Amsterdam 1993, no.64. Frensemeier 2001, under no.12, observes that the drawing was used for the man on the far right in *The Ferry* in the Staatliches Museum, Schwerin.

8 "*Wie in het Rijksmuseum de geheel in Bologneeschen trant geschilderde Annonciatie van Adriaen van de Velde aanschouwt, verbaast zich dat deze aristocraat onder onze landschapschilders ooit zóó iets heeft willen maken*": Martin 1936, I, pp.110–11.

9 "*Wie het beste daaruit, de 'Annunciatie' (in het Rijksmuseum, Amsterdam) leert kennen, zal ongetwijfeld verbaasd zijn over de noblesse en den smaak, waarmede deze geschilderd is. Als er niet een zekere kilheid in uitdrukking en kleur heerschte, dan zou men aan een Italiaansch werk denken. Want hier is naar het Italiaansche ideaal van schoonheid en bevalligheid gestreefd, dat allen bezielde die niet in den ban van den afvalligen Caravaggio waren geraakt. Had Adriaen van de Velde verder niets aan religieuze doeken geschilderd, dan zou men hem in staat geacht hebben op dit gebied een rol van beteekenis te spelen*": Heppner 1948, p.119.

22

Portrait of a family in a landscape, 1667

Oil on canvas, 148 × 178 cm
Signed and dated, lower left: *A.V.Velde.f.1667*
Rijksmuseum, Amsterdam. On loan from the
City of Amsterdam (A. van der Hoop Bequest),
inv. no.SK-C-248

23

Seated woman with a child on her lap

Red chalk, over traces of a sketch in graphite
or black chalk, 19.8 × 16 cm
Rijksprentenkabinet, Rijksmuseum, Amsterdam,
inv. no.RP-T-1888-A-1523

24

A dog

Black chalk, heightened in white, on greyish-brown
paper, 15.1 × 20.7 cm
Signed and dated, lower right: *A.V.Velde 1670*
(pen and brown ink)
The Fitzwilliam Museum, University of Cambridge,
inv. no.PD.758.1963

Nineteenth-century writers were unanimous in their verdict: *Portrait of a family in a landscape* was a masterpiece; it was Adriaen van de Velde's magnum opus. John Smith, who probably studied the painting first-hand when it was put up for auction in London in 1833, set the tone. His description of the work, which he assumed, along with his contemporaries and many who came after him, to be a self-portrait of the artist with his family, concluded with the words: "This is unquestionably the most capital production known by the master; and from the careful attention which he has bestowed on every part, together with the portraits of himself and family being introduced, it may reasonably be supposed that he intended it to be his *chef-d'oeuvre*. Be this as it may, it must ever possess very considerable interest, on account of the agreeable recollections it gives of so eminent a painter, independent of its excellence as a work of art."[1] All those who wrote about the painting in the nineteenth century admired it for the same reasons – its impressive format and the loving attention with which the humblest of details were painted. Every writer was conscious that he was gazing at the artist himself, surrounded by his loved ones. The eccentric Lord Ronald Gower went furthest in his empathic interpretation: "... the rather pensive and melancholy-looking artist bears on his features that look of a short life which we fancy can also be traced in Paul Potter's portraits, the anxious and somewhat harassed look we think we see in both these over-hardworking painters, who during their brief lives created so much that cannot cease to please all who love nature for its own sake, in reality as in art".[2]

In spite of all this, the identification of the painting as a self-portrait is a nineteenth-century invention; it is first mentioned in the catalogue of the 1824 sale of the paintings of the Rotterdam collector Gerrit van de Pals (1742–1839). Curiously enough, four years earlier, Adriaan van der Willigen, writing about Van de Pals's "splendid little collection of paintings", described this work as: "An elegant family, scions of the current owner of the scene, depicted in a charming landscape; this great master thus shows himself here in the capacity of a portrait painter".[3] The author had obtained his information from first-hand sources. On 4th March 1820, Van der Pals's son-in-law Gerardus Johannes Verburgh wrote to Van der Willigen: "And there is a delightful landscape by A. v de Velde, its staffage consisting of a family in which the small child that sits on the lap of a maid or wet nurse must have been his great-great-grandmother".[4] The painting is believed to have ended up in the possession of Gerrit van de Pals through the female line; his maternal grandmother was Elisabeth de Clercq, who came from an affluent Amsterdam family of Mennonite merchants.[5] That was probably the circle in which the portrait was made. The question that remains is why Van der Pals should have decided to sell this painting – an heirloom – in 1824. Was the owner in such dire financial straits that the family's interests had to be set aside? And why was the work marketed with a new, completely unfounded, identification? Was the new description expected to boost the price? If so, it was a successful strategy: the painting fetched 10,000 guilders, an astonishing sum for the time.

PROVENANCE

The marks of John Barnard (Lugt 1420), Jacob de Vos Jbzn (Lugt 1450), the Vereniging Rembrandt (Lugt 2315) and the Rijksprentenkabinet, Rijksmuseum (Lugt 2228), that are mentioned in exh. cat. Amsterdam and Washington 1981–82 are not on the drawing itself but were evidently on an old mounting board that can no longer be found; Jacob de Vos Jbzn sale, Amsterdam, 22nd–24th May 1883, lot 540; purchased with the support of the Vereniging Rembrandt, 1888

EXHIBITIONS

New York, Chicago, Boston and Amsterdam 1972–73, no.97; Amsterdam and Washington 1981–82, p.118 and no.93; Vancouver 2009, pp.196–97; Paris 2009–10, no.122

REFERENCES

Robinson 1979a, no.D-12

23

PROVENANCE

Gerrit van der Pals sale, Rotterdam, 30th August 1824, lot 40, bought by Christianus Johannes Nieuwenhuys (fl. 10,000);[6] his sale, London, 10th May 1833 and following days, lot 131, bought in (£1,375 10s); bought from Christianus Johannes Nieuwenhuys, London, by Adriaan van der Hoop in 1834 (£958) and bequeathed to the City of Amsterdam in 1854; Museum Van der Hoop, 1854–85; on loan to the Rijksmuseum, Amsterdam, since 1885

EXHIBITIONS

Amsterdam 1845, p.11, no.27; Amsterdam 1876, no.3384; Eindhoven 1948, no.69; Bolsward 1950, no.58; Tilburg 1953, no.93; Zürich 1953, no.161; Rome and Milan 1954, no.166; New York, Toledo and Toronto 1954–55, no.83; Amsterdam 2004–05, p.101 and no.187; Melbourne and Kobe 2005–06, pp.188–89; Shanghai 2007–08, no.60; Vancouver 2009, pp.196–97; Paris 2009–10, no.98; Boston and Kansas City 2015–16, no.15

REFERENCES

Van Eijnden and Van der Willigen 1816–40, III, p.477; Murray 1824, pp.21–22; Smith 1834, no.100; Smith 1842, no.23; Immerzeel 1842–43, III, pp.162–63; Oltmans 1845–46, p.10; cat. Amsterdam 1855, no.126; Texier 1857, pp.200–01; Kramm 1857–64, V, p.1687; Thoré-Bürger 1858–60, II, pp.2 and 89–92; Waagen 1860, pp.410–11; Van Vloten 1874, pp.330–31; Gower 1875, pp.116–17; Woltmann and Woermann 1888, II, p.747; Michel 1888, p.282; Bode 1906, p.14; Hofstede de Groot 1912, no.29; Bode 1917, p.224; Wiersum 1922, p.10; Zoege von Manteuffel 1927, p.71; Martin 1936, II, p.337; Goldscheider 1936, p.39; Van Hall 1963, no.2146:1; Stechow 1966, p.32; exh. cat. Amsterdam 1973, under no.97; Van Thiel 1976, p.557; De Zeeuw 1979, p.529; Robinson 1979a, under no.D-12; Robinson 1979b, p.495; exh. cat. Amsterdam and Washington 1981–82, pp.116 and 118; Fromentin 1984, p.1166; exh. cat. Amsterdam, Boston and Philadelphia 1987–88, p.11; Hoogenboom 1993–94, p.143; Gibson 2000, p.110; Frensemeier 2001, no.19; Middelkoop 2008, p.251; Sebag Montefiore and Armstrong-Totten 2013, p.169

22

24

PROVENANCE

Sale, London, Christie's, 31st July 1947, lot 218,
bought by Colnaghi for Sir Bruce Ingram (£5 5s);
bequest of Sir Bruce Ingram, 1963

EXHIBITIONS

Washington etc. 1959–60, no.79; Rotterdam and
Amsterdam 1961–62, no.91

For most of the nineteenth century, the painting enjoyed considerable fame. However, as the realisation took hold that the figures depicted could not possibly be the artist and his family – if only because of the group's composition – it gradually fell from grace. Even Wilhelm Martin, who greatly admired Adriaen van de Velde, mentioned it only in passing, to substantiate his claim that Van de Velde felt less at home in large formats than in cabinet paintings. The painting has been exhibited recently on several occasions, and the accompanying publications chiefly emphasize its importance as a document of social history. This rather sells the painting short: in fact it occupies a special place in the history of seventeenth-century Dutch painting. While group portraits in the open air are not uncommon in Holland's Golden Age, in most cases the landscape functions solely as the backdrop in a theatrical setting.[7] Van de Velde has clearly made an effort to incorporate his figures in a natural manner into the landscape. This has been particularly successful in the case of the boy with the dog. The boy – who appears to be about eight years old – is only just strong enough to control the dog, which is energetically pulling and sniffing its way along the path. While larking around with the dog he has lost his hat, which has fallen on the ground. The boy looks sideways at his little sister, who is sitting on the nursemaid's knee, hoping that she sees how well he is managing the dog. She does not notice, but looks the viewer straight in the eye. Her parents too are mainly preoccupied with posing, although the mother does seem a bit distracted by the goings-on with the dog.

The clothes of those portrayed merit further consideration.[8] The man wears a *kasack*, a coat that reaches to just above the knee, made of thick brown material – a windproof, weatherproof garment that was often used for horse riding. In a similar vein he has sturdy chamois gloves trimmed with black fur. Contrasting with these items are his rather dandyish lace jabot with a black velvet ribbon, silk stockings and low black shoes. The outfit is a mix of 'sensible' clothes chosen for country life and elegant (though unpretentious) city apparel. To some extent, the woman's clothes display a similar mix. Over a red underskirt she wears a skirt of a somewhat brighter red, which is slightly raised all around, evidently to prevent the hem from getting muddy during the walk. She wears a close-fitting brown bodice over a white blouse, and over it a large, simple-looking black shawl. On her head she has a simple white cap. Thus far her costume makes a fairly rural impression; and yet her light gloves are strikingly elegant city garments. The boy, like his father, is dressed in 'sensible' brown clothes, but he is the most fashionable member of the group. He wears an extremely short jacket, whose bottom buttons have been left undone, revealing his white shirt, and very loose-fitting, fashionable knee breeches. The maid or wet nurse is the figure who is posing most emphatically in her Sunday best. The bright blue skirt and attractive lace bonnet were surely the best items in her wardrobe, and her apron has come straight from the linen-press, judging by the sharp creases in the material. The apron is marked with the initials *CL*, embroidered in red. Marks like this were used to identify linen when it was sent to the washerwoman. Aprons would have been part of a household's linen, so these initials may assist some future investigation into this family's identity. The child sitting on the maid's lap is dressed in miniatures of the maid's own costume – a skirt, an apron, a short jacket and a cap. Still, class distinctions are *de rigueur*: the little girl wears bracelets of precious pearls with a bright red ribbon on both wrists. In short, these are wealthy folk, but they are not overly ostentatious. They belong to the urban patrician class, but sometimes spend time outside the city. When in the countryside, they adopt an air of rural simplicity; that is also clear from their chosen mode of transport – not a closed carriage, but an open farmer's cart, drawn by two patient grey horses.

The landscape in which the family poses was described in the 1824 auction catalogue as "in Brabant, in the vicinity of Antwerp". Later authors have generally taken a different view, placing it in the dunes around Haarlem. The city skyline bears little resemblance to that of seventeenth-century Haarlem. However, this need not be a portrait of a specific location at all; the artist may well have built up his composition from diverse heterogeneous observations. The landscape is awash with allusions to death and decay. The nursemaid sits on the trunk of a tree that has been felled by a storm, and some distance away we see more dead or decaying wood. The wooden fence behind the nursemaid is almost falling apart. The square mansion glimpsed between the trees appears not to have escaped the ravages of time. 'All things on earth will pass away' appears to be the painting's message.[9]

During restoration in 2008–09, X-ray and infrared photographs were made of the painting.[10] The X-rays show cusping on three sides of the canvas – that is, the edges of the linen have been pulled out of shape where the canvas was pulled taut and attached to the stretcher. On the left side there is no such cusping. This means that a strip must have been cut off along the left at some point. Comparison with the distortions on the other sides suggests that the canvas must have been at least 15 cm wider on the left. Furthermore, in the sky along the left edge, old overpainting emerged that concealed the remnants of a group of trees that had been cut off awkwardly. The vegetation in the left foreground contains some leaves that appear to sprout from nowhere. In other words, the painting did not originally have its current, rather unusual – almost square – shape. The cropping must also have affected the composition: the wet nurse and child were initially almost at the centre of the image.

From infrared photographs it can be inferred that all the figures were painted over the existing landscape. Where this is most clearly visible – such as around the gentleman's legs – it appears that the figures were painted on to a detailed, fully finished painting. The normal practice was to leave space in the painting's background in which the large figures could be inserted afterwards; seventeenth-century painters were not fond of unnecessary work. It is therefore possible that the group portrait was added later to a landscape that was initially regarded as finished – or virtually finished. This is an interesting idea, since it would mean that the figures and the surrounding landscape may have nothing to do with one another.

Particularly in the case of a painting like this, we are left wishing that a set of drawings had been preserved that would shed more light on the development of this work – a sketch of the composition, a detailed design, figure studies and a series of portraits. Sadly, however, there is only one drawing that can be directly linked to the painting, the study of the seated wet nurse with the little girl on her lap in the Rijksmuseum (cat. no.23). Over an extremely cursory sketch in graphite or black chalk, the drawing is worked-up only in red chalk. Only the figure of the nursemaid is rendered in detail; the child's contours are roughly indicated, her head turned three-quarters to the right. Van de Velde would eventually paint the girl *en face*. In the drawing the woman sits on an ill-defined rectangular object that is indicated only with a few straight lines. Evidently Van de Velde already knew precisely where she would end up in the painting when he started drawing, since he has drawn a piece of a broken branch behind the woman's knee. For anyone familiar only with the drawing, this is a fairly incomprehensible detail; as soon as one holds the drawing beside the painting, however, all becomes clear. Further comparison of the nursemaid in the drawing and the painting shows that, in spite of this clear plan, Van de Velde changed all sorts of tiny details while he was painting. The maid sits in a different pose in the painting: her back is slightly more bent, her neck has become a little longer, and she makes a rather more youthful impression. The large collar that hangs over her jacket right down her back has disappeared.

A study of the little dog that occupies such a prominent place in the scene has also been preserved, but the drawing does not show the dog in the same pose as in the painting (cat. no.24). The drawing bears the date 1670 and might therefore have nothing to do with the painting, but we should probably not attach too much weight to this date. Studies such as this were rarely signed or dated, and Van de Velde may well have added the inscription later on, in the hope of selling his drawing. That the drawing shows the same creature as that in the painting is beyond doubt, since the animals' markings are in every respect identical. Whether the dog – probably a *kooikerhondje*, an old Dutch breed – really belonged to the household of the couple and their children depicted here is impossible to say. Just as the landscape may have sprung from the artist's imagination, the dog too may have entered the stage to play a supporting role at the painter's initiative. M.S.

NOTES

1 Smith 1834, p.203.
2 Gower 1875, p.116.
3 "*Een deftig gezin, voorzaten van den tegenwoordige Bezitter des Tafereels, wordt daarop in een bevallig Landschap verbeeld; deze groote Meester komt hier alzoo als Portret-Schilder voor*": Van Eijnden and Van der Willigen 1816–40, III, p.477.
4 "*En de A. v de Velde is een Fraaij Landschap gestoffeerd met eene Famielle waar van het kleijne kind, dat op de schoot van eene Meyd oft minne zit, zijn Bed-over Grootmoeder moet geweest zijn.*" The letter is preserved at the RKD-Netherlands Institute for Art History, The Hague, in the Van der Willigen archives. With thanks to Robert-Jan te Rijdt, curator of drawings at the Rijksmuseum, who alerted me to the existence of this letter and provided me with a photocopy of the relevant passage.
5 *Nederland's Patriciaat* 16 (1926), p.238 (Van der Pals), and ibid., 84 (2002), p.31 (De Clercq).
6 See Nieuwenhuys 1834, p.249.
7 It may be added that there is a *Family portrait in a landscape* by Adriaen van de Velde, dated 1655, whose landscape background is purely decorative: see Frensemeier 2001, no.18. The current whereabouts of this youthful work are unknown; it was last recorded in 1999, when it was with Hoogsteder & Hoogsteder, The Hague.
8 With thanks to Sara van Dijk, junior curator of textiles at the Rijksmuseum, who patiently studied the items of clothing worn by the family depicted in the painting.
9 Bruyn 1987, pp.86–88.
10 With thanks to Ige Verslype, conservator of paintings at the Rijksmuseum, who generously shared with me the findings of her research.

25

Colf players on the ice, 1668

Oil on panel, 30.3 × 36.4 cm
Signed and dated, lower left: *A.V.Velde. f / 1668*
The National Gallery, London, inv. no.NG 869

26

Ice skating outside the city wall, 1669

Oil on canvas laid down on panel, 33 × 40.5 cm
Signed and dated, lower left: *A.V.Velde f / 1669*
Gemäldegalerie Alte Meister, Staatliche
Kunstsammlungen, Dresden, inv. no.1659

Van de Velde painted only a handful of winter landscapes. It has always been recognized that they fall into two distinct groups. One consists of works with a low horizon and the viewer at a considerable distance from the scene, so that the figures populating the landscape are relatively small. The other includes works in which the spectator moves closer to the scene and the figures loom much larger. In these works the landscape plays a subordinate role, with the result they are genre scenes as much as they are landscapes.

Both groups were always thought to date from the late 1660s, but there can be no doubt that the first group (figs.131–33) instead dates from the early 1660s because they chime perfectly with Van de Velde's other works of that period, which tend to emphasize the landscape more than its inhabitants. Although of a crystalline clarity that is all their own, their compositions relate to earlier winter landscapes by artists such as Aert van der Neer and Jan van de Cappelle.[1]

Some of the confusion arising over the dating of Van de Velde's winter scenes stems from the fact that the date on the Louvre painting (fig.132), which is not easy to decipher, was for a long time misread as 1668, probably because the works from London and Dresden under discussion here are dated 1668 and 1669. But when the picture is studied closely, it becomes clear that the date most probably reads 1662, and, once the idea that Van de Velde's winter scenes should all date from the late 1660s is let go, it is evident that the small panel in the Harold Samuel Collection, London (fig.131), and the winter scene in Philadelphia (fig.133) must also be dated earlier than was thought. The first gives the impression of a relatively inexperienced attempt at the subject and might even date from the second half of the 1650s. Like Van de Velde's other early landscapes, these works are characterized by a light tonality and a cheerful mood.[2] In the course of the 1660s Van de Velde emphasized the figures more, introduced more dramatic contrasts between light and dark and created an altogether more brooding atmosphere in his paintings.

These first two traits are found in the two winter scenes from London (cat. no.25) and Dresden (cat. no.26). The former has recently been cleaned and its brilliant evocation of a late afternoon on a cold but crisp winter's day can be appreciated once again in its full glory. In both paintings people from various social backgrounds have come together to enjoy the pastimes of winter, including the game of *colf*. Its origins can be traced to the thirteenth century, but *colf* became increasingly popular in the seventeenth century. It could be played all year round, but in winter frozen canals or rivers provided both a useful smooth surface and a wide expanse, even if passing skaters introduced an extra challenge. One of the variants of the game was not that different from today's golf in that players needed to hit a target, such as a pole, in as few strokes as possible. There is hardly a winter scene in seventeenth-century Dutch painting in which the game does not play a role of some sort, even if it is sometimes only alluded to through the presence of a discarded *colf* club.

In the Dresden painting we see a glorious detail of a young man getting ready to play the game by putting on a skate, his other skate and his club

25

26

PROVENANCE

Collection of Jean Gaillard de la Bouëxière
(1676–1759), from whom acquired in 1754
through the agency of Le Leu for Augustus III

EXHIBITION

The Hague 2001–02, no.30

REFERENCES

Smith 1834, no.121; Nagler 1835–52, XX, p.29;
Hübner 1856, no.1439; Waagen 1860, p.411;
Parthey 1863–64, II, p.705, no.33; Woermann 1887,
no.1659; Hofstede de Groot 1912, no.369; Bode
1917, p.230; Zoege von Manteuffel 1927, pp.73–74;
Martin 1936, II, p.338; Stechow 1966, p.98; Haak
1984, p.472; exh. cat. Amsterdam, Boston and
Philadelphia 1987–88, p.496; Frensemeier 2001,
no.173

FIG.131
Adriaen van de Velde, *Winter landscape with skaters*. Inscribed, lower right: *A.V.V.* Oil on panel, 21.7 × 21.1 cm. Guildhall Art Gallery, City of London. Harold Samuel Collection

FIG.132
Adriaen van de Velde, *Frozen river with skaters and colf players*. Signed and dated, lower left, on slats of building: *A.V.Velde 166[2?]*. Oil on canvas, 23 × 30 cm. Musée du Louvre, Paris, inv. no.1920

FIG.133
Adriaen van de Velde, *Winter landscape*, early 1660s. Oil on panel, 30.6 × 37 cm. Philadelphia Museum of Art, inv. no.603

FIG.134
Hendrick Avercamp, *Ice scene with colf players*, c.1625. Signed, lower right: *HA*. Oil on panel, 28.5 × 51.2 cm. The Museum of Fine Arts, Houston, The Edward and Sally Speelman Collection

FIG.135
Salomon van Ruysdael, *Skaters on the frozen river Lek, the town of Vianen beyond*. Signed and dated, on the back of the central sledge: *S.VR / 1653*. Oil on canvas, 75.2 × 110 cm. Private collection

resting beside him. He is beautifully echoed diagonally across the ice in the far distance by another man near the city wall who is also putting on his skates. A boy is waiting for his companion to get ready and is distracted by another who is using poles to propel himself forward on his sledge. The entire spectrum of society is gathering outside the city walls, from the well-to-do couple travelling in an impressive shell-shaped sledge pulled by a horse wearing a luxurious caparison to the man and boy on the left offering an elegantly dressed couple a ride in a push-sledge, their hats taken off not so much in deference but in expectance of a donation.[3] Two beautifully characterized figures on shore to the left 'introduce' the scene that unfolds in the rest of the picture. The artist's keen observation is borne out by details such as the snow sticking to the men's shoes or the dog behind them eating snow, while Van de Velde's total command of tonal values can be seen in the bluish hue of the shadows cast on the snow, both on the ground and on the roof of the gatekeeper's house on the city wall, a tone that is extremely difficult to get right.

The entire conception of Van de Velde's Dresden winter landscape is original. While there are many genre-like elements in seventeenth-century Dutch winter landscapes, they are rarely depicted in such a resoundingly natural manner. Van de Velde understood that the secret of a convincing genre scene is that it should not look too anecdotal or contrived. Instead he lets the beautifully observed details take the viewer on a quiet journey across the canvas. There is an attractive and engaging intimacy in this scene that is invariably expressed in unerring brushstrokes.[4]

The same qualities are found in the London picture, where we see how the game of *colf* is played, the man in the foreground about to strike the ball towards the pole by the person who has just set it up as the target. This painting follows a more traditional pattern. Telling comparisons can be made, for example, with a picture by Hendrick Avercamp of c.1625 (fig.134) and one by Salomon van Ruysdael of 1653 (fig.135). In the former

ABOVE: FIG.136
Jean Jacques Aliamet after Adriaen van de Velde,
Les amusemens de l'hiver, 1750. Etching,
32.7 × 38.2 cm. Teylers Museum, Haarlem,
inv. no.KG 13550

FIG.137
Francesco Guardi, *Dutch landscape with a frozen
lagoon and classical ruins*, 1770s. Oil on panel,
24 × 36 cm. Present whereabouts unknown

BELOW: FIG.138
Jacques-Philippe Le Bas after Adriaen van de
Velde, *Petite Marine*. Etching, 27.7 × 35.6 cm.
Amsterdam Museum, inv. no.A 11538

FIG.139
Francesco Guardi, *Dutch landscape with
a beach and classical ruins*, 1770s. Oil on panel,
24 × 36 cm. Present whereabouts unknown

we encounter almost the same motif, while in the latter we see many of the
same elements and an entire composition that foreshadows Van de Velde's,
including the view of a distant town on the horizon.[5] And yet the comparisons
also brings out Van de Velde's highly original approach. While in Avercamp's
painting we are – quite exceptionally for a painting of that date – very close
to the scene, the composition is rather static, with the figures perhaps too
evenly distributed across the ice, while the placing of the figures in Van de
Velde's painting, although they are carefully choreographed, seems almost
accidental, making ingenious use of overlap.[6] In Ruysdael's picture there is
plenty of overlap, but we hardly know where to direct our attention and feel
slightly lost in the accumulation of detail. In Van de Velde's painting we feel
we are part of the crowd, observing the man striking the ball from a distance
comparable to that of the little boy watching the same crucial moment, while
our eyes are gently directed along receding diagonals towards the horizon.

In 1834 John Smith wrote of the London scene that "This picture has
always been deservedly esteemed as a bijou of the rarest excellence", and
added that "Aliamet has executed a faithful engraving, entitled *Amusement*

FIG.140
Adriaen van de Velde, *Winter landscape*. c.1670.
Oil on canvas, 41 × 52 cm. Gemäldegalerie,
Staatliche Museen zu Berlin, inv. no.1999

d'Hiver".[7] The print mentioned by Smith (fig.136) helped to spread the picture's fame and evidently reached Francesco Guardi (1712–1793), as can be seen in his eccentric *Dutch landscape with a frozen lagoon and classical ruins* (fig.137). This bizarre scene is only surpassed by its pendant (fig.139), in which we see how classical ruins have landed on Van de Velde's distinctly Dutch beach, which Guardi copied from a similar print known as the *Petite Marine* (fig.138) after a beachscape by Van de Velde discussed under cat. no.5.[8]

Probably the last winter landscape that Van de Velde painted is a picture in Berlin (fig.140). It can be compared to our cat. no.46, which is dated 1670, and it is probable that the Berlin picture was executed around the same time. But where the drawing succeeds, the picture somehow fails. It is strongly influenced by the dark and dramatic winter landscapes painted by Jacob van Ruisdael in the 1660s, but the threatening aspect of winter weather clearly did not suit Van de Velde's artistic temperament as well as its more playful and peaceful moods, so brilliantly evoked in the pictures from London and Dresden.[9] B.C.

NOTES

1 There are countless examples by Aert van der Neer. For Jan van de Cappelle, see especially his *Winter scene with thatched cottages and a frozen river spanned by a wooden bridge* in Manchester Art Gallery (inv. no.1979.455), which is relevant for Van de Velde's winter landscape in the Louvre (fig.132); see Frensemeier 2001, p.44.

2 Frensemeier 2001, pp.42–44, was the first to propose an earlier date for these pictures (her cat. nos.168–70). The later date for the Philadelphia painting is still mentioned on the website of the Philadelphia Museum of Art. For the Harold Samuel picture, see Sutton 1992, no.73. For the Louvre painting, see Foucart 2009, p.282, where Frensemeier's redating is duly noted. Mention should be made here of three comparable winter landscapes that are given to Van de Velde (they are rarely, if ever, discussed in the literature; indeed none of them is even mentioned in Frensemeier 2001) but whose attribution is doubtful: *Winter landscape with colf players, skaters and a horse-drawn sledge on a frozen river*, signed and dated, lower right:

A.V.VELDE / 1662, oil on panel, 30 × 39 cm (Koninklijk Museum voor Schone Kunsten, Antwerp, inv. no.733); *Winter landscape with colf players on a frozen river*, unsigned, oil on panel, 22.4 × 28.4 cm (Manchester Art Gallery, inv. no.1979.508); *Winter landscape*, unsigned, oil on panel, 38 × 30 cm (The Edward and Sally Speelman Collection; see Wheelock *et al.* 2000, p.38). They may originate in Van de Velde's orbit but are difficult to accept as by him.

3 The same motif is seen on the left in fig.165 on p.176 below.

4 Mention should be made here of a poor copy of the Dresden painting in the Royal Collection, probably dating from the nineteenth century. Its source is not recognized in White 1982, no.260, nor in White 2015, no.260, where the copy is mistakenly catalogued as 'Imitator (?) of Philips Wouwermans'.

5 This is claimed to be Haarlem in MacLaren 1991, p.441, no.867, on account of the characteristic shape of Haarlem's church, which has a central tower sitting over its crossing.

6 That Van de Velde took great care in positioning his figures is borne out by the fact that there are pentimenti in the hat, arm and club of the man about to strike the ball, the man leaning on his club and the outline of the boy and girl to the right of the sledge, all visible to the naked eye; see MacLaren 1991, p.441, no.867.

7 Smith 1834, no.31.

8 For Guardi's pendants, see exh. cat. Venice 1993, nos.61 and 62, where the source is correctly identified as Adriaen van de Velde but no mention is made of the prints that obviously served as Guardi's model. See also De Klerck 2009, pp.24–25.

9 Frensemeier 2001, p.84, dates the painting to the mid-1660s, but fails to note its relationship to our cat no.46, dated 1670. A poor copy after the painting was recently on the art market: sale, Pierre Bergé & Associés, Paris, 13th June 2014, lot 19.

27

Landscape with horses and other livestock, 1669

Oil on panel, 21.5 × 28.5 cm
Signed and dated, lower centre: *A.V.Velde.1669.*
Fondation Custodia, Collection Frits Lugt, Paris,
inv. no.6381

Relatively unassuming compositions in which animals figure prominently but humans are either absent or barely noticeable form a specific group within Van de Velde's oeuvre. Early examples include his *View of an estuary* (1658; see cat. no.3) and *Meadow with horses and cattle* of 1660 in Copenhagen (fig.141).[1] Although in his early work Van de Velde often followed the example of Paulus Potter, whose precedent is not without significance here (fig.144), we find a more comparable focus on small groups of animals in the works of Van de Velde's slightly older colleague Karel Dujardin (fig.142).

In the picture of 1669 under discussion here the focus is also entirely on the animals, albeit that they are closer to the viewer. It is also a textbook example of the manner in which Van de Velde's early predilection for clarity and luminosity made way in his later work for far more dramatic effects of light and dark. No longer do the animals stand out against the bright blue sky of a summer's day but instead are silhouetted against billowing clouds that suggest that a massive storm will soon disturb the sunlit scene. The party travelling on a horse-drawn cart in the far distance, the only human element in this painting, seems to be aware of the imminent turn in the weather and hurry to find shelter.

We recognize some stock-in-trade elements, such as the cow lying down in the centre, which we have already seen in our cat. no.13 and will see again in cat. nos.30, 33, 35 and 52. The motif of two horses nibbling each other's withers, a form of mutual grooming, is also found in one of the artist's earliest dated works (1657, the Royal Collection);[2] in a related painting of 1663 (fig.143);[3] in a painting of horses and cattle on a river bank of 1664 in the Musée du Louvre, Paris (fig.22 on p.22);[4] and in a composition study for a painting of *Mercury and Battus*.[5] Although it could well be that Van de Velde had observed horses grooming each other from life, one suspects that the example of Dujardin must have played a role, as fig.142 suggests.

FIG.143
Adriaen van de Velde, *Two horses, cows, sheep and goats in a woodland clearing*. Signed and dated, lower centre: *a.v.velde. f/ 1663*. Oil on canvas, 36.8 × 33.6 cm. Courtesy of Johnny van Haeften Ltd, London

FIG.144
Paulus Potter, *Two horses near a gate in a meadow*. Signed and dated, lower centre, on gate: *Paulus / Potter. f. 1649*. Oil on panel, 23.3 × 29.6 cm. Rijksmuseum, Amsterdam, inv. no.SK-C-205

One of the hallmarks of Van de Velde's later works is their brooding character. Brightly lit elements of the composition catch our immediate attention and stand in stark contrast to those that are in deep shadow. It is this kind of drama that is a far cry from the unadulterated light that permeates the scenes in Van de Velde's early works, but the perfectly observed details and superb brushwork are still present, making this one of the artist's finest late works.[6]

The painting is perfectly in character with the collection in which it now resides. Bought in 1951 by the connoisseur and scholar Frits Lugt (1884–1970), whose bequest forms the core of the collection preserved at the Fondation Custodia, Paris, it exemplifies what could be dubbed a 'Lugt taste' for unusual pictures, in this case a work that has all the refinement and composure of the artist's early work but all the drama of his later output. Lugt was a great admirer of Adriaen van de Velde, whom he described as "one of the best landscapists of his period, a talent of great delicacy and distinction, at the same time an extraordinary painter of figures and animals, which always makes his landscapes agreeably lively".[7] B.C.

PROVENANCE

Friedrich Wilhelm Michael Kalkbrenner, Paris, sold, together with five other paintings, for 10,000 francs in or before 1849, and thus not included in his sale, Paris, 14th January 1850; Auguiot sale, Paris, 1st and 2nd March 1875, lot 29 (11,700 francs); Etienne H. sale, Paris, 9th March 1951, lot 58, bought by Frits Lugt

EXHIBITIONS

Paris 1960, no.286; Paris 1983, no.83; The Hague 2002, no.32; Paris 2012, no.74

REFERENCES

Hofstede de Groot 1912, no.303; Frensemeier 2001, no.56

NOTES

1 Hofstede de Groot 1912, no.191; Frensemeier 2001, no.52.
2 Hofstede de Groot 1912, no.336; Frensemeier 2001, no.43; White 1982, no.201; White 2015, no.201.
3 A preliminary composition study for this painting is in the Amsterdam Museum, inv. no.TA 10347 (not in Robinson 1979); see Broos and Schapelhouman 1993, no.135.
4 Hofstede de Groot 1912, no.120; Frensemeier 2001, no.155; Foucart 2009, p.282. A *modello* for this painting is in the Petit Palais, Paris (fig.163 on p.170); see Robinson 1979, no.C-3.
5 Robinson 1979, no.B-16. A painted version of this composition, not necessarily an autograph painting by Van de Velde, is in the National Gallery, Prague, inv. no.DO5680; see Ševčík 2012, no.431.
6 An early copy of the painting, not by Van de Velde, was sold from the collection of the New York Historical Society at Sotheby's, New York, 12th January 1995, lot 45.
7 Cited in exh. cat. The Hague 2002, p.168.

28

A hawking party setting out, 1666

Oil on panel, 50 × 46.9 cm
Signed and dated, lower left: *A.V.Velde. f 1666*
The Royal Collection / HM Queen Elizabeth II,
inv. no.RCIN 406966

29

The hunting party, 1669

Oil on canvas, 59.5 × 73 cm
Signed and dated, lower left: *A.V.Velde f / 1669*
Rijksmuseum, Amsterdam. On loan from the
City of Amsterdam (A. van der Hoop Bequest),
inv. no.SK-C-249

It is not too difficult to identify the examples that inspired most of Van de Velde's hunting pictures. As discussed in the entry for *Departure for the hunt* in the Schroder Collection (cat. no.11), improving on the work of Jan Blom was hardly an insurmountable challenge, but the example is of interest because it shows it clearly did not take a masterpiece to inspire one, while the resulting work, in its turn, inspired the slightly older Karel Dujardin. In other cases Van de Velde struggled to improve on his model; his Wouwermanesque *Hunting party in the grounds of a country house* (fig.102 on p.82) is flawless in its execution, but suffers from the same incoherence that so frequently plagues the compositions of Philips Wouwerman.

For the Royal Collection *A hawking party setting out* (cat. no.28) Van de Velde almost certainly took his cue from Paulus Potter, as is clear from a comparison with Potter's *Hawking party* at Woburn Abbey (fig.145).[1] Van de Velde's paint is applied more smoothly than Potter's, so much so that when Gustav Waagen described this picture in 1838 he judged it "almost too smooth".[2] But his technique is never enamel-like; when viewed up close, the brushstrokes are clearly visible. They are in Potter's work, but the difference is that while Potter's technique is very precise and therefore can seem a little harsh, Van de Velde carried over what he knew about gradations as a draughtsman into his painting technique. He was, one could say, always drawing in paint, a few supple flicks of paint indicating shadow making the difference between a flat surface and one that seems to exist in the round. *A hawking party* is a particularly good example of this.

Waagen was also not too impressed with the flamboyant costumes of some of the protagonists, noting that "the gay dresses disturb in some measure the general harmony".[3] Hunters are never knowingly underdressed, so the problem is inherent to the subject, while one could counter that in this case

FIG.145
Paulus Potter, *A hawking party*. Signed and dated, lower right: *Paulus Potter: / f: 1653*. Oil on canvas, 56 × 65 cm. The Woburn Abbey Collection

28

PROVENANCE

Louis-César-Renaud, duc de Choiseul-Praslin sale, Paris, 18th–25th February 1793, lot 86, bought by Alexandre-Joseph Paillet (7,021 livres); Hendrik van Eyl Sluyter sale, Paris, 25th–28th January 1802, lot 182, bought by Nicolas Lerouge (6,900 francs); Peter Isaac Thellusson, 1st Baron Rendlesham sale, 20th June 1806, lot 46, bought in (£315); same owner's sale, 17th–18th May 1809, lot 46, bought in (£210); same owner's sale, 28th May 1810, lot 32, bought by Francis Charles Seymour-Conway, 3rd

Marquess of Hertford, for the Prince of Wales, later George IV (£294)

EXHIBITIONS

London 1946–47, no.323; Hull 1961, no.101; London 1971–72, no.37; London 1988–89, no.37; Edinburgh and London 2004–05, pp.160–61; Edinburgh, London and Barnard Castle 2010–12, no.16

REFERENCES

Smith 1834, no.59; Nagler 1835–52, XX, p.29; Waagen 1838, II, pp.365–66; Jameson 1844, p.57, no.155; Waagen 1854, II, p.16; Waagen 1860, p.410; Hofstede de Groot 1912, no.154; Bode 1917, p.232; White 1982, no.206; Frensemeier 2001, no.37; White 2015, no.206

29

PROVENANCE

Collection of Jacob Pompejus Hoeufft van Velzen
(1779–1835), Velzen; acquired from his heirs by
the art dealer Jan de Lelie, Amsterdam; art dealer
C.J. Nieuwenhuys, London; art dealer Albertus
Brondgeest, Amsterdam; from whom bought
in 1838 by Adriaan van der Hoop (fl. 5,650) and
bequeathed to the City of Amsterdam in 1854;
Museum Van der Hoop, 1854–85; on loan to the
Rijksmuseum, Amsterdam, since 1885

EXHIBITIONS

Amsterdam 2004–05, no.188

REFERENCES

Smith 1842, no.15; exh. cat. Amsterdam 1855,
no.127; Thoré-Bürger 1858–60, II, pp.93–94; Gower
1875, p.110; Hofstede de Groot 1912, no.152; Van
Thiel 1976, p.558; Blankert and Ruurs 1979, no.462;
Fromentin 1984, p.1166; Van Thiel *et al.* 1992, p.88;
Dumas, Van Strij, 2000, p.111; Frensemeier 2001,
no.38; Middelkoop 2008, p.251

FIG.146
Jan Hackaert, *The avenue of birches*, 1665–70.
Oil on canvas, 66.5 × 53.5 cm. Rijksmuseum,
Amsterdam, inv. no.SK-A-130

FIG.147
Details of fig.146 and cat. no.28

they provide the colourful accents that make the picture so attractive. The painting is effectively an exercise in primary colours: red, yellow and blue are the eye-catching colours in the composition. There is a definite sense of movement in the picture – one feels that if the imaginary viewer would stand still and wait for a minute he would soon be looking at an empty clearing in the wood – and the bright colour accents help us to relish this brief moment, even if the actual viewer has all the time in the world to study the picture. These colours add immediacy to the scene, but they are also exquisitely employed: the purplish blue feathers worn by the woman riding side-saddle are the same colour as the fabric she carries over her shoulder, and both of them are beautifully set against the background green, although the real *tour de force* here is the combination with the bright blue of the grey's saddle: in painterly terms, placing a purplish blue next to a bright blue is a dangerous move, but Van de Velde seems to pull it off effortlessly. Meanwhile the red ribbons and trimmings of the outfit of the man pointing the way are superbly echoed not only in the ribbons worn by the bay horse but also in the highlights of the horse's coat, although these highlights are likewise slightly different in tone in that they are almost orange, and orange and red is another notoriously difficult combination to get right.

Comparing the picture to Potter's *Hawking party* of little over a decade earlier demonstrates how much more effectively Van de Velde integrated his figures into the landscape, making the composition look effortless and convincing. Van de Velde painted the figures and animals in the background in slightly broader brushstrokes, indicating their shape, volume and the contrasts between light and shade with mere flicks of paint: they are almost

out of focus. It is this use of aerial perspective that helps to push them into the background – in a manner quite unlike Potter's *Hawking party*, in which everything remains in sharp focus. These qualities clearly impressed Van de Velde's colleagues, who were keen to employ him to furnish their pictures with animals and figures. When the same subject was needed by Jan Hackaert (1628–after 1685) for his *Avenue of birches* (fig.146), Van de Velde managed to do exactly the same, even if this time the landscape was by another artist.[4] It was not only a matter of scale; although that was obviously crucial, it was as much about movement and choice of motifs. If it has been judiciously done, one seems to see a snapshot of an actual event, even if this kind of naturalism is achieved only through a careful choreography of the staffage. As always, Van de Velde was economical in his use of motifs: the man on horseback pointing in Hackaert's painting is closely related to his counterpart in *A Hawking party setting out* (fig.147), and one may assume that Van de Velde made a drawing for this figure that he kept for reference in his studio, although the drawing has not survived.

As has been noted with regard to Van de Velde's winter landscapes (cat. nos.25 and 26), in the latter half of the 1660s the artist introduced larger, genre-like figures into his landscapes. The Rijksmuseum's *Hunting party* (cat. no.29) is emblematic of that development. Impressive gates on the left of the scene indicate that the party is leaving a grand estate. They are accompanied by a large pack of hounds, but as yet relatively little is happening, so that one of them has decided that this is as good a time as any to lie down for a nap. Although different in conception from the *Hawking party setting out* in the Royal Collection, its composition is just as carefully orchestrated. There is a pleasing symmetry in the positions of the two grooms holding the horses, the one walking towards the viewer immediately catching our attention, after which we notice that he has a companion who is not only mostly hidden by the bay horse but also largely in shadow, his splendid red outfit only just catching the light. It is another example of Van de Velde's quest for a form of naturalism that goes beyond careful description; he always made sure his compositions would not look contrived, even if that involved 'accidentally' hiding a figure.

As has been mentioned under cat. no.11, in 1660 those who held important governmental functions had successfully challenged the aristocracy's exclusive right to pursue the hunt, which must account for the increasing popularity of hunting pictures. In his description of the painting in 1842, the art dealer John Smith maintained that "this exquisitely finished picture was doubtless painted for the owner of the horses and the adjoining lands". It is difficult to say whether he was right. The 'portrayal' of property in such a manner is commonly found in British painting – one only needs to think of the work of George Stubbs – and Smith's interpretation is likely to have its roots in this tradition. It is more plausible that in Van de Velde's time there was a healthy demand for hunting pictures and that he painted it speculatively. B.C.

NOTES

1 For this painting, see exh. cat. The Hague 1994–95, no.31.
2 Waagen 1838, II, p.366.
3 Ibid.
4 For this picture, see exh. cat. Amsterdam, Boston and Philadelphia 1987–88, no.42, where it is dated 1675–80. The figures are definitely by Van de Velde, so the painting can be no later than 1672. It probably dates from around the same time as the Royal Collection *Hawking party*.

30

The Hut, 1671

Oil on canvas, 76 × 65 cm
Signed, lower left: *A.V.Velde. f. / 1671*
Rijksmuseum, Amsterdam, inv. no.SK-A-443

31

A hut or sheepfold

Brush and grey ink over a sketch in black chalk;
framing lines with pen and grey ink, 18 × 27.6 cm
Verso, lower centre: *A. van de Velde* (pencil);
lower left: /:*v*- (pencil); upper right: *XV* (pencil)
Peck Collection, Boston

32

Shepherdess with sheep

Red chalk over a sketch in graphite or black chalk,
framing lines with pen and dark brown ink,
19.3 × 29.9 cm
Verso, lower left: *N°3.* and *205.* (pen and dark
brown ink) and stamp of Museum Fodor (Lugt 1036);
lower right: *228* (pencil)
Amsterdam Museum, C.J. Fodor Bequest, inv. no.TA
10345

33

Recumbent cow and three sheep

Red chalk over remnants of a sketch in graphite
or black chalk, framing lines with pen and dark
brown ink over red chalk, 19.5 × 30.8 cm
Verso, lower left: *N°2.* and *205.* (pen and dark brown ink)
and stamp of Museum Fodor (Lugt 1036);
lower right: *229* (pencil)
Amsterdam Museum, C.J. Fodor Bequest,
inv. no.TA 10346

34

Seated woman with basket

Red chalk, 28.3 × 20 cm
Inscribed, lower right: *A.V.V.*
Private collection

"With the exquisite decorum of the arrangement of figures, the peerlessly deliquescent brushwork and the splendid rendering of the sunlight, this work ranks among the Master's finest, in which all the perfections of his art seem to have come together."[1] Thus concludes the entry in the catalogue of the "celebrated Collection of Paintings, by the leading Netherlandish, Italian and other Masters, of the late Mr Josephus Augustinus Brentano",[2] whose sale took place on 13th May 1822 and following days. The words convey how greatly the painting was admired at the time. The price it fetched was entirely in accordance with this reputation: it went for fl. 8290, making it the most expensive painting in the sale. *The Hut* – an anecdotal title that the painting did not acquire until 1858 – was purchased for the Rijksmuseum. A comment by Cornelis Apostool, written a few years after its acquisition, is likewise brimming with superlatives: "Such are the wealth of detail, verisimilitude, and the superb draughtsmanship and expression of this outstanding Painting, one of the finest works by this peerless artist, that it leaves nothing to be desired, and may thus be celebrated as one of the greatest of all fruits brought forth by the Dutch School".[3] Non-Dutch authors dispensed similar encomia, though with a somewhat perfunctory air. In 1834 John Smith concluded his fairly bland description, void of hyperbole, with the mechanical statement, "This very capital and admirably-finished picture is dated 1671",[4] and in 1875 Lord Gower, who had devoted such tender words to the artist's presumed self-portrait with his family (cat. no.22), could not muster more than a single cursory phrase: "*The Hut.* A very fine example."[5] In 1858 Théophile Thoré, like Smith, furnished a fairly neutral description of the work, for the rest confining himself to a rather grudging remark about the composition, which was not entirely to his liking.[6] In the art-historical literature of the twentieth century, too, the painting plays little more than a supporting role; it was not included, for instance, in the major exhibition devoted to seventeenth-century Dutch landscape painting held in the Rijksmuseum in 1987.[7] And although *The Hut* featured in 2000 in the Rijksmuseum's bicentenary exhibition *The Glory of the Golden Age*, the authors of the accompanying catalogue did not devote a single sentence to the painting itself.[8]

Yet there is no reason at all to conclude that all that early nineteenth-century Dutch veneration was misplaced. The painting, provided it is hung so as to catch the light, sparkles like a gem. The yellow and blue of the woman's jacket and skirt, and the man's red coat, impart precisely enough colour to the scene to guard against monotony, the extremely sober and utterly uncontrived-looking composition creates the impression of a veritable 'slice of life', and Van de Velde's sheep are among the most cuddlesome creatures in seventeenth-century Dutch painting. The wooded ridge – or could it be a row of high dunes? – that bound the scene and the blue sky with its cumulus clouds chased along by the wind are among the best that Van de Velde ever produced. In short, the painting is in every respect a resounding success. Once more, Van de Velde presents here his own Dutch Arcadia, but he does not close his eyes to everyday reality and even allows himself a touch of humour: in the grass behind and to one side of the cow that lies placidly chewing the cud is a large cowpat.

31

PROVENANCE

Jacob de Vos sale, Amsterdam, 30th–31st October 1833, Kunstboek W, lot 5, bought by De Vries for Jacob de Vos Jbzn (fl. 100); his sale, Amsterdam, 22nd–24th May 1883, lot 550; Constant C. Huysman and A.J. van Wijngaerdt sale, Amsterdam, 21st–22nd June 1887, lot 222; August Sträter sale, Stuttgart, 10th–14th May 1898, lot 1207; Rudolph P. Goldschmidt sale, Frankfurt, 4th–5th October 1917, lot 593; H.C. Valkema Blouw sale, Amsterdam, 2nd–4th March 1954, among lots 725–34 (unspecified additional lots); Hans van Leeuwen sale, Christie's, Amsterdam, 24th November 1992, lot 204

EXHIBITIONS

Utrecht 1959–60, no.69; Laren 1963, no.13; Nijmegen 1965, no.39; Leeuwarden 1966, no.31; Bonn, Saarbrücken and Bochum 1968–69, no.138; Rheydt 1971, no.77; Amsterdam 1975–76, no.124; Bremen, Braunschweig and Stuttgart 1979–80, no.139; Chapel Hill, Ithaca and Worcester 1999–2001, no.34

REFERENCES

Schatborn 1975, pp.159–65, fig.6; Robinson 1979a, no.A-3; exh. cat. Amsterdam and Washington 1981–82, p.117, fig.6; exh. cat. Amsterdam 1987–88, under no.69; exh. cat. Paris 2009–10, p.136

PROVENANCE

Wouter Valckenier, Amsterdam; Elisabeth Valckenier-Hooft sale, Amsterdam, 31st August 1796, lot 39 (fl. 4,020); Josephus Augustinus Brentano, Amsterdam; his sale, Amsterdam, 13th May 1822, lot 344, bought by Jeronimo de Vries for the Rijksmuseum (fl. 8,290)

EXHIBITIONS

Rome 1956–57, no.307; Dordrecht and Leeuwarden 1988–89, no.32; Amsterdam 2000a, no.177

REFERENCES

Murray 1824, pp.147–48 and 152; Apostool 1825, pp.76–77; Smith 1834, no.15; Nagler 1835–52, XX, p.29; Dubourcq 1858, no.336; Thoré-Bürger 1858–60, I, pp.137–38; Waagen 1860, p.411; Gower 1875, p.88; Michel 1888, p.272; Hofstede de Groot 1912, no.79; Zoege van Manteuffel 1927, pp.68, 69 and 80, fig.68; Blankert 1968a, p.131; Schatborn 1975; Van Thiel 1976, p.558; Robinson 1979a, nos.A-3, D-17, D-18 and D-24; exh. cat. Amsterdam and Washington 1981–82, pp.116–17, fig.1; Bionda 1986, p.145; Bergvelt 1992, p.276; Bergvelt, Meijers and Rijnders 1993, p.344; Broos and Schapelhouman 1993, nos.143–44; exh. cat. Amsterdam 1997–98, p.18; exh. cat. Enschede 1998–99, p.38; Bergvelt 1998, pp.112–13; Filedt Kok *et al.* 2001, no.95; Frensemeier 2001, no.125

32

PROVENANCE

H. van Cranenburgh sale, Amsterdam, 26th
October 1858 and following days, Portfolio E, lot
98, bought by Lamme for C.J. Fodor (together with
lot 97, fl. 410); C.J. Fodor bequest, 1860

EXHIBITIONS

(Selection) Brussels 1961, no.143

REFERENCES

(Selection) Schatborn 1975, pp.161–62; Robinson
1979a, no.D-18; exh. cat. Amsterdam and
Washington 1981–82, pp.116–17, fig.4; Broos
and Schapelhouman 1993, no.143 (with earlier
literature)

A good many drawings provide insight into the genesis of *The Hut*. At the same time, the evidence shows that Van de Velde did not always prepare his paintings in the same way. This painting appears to have originated with an extraordinarily suggestive drawing of a dilapidated thatched hut or sheepfold, made primarily with the brush and grey ink 'after life' (cat. no.31). Van de Velde eventually incorporated this hut almost literally, complete with the play of light from the upper right, into his painting. The small dog lying in front of it on the right in the drawing was supplanted in the painting by the shepherdess. The tree that casts its shadow on the roof of the hut also ended up in the painting, though in slightly modified form and with a little foliage. Van de Velde probably started by making a rough sketch for the entire composition, but we cannot be sure about this, since no such 'initial idea' has been preserved. What we do have is a drawing in red chalk of the shepherdess with six sheep (cat. no.32). All six of these creatures have been incorporated into the painting, in which the sheep depicted from behind, lying with her lamb – in the far left of the drawing – was eventually moved still further to the left. Van de Velde based the figure of the seated girl on a counterproof of a drawing that belonged to his stock of motifs. Both the drawing (cat. no.34) and the counterproof have been preserved (fig.150).[9]

33

PROVENANCE

H. van Cranenburgh sale, Amsterdam, 26th
October 1858 and following days, Portfolio E,
lot 97, bought by Lamme for C.J. Fodor (together
with lot 98 for fl. 410); C.J. Fodor bequest, 1860

EXHIBITIONS

(Selection) Paris 1960, no.290

REFERENCES

(Selection) Schatborn 1975, pp.161–62; Robinson
1979a, no.D-24; exh. cat. Amsterdam and
Washington 1981–82, pp.116–17, fig.5; Broos
and Schapelhouman 1993, no.144 (with earlier
literature)

FIG.148
Dutch, 17th century, *Cow*. Polychromed
terracotta, 13.2 × 34.5 cm; base, 11 × 36.3 cm.
Musée du Louvre, Paris, inv. no.R.F. 1161

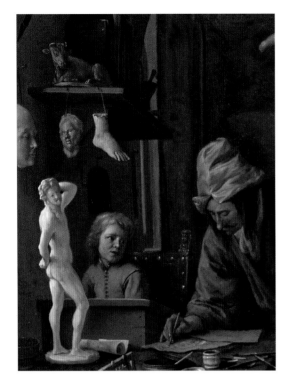

FIG.149
Detail of Jan Steen, *The drawing lesson*, c.1665.
Signed, lower left: *JSteen.* Oil on panel,
49.2 × 41.2 cm. J. Paul Getty Museum,
Los Angeles, inv. no.83.PB.388

Then there is another drawing, also in red chalk, featuring the cow and two sheep that are depicted prominently in the left foreground of the painting (cat. no.33). A third sheep, hastily sketched, can be seen in the drawing, but this animal was not included in the painting.

In discussions of Adriaen van de Velde, a passage from Houbraken's brief biography of the artist – a description that appears to have been strongly influenced by the memories of a loving daughter – is quoted ad nauseam. Houbraken writes that the meticulous Van de Velde "zealously drew and painted cows, bulls, sheep and landscapes and carried his equipment each day out to the countryside – a practice that he maintained until the end of his life once per week".[10] It is beyond dispute that Van de Velde sometimes drew animals and landscapes from life: his cows depicted from life are often recognizable by the absence of hooves – which were simply invisible in the tall grass.[11] But the artist sometimes had recourse to other means. The recumbent cow in *The Hut* – a creature that recurs in numerous other paintings and drawings – is probably based on a terracotta figurine, a specimen of which is preserved in the Musée du Louvre, Paris (fig.148).[12] This figurine is attributed there to Adriaen van de Velde, an attribution probably dating from the early nineteenth century, but this is a topsy-turvy view of things. Such items were standard elements of a painter's studio. Adriaen van de Velde evidently possessed one and often used it. In Jan Steen's *The drawing lesson* (fig.149) a small figurine of a cow is depicted on a shelf above the heads of the artist and his pupils.[13] M.S.

NOTES

1 *"De keurige zedigheid der ordonnantie, het onnavolgbaar smeltend penseel, en de treffelijke uitdrukking van het zonlicht, doen dit tafereel onder de fraaiste van den Meester rangschikken, welke al de volmaaktheden zijner kunst in hetzelve schijnt te hebben verenigd"*: Josephus Augustinus Brentano sale, Amsterdam, 13th May 1822, lot 344.

2 Ibid.: *"… beroemde Kabinet van Schilderijen, der voornaamste Nederlandsche, Italiaansche en andere Meesters, nagelaten door den wel-edelen Heer Josephus Augustinus Brentano".*

3 *"Dit uitmuntende Tafereel, een der voornaamste werken van dezen onnavolgbaren kunstenaar, laat niets te verlangen, wegens uitvoerigheid, waarheid, teekening en uitdrukking, en kan dus geroemt worden als een der voornaamste voortbrengsels uit de Hollandsche School"*: Apostool 1825, pp.76–77.

4 Smith 1834, no.15.

5 Gower 1875, p.88.

6 Thoré-Bürger 1858–60, I, pp.137–38.

7 Exh. cat. Amsterdam, Boston and Philadelphia 1987–88.

8 Exh. cat. Amsterdam 2000a, no.177.

9 Schatborn 1975, p.162.

10 *"torschende dagelyks met zyn gereedschapjes naar buiten in 't velt, 't welk hy tot het einde van zyn leven eens ter weeke onderhouden heeft"*: Houbraken 1718–21, III, p.90.

11 Broos and Schapelhouman 1993, no.142.

12 Exh. cat. Paris 1960, no.297 (as Adriaen van de Velde); Walsh 1996, p.68, fig.58 (as Adriaen van de Velde).

13 Walsh 1996, passim.

PROVENANCE

L. Dupper Wz sale, Dordrecht, 28th–29th June
1870, lot 379 (fl. 12)

EXHIBITIONS

Exh. cat. Almelo 1961, no.145; Amsterdam and
Washington 1981–82, p.116, fig.2, p.143, no.92

REFERENCES

Schatborn 1975, p.159; Robinson 1979a, no.D-17

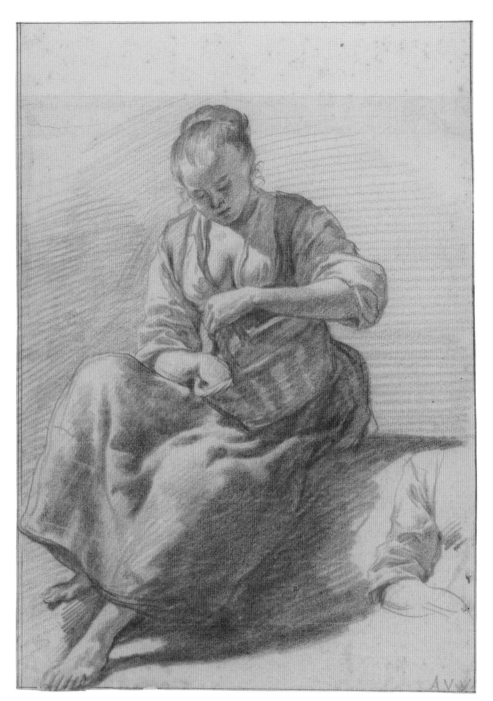

34

FIG.150
Adriaen van de Velde, *Seated woman with
a basket*. Counterproof of cat. no.34,
25.7 × 20.2 cm. Kupferstichkabinett,
Staatliche Kunstsammlungen, Dresden

35

A herdsman and a woman with cows and sheep by a river

Pen and brush and brown ink, 20.4 × 19.1 cm
British Museum, London, inv. no.Oo,11.258

36

A herdsman and a woman with cows and sheep by a river

Brush and grey and brown ink over a sketch in
black chalk, 26.1 × 24.9 cm
Albertina, Vienna, inv. no.17605

37

Two studies of a young woman with a bundle of washing

Red chalk, framing lines with pen and brown ink,
30.3 × 18.5 cm
Signed(?), lower left: *Adriaens / v.d. Velde f*. (red chalk);
verso: *H^s x,*[1] (pen and brown ink) and *6* (pencil)
Fondation Custodia, Collection Frits Lugt, Paris,
inv. no.4784

38

Two studies of a seated young man

Red chalk over a sketch in black chalk, framing
lines in black chalk, 22 × 29.6 cm
Inscribed, lower right: *A.V.V.* (red chalk); verso,
lower left: *S[...]* (illegible, pencil) and the mark of
Museum Fodor (Lugt 1036); numbered, lower right:
227 (pencil)
Amsterdam Museum, C.J. Fodor Bequest,
inv. no.TA 10344

Art history is a form of archaeology. From the documents and fragments of a more or less remote past, the art historian tries through detective work to construct a consistent story, always bearing in mind that only a small proportion of the evidence has been preserved. The detective who has uncovered most information in the research on Adriaen van de Velde is the American art historian William W. Robinson. Even today, his 1979 essay 'Preparatory Drawings by Adriaen van de Velde' remains essential reading material for anyone studying this subject. In his article, the four drawings discussed in this entry play a key role. The following paragraphs tell this story once again.

At the beginning of his essay, Robinson forces his readers to face the hard truth that much of the material that is mentioned in written sources has been lost. Still, this reminder of the "dismal record", as he calls it, is followed by the good news: so much – and such richly varied – material by Adriaen van de Velde *has* been preserved that we are able, up to a point, to reconstruct the genesis of his paintings from one stage to the next.

Each painting started off as a rapid sketch, generally executed with pen and brown ink and brush and grey ink. Of such initial designs, drawn in an instantly recognizable, characteristic 'shorthand', the drawing in the British Museum (cat. no.35) is a good example. In each such initial concept or *prima idea*, the artist surveyed the ingredients of the painting that was taking shape in his mind: the general plan of the landscape, the play of light – always a crucial element in Van de Velde's paintings – and the placing and poses of the human figures and animals that would populate the landscape. Van de Velde always devoted the greatest possible care to this staffage. His clients were keen to see well-painted human figures and creatures and Van de Velde was supreme in this regard: of all the landscape painters in seventeenth-century Holland, he had the greatest gift for drawing figures. In adding the staffage to his landscapes, Van de Velde could draw on an ever-expanding stock of figure and animal studies. Occasionally, when he needed something he did not yet possess in his treasury of motifs, he drew new studies with the aid of a hired model. We shall return to this presently.

We can assume that the first sketch was followed in most cases by a far more carefully worked-up drawing, executed in minute detail. For the composition under discussion here, one such drawing has been preserved in Vienna (cat. no.36).[1] Comparison of the drawings in London and Vienna shows the drastic changes that were made. Not so much was altered in the landscape itself; in the right distance the artist added some ancient-looking ruins to emphasize the scene's southern ambience. It is above all the animals that Van de Velde moved around his composition like pawns on a chessboard. The cow in the centre, whose head faces right in the first sketch, has been turned to look left in the second version. In fact the first sketch is rather overcrowded: Van de Velde evidently decided that the two human figures and the cow's head between them were a bit too much. Turning the cow the other way made the composition more serene. The second standing cow, which is partly hidden behind the central one in the initial sketch, was moved some distance to the right in the second version, thereby becoming

35

PROVENANCE

Bequeathed by Richard Payne Knight, 1824

REFERENCES

Hind 1931, p.77, no.17; Robinson 1979a, no.B-11;
exh. cat. Vienna 1993, under no.96; Frensemeier
2001, under no.117; exh. cat. Milwaukee 2005–06,
under no.105; Van den Eerenbeemd 2006, no.32

36

PROVENANCE

Cornelis Ploos van Amstel sale, Amsterdam, 3rd
March 1800 and following days, Kunstboek F,
lot 11, bought by "Mensart" (fl. 105); Duke Albert
von Sachsen-Teschen

EXHIBITIONS

Vienna 1993, no.96; New York and Fort Worth 1995,
no.85; Milwaukee 2005–06, no.105; Vienna 2009,
no.176

PROVENANCE

W. Baartz sale, Rotterdam, 6th–8th June 1860, Livre I, lot 222, bought by Lamme for C.J. Fodor (fl. 159); bequest of C.J. Fodor, 1860

REFERENCES

(Selection) Hofstede de Groot 1912, under no.126; Robinson 1979a, p.10 and no.D-6; Broos and Schapelhouman 1993, no.138 (with earlier literature and exhibitions); Frensemeier 2001, under nos.115 and 117

37

152

38

PROVENANCE

Henri Duval sale, Amsterdam, 22nd–23rd June 1910, lot 405, bought by Cornelis Hofstede de Groot (fl. 975); his sale, Leipzig, 4th November 1931, lot 246, bought by Frits Lugt (DM 300)

EXHIBITIONS

Paris 1970a, no.126; Paris 1974, no.115; New York and Paris 1977–78, no.108

REFERENCES

Hirschmann 1917, p.209; Becker 1923, no.47; Bernt 1957–58, II, no.595; Van Gelder 1958, pp.40 and 96; Robinson 1979a, no.D-7; Frensemeier 2001, under no.117

wholly visible. This meant that the cow lying on the ground that was so prominent in the initial sketch had to be jettisoned; two lambs lie in her place. The sheep that is drinking from the stream immediately to the left of the standing woman metamorphosed into a drinking dog. Of the two human figures, the woman is still standing in exactly the same position in the worked-up drawing as in the early sketch. Her pose corresponds entirely – aside from the angle of her head – to that of the small figure on the right in the sheet of studies in Paris (cat. no.37). However, the seated man was not left unchanged. In the preliminary sketch his left leg is dangling, partly in the water. In the finished drawing, his left leg is crossed over the right; his right hand rests on the instep of his left foot, while his left hand rests on his knee. This pose derives exactly from that of the figure on the left in a sheet of studies of seated boys that is preserved in the Amsterdam Museum (cat. no.38). From the fact that the woman is left unchanged but the seated boy is altered in the second drawing Robinson shrewdly concludes that in the case of the woman Van de Velde used a study he already had in his stock of motifs, whereas for the boy he needed a new 'custom-made' drawing. This explanation sounds highly plausible: in this way, the artist's stock of figure studies expanded organically over the years into an ever larger 'archive' that

FIG.151
Adriaen van de Velde, *A herdsman with animals by a river*. Oil on panel, 30.6 × 39.3 cm. Present whereabouts unknown

FIG.152
Adriaen van de Velde, *A couple with animals by a river*. Signed and dated, lower centre: *A.V.Velde 1667*. Oil on canvas, 33.7 × 28.6 cm Sale, London, Christie's, 9th July 1993, lot 161

he could use time and again. The study of the seated boy on the right was used in a painting whose current whereabouts are unknown (fig.151).[2]

Robinson rightly referred to the large, detailed drawings made in preparation for paintings as *modelli*. The word's literal meaning is simply 'example', and that is precisely what these drawings were – examples that could be consulted during the painting process. At the moment we do not know a great deal about the way in which Van de Velde transferred his compositions to panels or canvas; technical aids might shed more light on this in the future. In any case, the *modelli* did not serve as working drawings, used to transfer the image to canvas or panel: in that case, they would display traces of a grid. Possibly the drawings remained in the studio after they had served their purpose and the painting was finished, as useful illustrations of the artist's work to show to prospective clients. The Haarlem painters Salomon and Jan de Bray are known to have made their own copies after paintings that were about to leave the studio. These drawings could later be shown to clients as examples of their work.[3] In the case of Van de Velde, the *modelli* may easily have enjoyed a second life as advertising material.

The painting that eventually resulted from the deliberations described above was preserved. It once formed part of the famous Steengracht van Duivenvoorde collection and was last recorded at an auction in London in 1993, but since then it has disappeared from sight (fig.152).[4] Judging by the reproduction in the auction catalogue, the painting was quite dirty at that time; in any case some of the details are scarcely legible. As far as can be seen, Van de Velde adhered closely to his *modello* when making the painting. The only change appears to be that the painting became slightly less square, displaying rather more of the cloudy sky above the trees than in the drawing.
M.S.

NOTES

1 The drawing in Vienna, which was first published in exh. cat. Vienna 1993, no.96, was known to Robinson only from the facsimile print that Cornelis Ploos van Amstel had made after it (Laurentius, Niemeijer and Ploos van Amstel 1980, p.257, no.4).
2 Hofstede de Groot 1912, no.129; Frensemeier 2001, no.115.
3 See Giltaij and Lammertse 2001, passim.
4 See De Vries and Buvelot 2012, p.104, no.78.

39

Two studies of a resting shepherd

Red chalk over remnants of a sketch in graphite or black chalk, framing lines in graphite, 19.9 × 29.1 cm
Signed(?), lower left: *A.v.d.Velde.f:* (red chalk); verso, lower left, the mark of Jacob de Vos Jbzn (Lugt 1450); lower centre, the mark of the Rijksprentenkabinet, Rijksmuseum, Amsterdam (Lugt 2228)
Rijksprentenkabinet, Rijksmuseum, Amsterdam, inv. no.RP-T-1885-A-497

This sheet shows two studies of the same boy shepherd, reclining in rest: in one he is asleep, in the other awake. His legs were drawn only once: the same position could do service for either pose. Seventeenth-century artists were keen to avoid unnecessary work.

Van de Velde followed one of his standard procedures here, starting the drawing in black chalk and very soon switching to red chalk. The rationale underlying this rather curious method is not entirely clear. One consideration might have been that red chalk is harder to erase than black. Yet in this drawing Van de Velde first sketched the boy's legs in black chalk and then immediately corrected the sketch in red chalk, ostensibly without making the slightest attempt to erase the black lines. He did the same in the upper torso of the sleeping boy. Perhaps the artist considered such incidental black accents amid the red to be attractive.

This sheet of studies clearly belonged to Van de Velde's stock of motifs, the collection of figure drawings to which he could always have recourse when painting figures in his landscapes. We encounter the boy shepherd – this time awake – in a painting in Karlsruhe (fig.154).[1] He also makes an appearance, in miniature, in a drawing in Berlin, which gives the impression of having been an initial idea for a painting (fig.153).[2] There he lies in the sleeping pose, his head in the lap of a young shepherdess who is bending over towards him and seems to be lovingly caressing his curls. He crops up again, sleeping amid his sheep, in an anonymous painting that was put up for auction at Christie's, Amsterdam, in 2007 (fig.155). Finally, there is a rather enigmatic drawing in Chantilly (fig.156).[3] There too we encounter him fast asleep, and he is a meticulous hybrid of the two components of the Amsterdam sheet of studies – the torso of the sleeping shepherd combined with the legs of the waking boy. The drawing in Chantilly is clearly the work of a copyist, and some of the details have been botched: the face of the sleeping boy, in particular, has become a rather boorish square head.

FIG.153
Adriaen van de Velde, *Italian landscape with herdsman, herdswoman and animals.*
Pen in brown, brown wash, 16.5 × 21.5 cm.
Kupferstichkabinett, Staatliche Museen zu Berlin, inv. no.KDZ 1550

FIG.154
Adriaen van de Velde, *Resting herdsman with animals*. Signed and dated, centre left: *A.v.Velde. f/ 1671* (last two digits difficult to read). Oil on canvas, mounted on wood, 31.5 × 40.8 cm. Staatliche Kunsthalle, Karlsruhe, inv. no.292

FIG.155
Follower of Adriaen van de Velde, *A herdsman sleeping outside a shed among his herd in a wooded landscape*. Oil on canvas, 38.5 × 44 cm. Sale, Amsterdam, Christie's, 19th–20th December 2007, lot 793

The drawing technique too is unlike Van de Velde's. While it is true that the artist has worked in red chalk over an initial rough sketch in black chalk, in some places he has gone over the red chalk with a damp brush, creating a somewhat blurred effect, something that Van de Velde appears never to have done. Still, it is intriguing that the shepherd boy in the drawing in Chantilly is accompanied by a number of sheep that also appear in the painting offered at auction in 2007 (fig.155). This observation almost inevitably prompts certain new assumptions. Perhaps the painting is a copy after a lost original by Van de Velde; the drawing in Chantilly might then have been based on a drawing that was similar to, and had the same function as, the separate sketches that Van de Velde used for his painting of *The Hut* – the two drawings at the Amsterdam Museum (see cat. nos.32 and 33). Such a drawing could also have been used to make a counterproof. In an overdoor painting by Dirck van Bergen at Ham House in Richmond, Surrey, we encounter the same sleeping shepherd accompanied by the same animals in reverse image (fig.157). Van Bergen, whom Houbraken names as one of Adriaen's pupils, evidently had at his disposal a sheet showing this group in reverse.[4] Hypotheses of this kind

FIG.156
After Adriaen van de Velde, *The sleeping shepherd*. Red and black chalk, 14.8 × 25.6 cm. Musée Condé, Chantilly, inv. no.DE 1109 (373 bis)

FIG.157
Dirck van Bergen, *Landscape with nursing herdswoman, sleeping herdsman and a cow, a horse and sheep*, c.1675. Oil on canvas, 53.3 × 153.7 cm. Ham House (National Trust), Richmond, Surrey, inv. no.NT 1140135

always lead to the same slightly disconcerting conclusion: there must once have been far more than we know today.

While in the eighteenth and early nineteenth centuries it was above all Van de Velde's highly finished landscapes with figures – coloured or not – that were celebrated and coveted by collectors, in the second half of the nineteenth century the art-loving public gravitated more to his figure studies. This trend continued in the twentieth century; Van de Velde's figure studies were repeatedly praised as high points in seventeenth-century Dutch draughtsmanship. Even so, dissenting voices were also heard. When in 1955 K.G. Boon presented a concise overview of Dutch draughtsmanship in the seventeenth century, he occasionally adopted a rather cheerless tone. Presenting the sheet of studies in Amsterdam to support his appraisal, Boon expressed only reluctant admiration for it. Having first praised Van de Velde's animal studies for their monumentality, he wrote: "... in his other drawings too, whether they were figure studies drawn with fluid, supple transitions or studies of tree-lined meadows, Van de Velde was ahead of his time. Unfortunately he failed to renew his subjects, with the result that his drawings gradually became stale as pure specimens of virtuosity".[5] M.S.

PROVENANCE

Jacob de Vos Jbzn; his sale, Amsterdam, 22nd–24th May 1883, lot 545, bought by Carl Schöffer (fl. 600); purchased with the support of the Vereniging Rembrandt, 1885

EXHIBITIONS

London 1929, no.713; Washington etc. 1958–59, no.98; Amsterdam and Washington 1981–82, pp.118–19, fig.7, p.143, no.94; Amsterdam 1983, no.94; Amsterdam 2000b, no.67

REFERENCES

Moes 1905–06, I, no.82; Kleinmann 1913, I, no.58; Van Regteren Altena 1948, no.42; Boon 1955, pp.148 and 151; Lauts 1966, p.300; Stechow 1967, p.35, note 15; Robinson 1979a, no.D-21; Filedt Kok *et al.* 2001, no.96

NOTES

1 Lauts 1966, I, p.300, no.292; Hofstede de Groot 1912, no.206; Frensemeier 2001, no.126. For a copy of the Karlsruhe painting, see sale, Munich, 22nd and 23rd June 1932, lot 460 (ill.).

2 Bock and Rosenberg 1930, I, p.293; Zoege von Manteuffel 1927, p.71.

3 Exh. cat. Chantilly 2001–02, no.53. In this entry, David Mandrella tentatively attributed the

drawing to Dirck van Bergen, although in the realisation that the endeavour was unlikely to succeed.

4 The sleeping herdsman accompanied by the same animals in reverse image crops up once more in a painting that was sold as "Circle of Adriaen van de Velde" at Van Ham, Cologne, 16th November 2007, lot 805.

5 "*Ook in zijn andere tekeningen, hetzij figuurstudies getekend met vloeiende en soepele overgangen, hetzij studies van met bomen omzoomde weiden, was Van de Velde zijn tijd vooruit. Helaas wist hij zijn onderwerpen niet te vernieuwen, zodat zijn tekeningen langzamerhand in louter virtuositeit verstarden*": Boon 1955, p.151.

40

A young man playing the harp

Red chalk over remnants of a sketch in black
chalk, 21.5 × 27.4 cm
Fondation Custodia, Collection Frits Lugt, Paris,
inv. no.1174

The vast majority of Adriaen van de Velde's figure studies are 'neutral' – for want of a better word – in nature: that is, in most cases, it is impossible to tell what role they might end up playing in a composition. That the nudes are blank slates, as it were, is self-evident, but even the clothed figures are generally not identifiable as specific characters, since they have no attributes and their costumes are quite indeterminate. Occasionally a man may be recognizable as a shepherd, a woman perhaps as a farmer's wife or a shepherdess, and then there is the intriguing study with two villains in London (cat. no.41). One who was unmistakably cast in his role from the start is the overpowering figure of the mourning John the Evangelist (cat. no.21). A slightly more difficult case is the drawing under discussion here of a young man playing a harp.

There are really only two possibilities for a youth plucking a harp: he is either the mythical singer Orpheus, who bewitches the animals with his music, or the young David playing the harp for King Saul, who is afflicted by periodic bouts of madness. Initially, Orpheus seems the likeliest candidate. After all, the singer is traditionally depicted in a landscape, surrounded by a varied company of exotic and indigenous creatures. On the few occasions on which Van de Velde painted subjects from antique mythology he always opted for scenes set in a landscape, and within these he gravitated to those that could feature the kind of animals that appear in his other landscapes – *Mercury and Argus*, *Mercury and Battus* and *Vertumnus and Pomona*.[1] Furthermore, Van de Velde had a convenient example close to home: Paulus Potter, whose work he evidently held in high regard, painted an *Orpheus and the animals* in 1650.[2] Yet it does not quite fit. As already noted, Orpheus is always surrounded by a mix of domestic and exotic creatures, and Van de Velde very rarely depicted more outlandish animals. Even in his drawing of *The Golden Age* (cat. no.59), another subject that – albeit a little less compellingly than an *Orpheus* – invites the artist to assemble a varied fauna, he confines himself to some cattle, a goat and chickens.

Could the youth then be David after all, whose play assuages the tormented spirits of King Saul (1 Samuel 16:23)? This instantly conjures up visions of a different type of painting. The story takes place inside, and strictly speaking only two characters matter – the king and his harp-playing servant. Although one can find a great many interpretations of the scene depicting Saul amid an extensive royal household, Rembrandt showed convincingly in his *Saul and David* (fig.158) that an intense emotional scene could be built up with only the two protagonists.[3] With a little imagination, we might speculate that the harpist in the Paris drawing was intended to be used for the right half of a painting that was compositionally akin to Rembrandt's work. If we then recall Van de Velde's *Annunciation* – another scene with only two 'actors' – the picture takes shape: a painting about the same size as *The Annunciation*, with two large, colourful figures painted with virtuoso smoothness and set against a dark background. Unfortunately, such a vision can never be more than an enticing fantasy, since there is nothing now to suggest that Van de Velde ever produced such a painting.

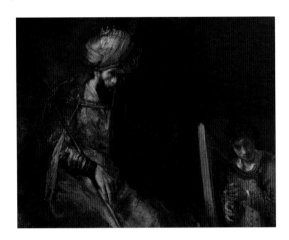

Whatever the drawing's original function, it is incontrovertibly one of the most attractive figure studies by Van de Velde to have been preserved. The harpist's concentration, his utter absorption in his play, has been captured magnificently: lips slightly parted, his eyes are intent on the movement of his hands. On the right Van de Velde drew another variant of the face, in which it is turned slightly more towards the viewer, the mouth closed. He also repeated the harpist's right hand, with only subtle modifications to the angle of the hand and the positions of the fingers, in addition to a slight alteration to the play of light. Minor details of this kind are characteristic of the almost obsessive concentration with which Van de Velde drew such figure studies.

A near-rectangular strip has been unceremoniously lopped off the lower right corner of the sheet and replaced by a blank piece of paper. The intervention appears fairly pointless and one wonders what might have prompted it. It is of course possible that there was some blemish here and that one of the past owners was attempting a form of damage limitation. There is another possible scenario, in which we should bear in mind that nothing is known about the drawing's early collecting history. It first appears at the auction of the Rosenheim brothers in 1923, in a lot of eight drawings, only two of which were furnished with attributions, the rest being curtly summarized as "and six others". Frits Lugt, who purchased the lot at the London sale, evidently recognized the drawing as a work by Adriaen van de Velde. The discarded strip of paper was exactly large enough to accommodate the kind of beautifully written 'signature' as found on some of Van de Velde's drawings, notably his figure studies (see cat. nos.21, 37, 39 and 42). It is not inconceivable that the drawing fell into the hands of someone who thought it might be sold more profitably under a greater name than Van de Velde's and who therefore had the inscription removed. M.S.

41

*A mounted horseman with a study
of a head and shoulders below*

Red chalk, 28.8 × 19.5 cm
Remains of an inscription, lower left:
.d. velde dess (?; graphite or black chalk)
British Museum, London, inv. no.1895,0915.1330

Many of Adriaen van de Velde's figure studies, especially those in red chalk, have a distinctly 'painterly' quality. He composed his studies employing large areas of parallel hatching, which is frequently so dense that the individual lines can scarcely be distinguished. He appears to have been less concerned to capture small details than to render the light that glances off the figures, the play of light and shade on faces, hands and clothing.

The London study of a mounted horseman is among the drawings in which this mode of composition, from almost exclusively parallel lines, has been taken to extremes. The light comes from the upper right, almost from behind the figure, and graces the brim of his hat, the left half of his nose, his left cheek, his left upper arm and his back. His face and hair are composed almost entirely from hatching that runs from the lower left to the top right; there is not a single sharp contour to be seen. His eyes, on which the wide brim of his hat casts a shadow, are barely visible. He seems to be peering into the distance and squinting against the glare of the sun. Leaning forward slightly, he appears rapt in concentration, every sinew of his body taut, poised for action. That he is mounted is suggested only by his left foot in a stirrup; the artist has not indicated his horse at all. Another head of a man has been drawn in the lower right corner of this sheet, wearing a similar wide-brimmed hat. This man too is squinting in the bright sunlight and appears to be waiting for something outside the viewer's field of vision. Part of the barrel of a rifle is visible in the lower right corner.

We are left in no doubt that these folk are up to no good. They certainly bear no relation to the jaunty world of fashionable hunting parties, the biotope of sumptuously dressed aristocratic ladies and gentlemen whose delightful existence is ruffled only by the occasional poor wretch who crosses their path to beg for a few pennies (see cat. nos.11 and 12). These men belong to the raw reality of desperadoes, mercenaries whose sole objective is survival. It is a world that Van de Velde evoked in more than one drawing.

The artist evidently produced these studies with a specific goal in mind; they are not the kind of sketches he made for his stock of figure studies to be used in future compositions. The men in the London drawing must have been intended to play a role in a scene such as that depicted in the drawing *Plundering soldiers at a peasant's dwelling* (cat. no.56), or a similar scene depicting robbers waylaying a carriage with terrified travellers. Unfortunately, there is not a single other drawing or painting that can be linked to the London drawing. For the present, the precise purpose for which it was made remains a mystery. M.S.

PROVENANCE

P.H. Lankrink (Lugt 2090); John Malcolm of
Poltalloch (1805–1893); purchased from John
Wingfield Malcolm, 1895

REFERENCES

Hind 1931, pp.74–75, no.1; Royalton-Kisch,
Chapman and Coppel 1996, no.98; Taylor 2008,
pp.155, 156, fig.3, and pp.159–61

42

Standing male nude

Red chalk over remnants of a sketch in black
chalk or graphite, framing lines in light red chalk,
32.2 × 23.2 cm
Signed(?), lower left: *A.v.d. / Velde. f* (red chalk);
verso, upper right: *XVI* (pencil)
Rijksprentenkabinet, Rijksmuseum, Amsterdam,
inv. no.RP-T-1954-107

In many of his figure studies, both nude and clothed, Adriaen van de Velde
placed his models in a pronounced raking light, enhancing the relief of the
figures and giving them a more sculptural quality. We can see this here: the
light comes from the upper left, and the man's raised right arm casts a sharp
shadow on his body. The entire figure is drawn in red chalk, but traces are
visible here and there of a very rough initial design in graphite or black chalk
– in the profile of the face, the right arm and hand, the loins and the right leg.
Tentative sketches of this kind in black are quite common in Van de Velde's
figure studies; another example can be found in the sheet with two studies of
a resting shepherd (cat. no.39). It has to be said that the practical advantage
of this method is not entirely clear.

Unlike most of Van de Velde's other studies after male nudes, the model
in this drawing is completely naked. Virtually all the other male nudes he
depicted are draped with fairly voluminous loincloths. There is one other
drawing, a study of a kneeling man (fig.159), in which the figure is likewise
completely nude.[1] Indeed, judging from the facial features and the luxuriant,
somewhat tangled mass of shoulder-length hair in both, it seems more than
likely that the same model posed for both drawings. Evidently most male
models balked at posing completely naked but this man had no objection.
Van de Velde made his studies – whether nude or clothed – with two different
aims. Some were produced, as can be inferred from their highly specific
pose, as preparatory studies for figures in particular paintings, while others
were clearly intended to be fitted into a composition at some later stage; they
were added to a stock of motifs that the artist could draw on when needed.
Whether the Amsterdam drawing belongs to the first or second category is

FIG.159
Adriaen van de Velde, *Kneeling man*. Signed(?),
upper right: *A.v.d. Velde.f*. Red chalk, 32 × 24 cm.
Leiden University Library, inv. no.PK-T-AW-294

FIG.160
Adriaen van de Velde, *Standing male nude*.
Counterproof of cat no.41, 33.8 × 24.6 cm.
Die Lübecker Museen, Museum Behnhaus
Drägerhaus, inv. no.AB 397

not easy to say. The gesture and facial expression are fairly specific: the man appears to be recoiling in fear or surprise, while pointing at something or someone. If you dressed him in royal robes, he might be King David, trying to defend himself from the accusations of the prophet Nathan. Clad in a sheepskin, he might pass for a shepherd engaged in a heated exchange with a traveller. A counterproof of the drawing is preserved in Lübeck (fig.160).[2] The existence of such a counterproof might in itself be construed as evidence that the drawing belonged to Van de Velde's stock of motifs: the man's arm could point left or right according to the needs of the composition.

Drawings of which a counterproof was made have a somewhat lacklustre, faded appearance; this is because the procedure deprived them of some of their pigment. Van de Velde often retouched such drawings afterwards to brighten them up a little. He did so in this case – so successfully that if we did not possess the irrefutable evidence for it, no one would probably ever have guessed that the sheet had passed through the press. Especially in the face, the hands and the feet, Van de Velde has enhanced all sorts of details with short, angular strokes, giving the drawing a remarkably vibrant appearance. In the lower left corner, the drawing has an inscription penned in splendid handwriting; whether it is a signature or a later addition is not entirely certain. Characteristic details include the fine regular handwriting, the tall, slim capital A with a little 'foot' on its right 'leg', the horizontal dash above the first letter v, the abbreviation for *fecit* written as an elegant monogram, and the long horizontal stroke at the end. Inscriptions of this kind appear mostly in certain of Van de Velde's figure studies (see cat. nos.21, 37 and 39). In the case of the present nude study, it is clear that the inscription was not added immediately after the drawing's completion, since it does not appear in the counterproof in Lübeck. It is conceivable that Van de Velde himself signed some of his finest figure studies at a later stage, in the hope of being able to sell them to collectors. Another possibility is that, after Van de Velde's death, his widow or – later still – the daughter who provided Houbraken with information about her father furnished some of the drawings with inscriptions, with the same purpose of making them more attractive to collectors. M.S.

PROVENANCE

H.C. Valkema Blouw sale, Amsterdam, 2nd–4th March 1954, lot 490, bought by the Rijksmuseum (together with lot 491, for fl. 150)

EXHIBITIONS

Amsterdam and Washington 1981–82, pp.118–19, fig.11, pp.143–44, no.95

NOTES

1 Exh. cat. Amsterdam 1956, no.127.
2 Hasse 1969, pp.56–57. The height of the counterproof measures 1.6 cm. more than the drawing. The drawing was probably cropped along the top, since the man's head grazes the framing line there.

43

A path by sand hills and trees

Black chalk, brush and grey ink, framing lines
with pen and dark brown ink, 20.4 × 32.1 cm
Signed, lower right: *A.v.de velde.* (pen and brown ink);
verso, lower left, the mark of Jacob de Vos Jbzn
(Lugt 1450)
Rijksprentenkabinet, Rijksmuseum, Amsterdam,
inv. no.RP-T-1886-A-622

AMSTERDAM ONLY

The vast majority of Adriaen van de Velde's landscape drawings can be assumed to have been produced within the four walls of his studio, for most are idealized landscapes, some of them composed with the aid of motifs drawn from direct observation, but still largely products of the artist's imagination. There are a handful of drawings of a highly topographical nature – *Skittle players in a clearing* (cat. no.55) being a case in point – that Van de Velde did make from life, wholly or largely on the spot: possibly he produced a sketch in chalk in the open air, later elaborating it with his pen in the studio. Drawings that were created entirely outside are scarcer still; however, there are several strong indications that *A path by sand hills and trees* was made in its entirety *en plein air*.

First and foremost, of course, there is the simple, informal composition depicting an unpaved road with cart tracks that curves gently away from the right foreground to the left, a few low sand hills on the right and behind them a row of trees among which, here and there, we glimpse the roofs of houses. On the left the image is bounded by a tree that is partly cut off by the edge of the sheet. It is such an utterly everyday scene, if not downright commonplace: this is not the stuff of imagination but something seen and registered. Van de Velde began by sketching the scene in black chalk, after which he finished it with the brush and grey ink. That is a method with which we are familiar from some of his initial ideas for paintings that sprang *uyt de geest* (from the mind) – see *Herdsman with livestock and passing travellers* (cat. no.50); yet here the relationship between the initial design in black chalk and the drawing in grey ink is fundamentally different. In the drawings originating *uyt de geest*, the sketch in black chalk is cursory in the extreme, almost nonchalant, and as soon as he sets about working it up the artist allows himself to make major changes to his original plan. In the *Path by sand hills and trees*, the chalk drawing, though sketch-like, is far more precise: it is clear that the draughtsman's hand was registering what his eyes saw. Here, the chalk drawing and wash areas do not just supplement each other but form a unified whole – they are interdependent. This is clearest in the way in which Van de Velde has drawn the light-coloured sand hills, blinking in the sunlight. He has suggested the volume of those mounds of sand almost exclusively by indicating the shaded parts. He began by sketching the contours of the little hills very lightly in chalk, after which he delineated only the upper edges of the shaded sections, also with the barest of chalk lines. Finally, he drew the complete shape of the shadows purely with brush and grey ink. Given that the chalk sketch and the sections in grey ink are connected so organically, the only possible conclusion is that the drawing was produced in its entirety on the spot *en plein air*.

Landscape drawings of this type, as already noted, are extremely rare. The only other one to display a similar, completely straightforward approach, without the slightest desire to idealize, is a landscape in Munich (fig.161).[1] In a drawing in the Amsterdam Museum (fig.162), whose unpretentious primary motif – a gently rolling landscape with a few clumps of trees – was probably drawn from direct observation, the artist appears nonetheless to have taken a few steps in the direction of pleasant embellishment: in the foreground a

FIG.161
Adriaen van de Velde, *Wooded landscape*.
Brush and grey ink, 17.5 × 29.9 cm. Staatliche
Graphische Sammlung, Munich, inv. no.2034 z

FIG.162
Adriaen van de Velde, *Panoramic landscape with
a cow and sheep*. Black chalk, brush and grey
ink, 16.7 × 28.1 cm. Amsterdam Museum,
C.J. Fodor Bequest, inv. no.10349

cow and a few sheep have been added as staffage, a pollard willow on the left works emphatically as a repoussoir, and clouds chase across the high-arching sky.[2]

In nineteenth-century auction catalogues, the drawing in the Rijksmuseum is called *Vue des dunes de Haarlem*. It seems likely that 'Haarlem' was added purely because Houbraken had written that Adriaen van de Velde was a pupil of the Haarlem landscape painter Jan Wijnants and so he must therefore have wandered around the Haarlem dunes. It is quite possible that Van de Velde did make his drawings in Holland's coastal dunes; alternatively, he may have made them in the Gooi, the sandy region with heath and woodland to the south-east of Amsterdam. M.S.

PROVENANCE

According to the catalogue of the Van Cranenburgh sale, the drawing originates from the Goll van Franckenstein collection. However, it is not listed in the Goll van Franckenstein sale catalogue (Amsterdam, 1st July 1833 and following days); Hendrik van Cranenburgh sale, Amsterdam, 26th October 1858 and following days, Portefeuille D, lot 79, bought by De Vries for Jacob de Vos Jbzn (fl. 35); Jacob de Vos Jbzn sale, Amsterdam, 22nd–24th May 1883, lot 541 (fl. 200); purchased with the support of the Vereniging Rembrandt, 1886

EXHIBITIONS

Amsterdam 1983, no.93

NOTES

1 Wegner 1973, I, p.136, no.977.
2 Broos and Schapelhouman 1993, no.136.

44

A huntsman with his dog by a pond in the woods

Black chalk, brush and grey and brown ink,
23.4 × 36.6 cm
Signed, lower left: *A.v.d.Velde f.* (black chalk); the
signature is repeated below in a different hand
(pen and brown ink)
Petit Palais, Musée des Beaux-Arts de la Ville
de Paris, inv. no.D-DUT 1132

FIG.163
Adriaen van de Velde, *Landscape with cattle and
an angler on the bank of a pond*. Signed and dated,
upper left: *a. v. velde: fᵉ 1671*. Pen and brown ink,
brush and grey ink worked up, 19 × 31.5 cm. Petit
Palais, Musée des Beaux-Arts de la Ville de Paris,
inv. no.D-DUT 1133

A great deal of money changed hands in the week of 30th October 1833, during the sale of Jacob de Vos's collection of drawings at the 'Huis met de Hoofden' on Keizersgracht in Amsterdam. In the Rijksmuseum's library is a copy of the auction catalogue in which an eye witness noted down the purchasers' names along with the winning bids. Anyone who leafs through the book will be surprised by the small number of purchasers. The same names recur again and again – in first place, those of the brokers Jeronimo de Vries, Albertus Brondgeest, Engelbert Michael Engelberts and Cornelis François Roos, who probably made most of their purchases on commission for a host of clients. In addition, we frequently encounter the names of Johannes Hulswit and Gerrit Jan Michaëlis, both of whom were artists as well as dealers. Michaëlis was also the curator and superintendent of Teylers Museum, Haarlem. The name "Booymans" also occurs a few times; this was undoubtedly the collector Frans Jacob Otto Boijmans (1767–1847). The only foreigners attending the auction appear to have been the famous English art dealer Samuel Woodburn and the French connoisseur and collector Ignace-Joseph Chevalier de Claussin. The auction was clearly dominated by a small coterie: outsiders had no chance.

Prices were high, and for three drawings by Adriaen van de Velde, in particular, the buyers dug deep into their pockets. Michaëlis paid 1,730 guilders for the *Landscape with livestock crossing a river* for Teylers Museum (see cat. no.49). A *Landscape with cattle and an angler on the bank of a pond* (fig.163),[1] lot 2 in Kunstboek C, went for 1,190 guilders to De Vries, who purchased it for a nephew of the deceased collector Jacob de Vos Wzn (1774–1844). De Vos may also have hoped to acquire the *Huntsman with his dog* discussed here, but this drawing was bought by Hulswit for 1,350 guilders. Both drawings would eventually end up in the collection of Jacob de Vos Jbzn (1803–1878), Jacob de Vos Wzn's son. This youngest Jacob de Vos inherited the former from his father and purchased the latter at the Van Cranenburgh sale in 1858. At the sale of the estate of Jacob de Vos Jbzn in 1883, both drawings were purchased by the Parisian art dealer Clément, acting on behalf of the brothers Eugène (1807–1886) and Auguste Dutuit (1812–1902).

In the auction catalogue of the eldest Jacob de Vos, *A huntsman with his dog* is described in the customary flowery language: "A first-rate and outstandingly beautiful woodland view, with a clear pond, beside which a huntsman and his dog have paused to rest. The diverse species of trees and the bright sunlight on them are depicted in an astonishingly natural manner, and this drawing, worked up in great detail and furnished with a thin brown wash, is among the best works produced by this renowned master."[2] The text is interesting less for what it says than for what it omits – that the drawing was completed by an unknown artist at a later stage. It was indeed standard practice in the eighteenth century for artists to add staffage to drawings that were unfinished, or that were little more than sketches. In those days collectors had a strong preference for meticulously worked, 'finished' drawings. If a drawing fell short of the prevailing aesthetic ideal, it was considered entirely acceptable to enlist the services of someone who

could brighten it up and if needs be add staffage. Such interventions were never seen as violations of the work's integrity. On the contrary, they were welcome embellishments, and auction catalogues generally referred to them expressly.[3] It is therefore odd that the description of *A huntsman with his dog* says nothing about the later additions. True, the artist who modified the drawing did so with taste and discretion. It is therefore possible that his efforts were honestly not recognized as such. In any case, he did not do all that much. In the foreground he brushed in brown ink perhaps a little too emphatically in his attempt to enhance the repoussoir effect of the strip of grassland. For the rest, only the long shadow under the large tree on the left has been accentuated a little, and the unknown artist also added some dark accents in the foliage of the trees on the right, possibly to counterbalance the effect. The seated huntsman and his dog also appear to be later additions. Although rather small, they are not bad efforts, and the dog is certainly in the spirit of Adriaen van de Velde. Still, the execution is rather too finicky and lacking in verve to be taken for the master's own work.

What remains if we try to imagine how the drawing looked without the additions? A woodland scene, somewhat akin to *Skittle players in a clearing* in Berlin (see cat. no.55), that was probably based on studies drawn from life, but – given the rather formal composition – produced in the studio. It is a work executed with more refined, cautious draughtsmanship than the *Skittle players*, and done entirely with the tip of the brush. In style it is closer to the *Landscape with sleeping shepherd* of 1670 in the Amsterdam Museum (fig.164).[4] We must resign ourselves to the later additions; they are part of the drawing's history, and even with these 'improvements' it remains an impressive, masterly drawing. M.S.

REFERENCES

Lugt 1927, p.34, no.79

NOTES

1 Lugt 1927, pp.33–34, no.77.
2 *"Een kapitaal en uitmuntend fraai Boschgezigt, met een heldere waterplas, waarbij een rustende jager en een hond. De onderscheidene soorten van boomen en het heldere zonlicht op dezelve zijn verwonderlijk natuurlijk voorgesteld, en deze zeer uitvoerige en dun met bruine inkt gewasschen Teekening, behoort tot de beste van dezen beroemden Meester"*; Jacob de Vos sale, Amsterdam, 30th October 1833 and following days, Kunstboek D, lot 1.
3 See Broos 1989.
4 Broos and Schapelhouman 1993, no.140.

45

A hut in the woods

Black chalk, brush and grey and black ink, heightened
in places with white body-colour, on paper discoloured
to light brown, framing lines with pen and black ink,
18.4 × 29.1 cm
Verso, lower left: *N.° 585* (graphite); behind this: *de 2 f
1241,0* (for the rest illegible); roughly in the centre of
the sheet: *n° 2* (pencil, nineteenth-century); lower right,
twice, the mark of William Pitcairn Knowles (Lugt 2643);
centre right: *4–4* (pen and brown ink, seventeenth- or
eighteenth-century)
Rijksprentenkabinet, Rijksmuseum, Amsterdam,
inv. no.RP-T-1902-A-4603

"... he sat all in a heap, with a board in his lap, and a
magnifying or spectacle glass in his hand; on his head he had a night-cap
almost down to his eyes, with his left leg over his hat, possibly to save it from
the wind; a small light coming from between the trees shone on his lap".[1]
This was how Gerard de Lairesse described an artist sitting drawing from
nature in the woods in his *Groot schilderboek* (1707). The passage comes from
a chapter that bears the ominous title: 'Of Things Deformed and Broken,
Falsely Called Painter-Like'. Lairesse wrote as if relating a bad dream; the
passage is essentially one long tirade against the painting of picturesque
decay. After the narrator has left the first draughtsman in his dream, he
encounters another, "... who stood and drew after a small rivulet full of big
and little clods of earth and pebbles, which he neatly designed on drawing
paper [*gegrond papier*], and marked with their different colours. His whole
portfolio was full of such painter-like trumpery; such as muddy water,
decayed and broken stones, pieces-of wood, barren shrubs and bushes,
rough grounds, toads, snakes, &c".[2] The text is interesting for several reasons.
It reveals that in De Lairesse's day – which was also Adriaen van de Velde's
day, since the two were only about four years apart in age – it was evidently
very common to go out with a drawing board and an inkpot to draw from
nature. The second draughtsman used "*gegrond papier*", paper that had been
covered with a coloured preparatory layer, and we can assume that he worked
with black and white chalk. The phrase "and marked with their different
colours" probably meant that this artist furnished his drawing with notes
indicating colours. In any case it is clear that both these artists did a great
deal more than scrawl a few rapid observations in a sketchbook.

Looking at a drawing such as *A hut in the woods* with De Lairesse's text
to hand raises all sorts of questions. Could such a highly detailed drawing
have been made entirely outside, from nature? Or did the draughtsman
merely sit outside drawing with chalk, later working up the details in his
studio? Or did the artist go through the entire process within the walls of his
workshop, making use of small sketches he had previously drawn *en plein
air*? We do not know the answer, but a few considerations can help us to
form a theory. Given its extreme simplicity, the composition initially creates
the impression that the artist plumped himself down on a fallen tree trunk
and dashed off his sketch. Simplicity can be misleading, however: even a
coloured drawing such as *Summer landscape* (see cat. no.48), which we can
surely assume to have been produced entirely in the studio, is deceptively
simple and informal in its composition. Let us look at the other extreme: it is
entirely possible that Adriaen van de Velde never set foot outside his studio
for this drawing. The hut, or sheepfold, or shed, or however one might wish
to label the little structure, appears to be the same as the one in the painting
from 1671 (see cat. no.30). Van de Velde painted that hut with the aid of a
drawing that gives a strong impression of having been made from the life
outside (see cat. no.31). In spite of its large format, it might well come from
a sketchbook; we know of even larger sketchbooks from the seventeenth
century.[3] A logical explanation would be that Van de Velde made a number
of sketches of the same hut from different angles and used one of these

for the drawing described here. And on further inspection, in spite of the ostensibly nonchalant way in which the hut is cut off by the right-hand edge, every aspect of this drawing is in complete equilibrium. The three trees on the left lean slightly to the left, thus forming a pleasing contrast with the hut's hump-backed roof. The tree behind the hut leans very slightly to the right: had the draughtsman decided to have this tree lean left as well, the image would have been rather lifeless. Then there is the extremely refined style of draughtsmanship. First came the chalk sketch, over which Van de Velde laid in the lightest grey hues, followed by successive layers, each one darker than the one before, before finally adding the details of grass stalks, twigs and leaves with the tip of the brush. Using white body-colour, he made the sunny space in the woods in which the herdsman and his dog are driving along a cow, two sheep and a goat even sunnier than it already was, and here and there he has touched up a few leaves with white. In short, most of the evidence points in the direction of the studio.

What would Gerard de Lairesse, the man whose *Groot schilderboek* was regarded as the touchstone of good taste for about a century and a half, have thought of a drawing that casts a dark, draughty and dilapidated shed in the leading role? We can hazard a guess that he would have found the subject not so 'pleasant', and many would have agreed. In any case, the drawing was never among the works that were passionately coveted by devotees of drawings in the eighteenth or nineteenth centuries. It did not surface until the end of the nineteenth century, at the Knowles sale, where it fetched the modest sum of thirty guilders. M.S.

PROVENANCE

William Pitcairn Knowles; his sale, Amsterdam, 25th–26th June 1895, lot 661 (fl. 30); purchased with the support of the Vereniging Rembrandt, 1902

EXHIBITIONS

Amsterdam 1987–88, no.69; Vancouver 2009, pp.156–57; Paris 2009–10, no.61

NOTES

1 Lairesse 1707, I, Chap. XVII ('*Van het onschoone en verbrokene, te onregt Schilderachtig genoemd*'), p.429: "*Hy zat nedergeboogen en in een gedrongen, met een bord op de schoot en een kleene inktkoker in de hand, nevens een vergrootglas of stuk van een bril, een slaapmuts tot aan zyne oogen neêrgetrokken, het linker been over zynen hoed, mogelyk om dat de zelve niet zoude weg waaijen. Een kleen lichtje, tusschen de boomen van daan komende, scheen hem op de schoot.*" The English translation has been taken from Lairesse 1817, I, p.293.

2 Lairesse 1707, I, p.430: "*... welke een kleen loopend riviertje, al staande, natekende, vol groote en kleene kluiten en keisteenen, die hy netjes op gegrond papier namodelde, en met hunne verscheidene koleuren aanwees. Deze had zyn gantsche portefeuilje vol zulke verbeeldingen van schilderachtige prullen, als modderig water, vervallene en gebrokene steenen, stukken houts, dorre takken, afgehakte gronden, padden, slangen, enz;*" English translation from Lairesse 1817, I, p.293.

3 For example, a sketchbook from 1645–46 belonging to Pieter Monincx, which measures 19.5 × 30 cm (Rijksmuseum, Amsterdam, inv. no.RP-T-1976-27; Schapelhouman and Schatborn 1987, no.36).

46

Autumn landscape with travellers and a ferry-boat, 1670

Pen and brown ink, brush and grey and brown ink over
traces of a sketch in graphite, on white paper, discoloured
to light brown; framing lines with pen and brown ink,
17.4 × 26.7 cm
Signed and dated, lower left: *A.v.Velde.f* / *1670*
(pen and grey ink)
Verso, lower left, in the hand of Cornelis Ploos van Amstel
(see Lugt 3002–04): *Ad: van de Velde f.* / *h. 6¾ d* / *b. 10¼ d.*
The work also bears inscriptions added in the nineteenth
and twentieth centuries and the mark of Museum
Fodor (Lugt 1036)
Amsterdam Museum, C.J. Fodor Bequest,
inv. no.TA 10352

AMSTERDAM ONLY

The minute clues we can garner suggest that Adriaen van de Velde's final years were not prosperous ones. He started designing decorations for maps (see cat. nos.57 and 58), the kind of work that an artist would tackle mainly to earn some money, and he certainly appears to have produced more and more drawings for the open market. This too is indicative of an acute shortage of funds. Van de Velde's signed and dated *Autumn landscape* is probably one of these drawings, intended for sale to a collector, though it is not impossible it was made on commission.

The wind is all-powerful here: nature and people alike are being buffeted by a furious gale. The horseman and his mount are leaning into the wind; the travellers making their way on foot are trying to stay upright as their cloaks flap around them. A woman in the ferry, her body encased in her cloak, makes herself as small as possible. The only creature that seems to be enjoying himself is the small dog on the left, which appears to be barking cheerfully while jumping up into the wind.

It seems likely that the drawing was initially one of a series of four, depicting the four seasons. This one, of course, is *Autumn*; Teylers Museum in Haarlem has a drawing of a winter scene which closely resembles the Amsterdam drawing in style and technique and may have belonged to the same set (fig.165);[1] the dimensions of the two drawings are nearly identical. *Spring* and *Summer* have thus far failed to surface.

In the eighteenth and nineteenth centuries, collectors doted on drawings of this kind. They loved the meticulous execution and the abundance of anecdotal detail. The popularity of such drawings translated unequivocally into money. At the sale in 1800 of Cornelis Ploos van Amstel's renowned collection, Van de Velde's *Autumn landscape* fetched 1,000 guilders, making it the third most expensive drawing in the sale. Only a coloured flowerpiece by Jan van Huysum and a coloured drawing by Adriaen van de Velde himself, *The Ferry* (see cat. no.47), fetched even higher prices.

In 1858, Carel Joseph Fodor purchased the *Autumn landscape* for fl. 1010 at the Cranenburgh sale. Fodor was a collector with a fairly conservative

FIG.165
Adriaen van de Velde, *Winter landscape with a lady and a gentleman*. Pen and brown ink, brush and grey ink, 17.6 × 26.5 cm. Teylers Museum, Haarlem, inv. no.R 048

taste, a devotee of carefully wrought, finished drawings. In the course of the nineteenth century the tide turned: around 1892, the painter and critic Emile Michel, referring explicitly to the *Autumn landscape*, stated that, although he admired the luminous quality of such drawings, and indeed the sureness of touch and ease with which they had been made, he nonetheless greatly preferred "sketches made simply by the artist, in black and red chalk, from nature".[2] Nothing much has really changed in the appreciation of Van de Velde's draughtsmanship since the end of the nineteenth century: even today, it is figure studies in black or red chalk that fetch the highest prices at auction.

At the Saportas sale in 1832, Van de Velde's *Autumn landscape* was accompanied by a "highly accurate and well-executed copy after the preceding drawing".[3] The original and the copy were both purchased by Johannes Hulswit, acting on behalf of Hendrik van Cranenburgh. The copy turned up again at the Van Cranenburgh sale, this time furnished with an attribution to "Cats".[4] The absence of a first name or initial in this attribution suggests, perhaps, that the attribution to Jacob Cats (1741–1799) need not be taken too seriously. In any case, no copy after the *Autumn landscape* that is demonstrably by Cats is known today.[5] Although Cats probably never copied Van de Velde's *Autumn landscape*, he certainly knew and admired such drawings. Indeed, a drawing such as Cats's *A windy day* in the Fitzwilliam Museum in Cambridge would appear scarcely imaginable without the example of Adriaen van de Velde (fig.166). M.S.

PROVENANCE

Probably Michiel Oudaan sale, Rotterdam, 3rd November 1766 and following days, Konstboek G, lot 73, bought by Metayer (fl. 166); Cornelis Ploos van Amstel sale, Amsterdam, 3rd March 1800 and following days, Kunstboek F, lot 1, bought by Bernard (fl. 1,000); Abraham Saportas sale, Amsterdam, 14th May 1832, Kunstboek A, lot 1, bought by Johannes Hulswit (fl. 800); Hendrik van Cranenburgh sale, Amsterdam, 26th October 1858 and following days, Portefeuille F, lot 121, bought by Lamme for C.J. Fodor (fl. 1,010); C.J. Fodor bequest, 1860

REFERENCES

Ploos van Amstel and Josi 1821, under Adriaen van de Velde; cat. Amsterdam 1863, p.42, no.235; Michel 1892, pp.120, 128; Mellaart 1926, no.31; Laurentius, Niemeijer and Ploos van Amstel 1980, p.21; Broos and Schapelhouman 1993, no.141

NOTES

1 Scholten 1904, p.258; Van Regteren Altena 1972, no.91. The drawing bears a curious inscription on the verso: *door A: V: de Velde getekent den 8 Januarij 1672 / Dit heeft hier bove van hem selfs geschreve gestaan do . .* (drawing by A: V: de Velde on 8 January 1672 / this was written above by himself b . .). If this is truly the transcript of an inscription in his own hand, it would mean that Van de Velde produced the drawing barely two weeks before his funeral. The text is probably

a romantic falsification, and the drawing, like *Autumn landscape*, must date from 1670.

2 "*... les croquis faits simplement par l'artiste, à la pierre noire et à la sanguine, en face de la nature*": Michel 1892, p.120.

3 "*Een zeer accurate en goed uitgevoerde Kopij naar de voorgaande tekening*": Abraham Saportas sale, Amsterdam, 14th May 1832, Kunstboek A, lot *1.

4 Hendrik van Cranenburgh sale, Amsterdam, 26th October 1858 and following days, Portefeuille F, lot 122.

5 However, a copy after Van de Velde's drawing by Jean Bernard (1765–1833) is preserved in the Rijksprentenkabinet, Rijksmuseum, Amsterdam, pen and brush in brown ink over a sketch in black chalk, 18.1 × 28.3 cm., inv. no.RP-T-1904-415.

47

The Ferry

Brush and watercolour over a sketch in black chalk,
17.5 × 31.2 cm
Signed, lower left, on the two wooden posts: *Adriaen / vande velde*; verso: *N° 3964* (inv. no.Goll van Franckenstein, pen and brown ink) and *J. Nieuwenhuys 1840*; numbered *N° 248*
Fondation Custodia, Collection Frits Lugt, Paris, inv. no.4776

48

Summer landscape with wheatfield, 1662

Brush and watercolour over a sketch in black chalk,
18.6 × 27.7 cm
Signed and dated, lower right: *a. v. velde f / 1662.* (pen and brown ink)
Kupferstichkabinett, Staatliche Museen zu Berlin, inv. no.KdZ 2424

To possess a coloured drawing by Adriaen van de Velde will have been the dearest wish of a good many early nineteenth-century Dutch collectors. Unfortunately, however, such drawings were rare and therefore expensive. Only the wealthiest of those who dreamt of owning one or more of these coveted items could turn this dream into reality. Christian Josi wrote in his commentary to the costly de luxe edition *Collection d'imitations de dessins d'après les principaux maîtres hollandais et flamands* of 1821 that he knew of only five or six coloured drawings by Adriaen van de Velde in the whole of the Netherlands. He singled out three of them for the highest praise: the first was a "*Vue du Rhin*", that is, the *Landscape with livestock crossing a river* that is now in Teylers Museum, Haarlem (see cat. no.49), and the second a drawing that Josi called "*Le charrette de foin*" (The haycart), which was owned at the time by the Amsterdam collector Johannes Hermanus Molkenboer. Molkenboer died in 1834. The following year, when his collection was sold at auction, the artist and the art dealer Albertus Brondgeest purchased *The Haycart* for fl. 950, but its subsequent whereabouts are a mystery. Josi's third favourite was a drawing that has been known ever since the Goll van Franckenstein sale in 1833 by the affectionate name of *Het Pontje – The Ferry*. Although Josi confessed himself incapable of saying which of the three drawings he loved most, he devoted the largest number of words to *The Ferry*: "This scene, as charming as it is simple, strikes us initially with its natural tone. The late afternoon sun bathes everything in a warm, harmonious light, which, handled by A. van de Velde's wide, virtuoso brush, produces the greatest possible illusion; see how skilfully that supreme tranquillity is contrasted with a simple incident: a few waterfowl that are swimming peacefully and in all innocence in front of the little vessel abruptly take flight, having been startled by a dog".[1] Rather unnecessarily, perhaps, the writer explains to his readers that the incident will strike the attentive viewer more than it would have struck those sitting in the boat, who would have been accustomed to the dog's antics. To read Josi is briefly to imagine oneself taking part in a nineteenth-century art appreciation evening. At these congenial gatherings, at which a group of friends and art lovers enjoyed a glass of wine while one of their number handed around items from his collection, there would be a fine mix of sophisticated discernment and joy at small anecdotal details. Those who were not so richly endowed with worldly goods as to be able to afford their own collection of drawings might always consider purchasing Josi's *Collection d'imitations de dessins*. This work consisted of a hundred beautiful facsimile prints after drawings, made using a complicated graphic procedure that had been developed – and kept a zealously guarded secret – by Cornelis Ploos van Amstel. After his death, the material from his workplace came into the possession of Josi. He added to the series until it contained a hundred prints and then marketed it, accompanied by the lengthy introduction from which the above quotation is taken. The series contains facsimiles of both *The Ferry* (fig.167) and *Landscape with cattle crossing a river* (fig.168). For the 'man in the street', the *Collection d'imitations de dessins* was just as unattainable as an original drawing: in 1821 the full series cost fl. 400.[2]

47

PROVENANCE

Jeronimus Tonneman sale, Amsterdam, 21st October 1754 and following days, Konstboek N, lot 21, bought by Hendrik de Wacker van Zon (fl. 230); his sale, Amsterdam, 26th October 1761 and following days, lot 178, bought by Lequien (fl. 257); Cornelis Ploos van Amstel sale, Amsterdam, 3rd March 1800 and following days, Kunstboek E, lot 1, bought by Willem Philip Kops (fl. 1,050); his sale, Amsterdam, 14th March 1808 and following days, Kunstboek A, lot 1, bought by

Yver for Jonkheer Johan Goll van Franckenstein (fl. 1,500); his sale, Amsterdam, 1st July 1833 and following days, Kunstboek A, lot 1, bought by I. van Idsinga (fl. 1,305); not in his sale, Amsterdam, 2nd November 1840; J. Nieuwenhuys; Robert Stayner Holford sale, London, 11th–14th July 1893, lot 674, bought by Joseph Meder; Valentin Weisbach; Werner Weisbach, 1924; E.A. Veltman; acquired by Frits Lugt, 1931

EXHIBITIONS

Brussels, Rotterdam, Paris and Berne 1968–69, I, no.153; Haarlem and Paris 2001–02, no.86

REFERENCES

Ploos van Amstel and Josi 1821, under Adriaen van de Velde; Lugt 1956, p.380, under no.2659a; exh. cat. Berlin 1974, under no.187; Laurentius, Niemeijer and Ploos van Amstel 1980, p.16, fig.9

48

PROVENANCE

Acquired in 1882

EXHIBITIONS

Munich 1972–73, no.75; Berlin 1974, no.187

REFERENCES

Zoege von Manteuffel 1927, p.66; Bock and Rosenberg 1930, I, p.293; Möhle 1948, pp.75, 77, pl.43; Bernt 1957–58, II, no.589

FIG.167
Christiaan Josi after Adriaen van de Velde, *The Ferry*. Etching, 17.4 × 31.1 cm. (no.66 in C. Ploos van Amstel and C. Josi: *Collection d'imitations de dessins d'après les principaux maîtres hollandais et flamands*, London 1821). Rijksprentenkabinet, Rijksmuseum, Amsterdam, inv. no.RP-P-OB-47.812

FIG.168
Christiaan Josi after Adriaen van de Velde, *Landscape with cattle crossing a river*. Etching, 15.8 × 23.3 cm. (no.67 in C. Ploos van Amstel and C. Josi: *Collection d'imitations de dessins d'après les principaux maîtres hollandais et flamands*, London 1821). Rijksprentenkabinet, Rijksmuseum, Amsterdam, inv. no.RP-P-OB-47.813

The Ferry belonged at various times to collections that were seen as the finest and richest of their day. It first appeared in the catalogue of the famous collection of Jeronimus Tonneman in 1754, where it was described rather dispassionately as a "A ditto [landscape] in which a boat is crossing the water, drawn with colours, by the same [Adriaen van de Velde], 7 inches high, 12 inches wide".[3] It fetched fl. 230, making it one of the more expensive drawings in the sale. It was not the most expensive, however: higher prices were paid for a flower still-life by Jan van Huysum, a few "first-rate drawings" by Nicolaes Berchem, and even for an "uncoloured" drawing by Adriaen van de Velde himself. After that, the price rose dramatically. In 1800 Willem Philip Kops paid fl. 1,050 for the drawing, and eight years later, when Kops's collection came up at auction, Jonkheer Johan Goll van Franckenstein found himself paying fl. 1,500 for it. That was the peak, however: at the Goll van Franckenstein sale in 1833, the drawing was sold for fl. 1,305.

Goll van Franckenstein possessed another coloured drawing by Adriaen van de Velde, which was described in the 1833 catalogue as "An expansive view of landscape and fields; near a tree in the foreground we see two shepherds and sheep; for the rest a field that has been sown with seed and an agreeable background. This Drawing, known as the Little Field [*Het Akkerlandje*], is exceedingly beautiful in tone, and is very detailed in its handling."[4] In 1776, *The Little Field* was offered for sale – together with *Landscape with cattle crossing a river* and *The Haycart* – at the Neyman sale in Paris. The broker responsible for selling them, Pierre François Basan, evidently regarded it as one of the best pieces in the sale, for he had it immortalized in an etching by Karl-Wilhelm Weisbrod – along with *Landscape with cattle crossing a river* – and bound in the catalogue as a foldout plate.[5] In the Goll van Franckenstein sale, *The Little Field* was purchased by Johannes Hulswit for fl. 900. After that it disappeared from sight, until it resurfaced in 1920 in the sale of the collection of Alfred Beurdeley.[6] Since then there has been no trace of its whereabouts.

This means that there are at least two coloured drawings by Adriaen van de Velde that are mentioned in old sources and that appear to have now vanished. However, the opposite also occurs. As far as we know, *Summer landscape with wheatfield* in Berlin is not mentioned in eighteenth- or nineteenth-century sources, but appears out of the blue in 1882, when it was purchased by the Kupferstichkabinett, Berlin. The two drawings are very similar in both style and technique. Both are characterized by an extremely simple composition that is primarily dominated by horizontals. The foliage of the trees is rendered with innumerable minuscule dashes made with the tip of the brush, but the other areas have been laid in with broad strokes, and the cloudy skies in particular have been splashed down with great self-confidence wet-in-wet on the paper. No pen was used at all; even the minuscule figures were drawn in colour straightaway with the tip of the brush. *Summer landscape* is dated 1662 and there is therefore every reason to assume that *The Ferry* was produced in the same year. Of the two drawings, the one in Berlin is unmistakably the better preserved. *The Ferry* is clearly the worse for wear: the paper displays quite a few light brown stains, and the colours have lost some of their original freshness. *Summer landscape* creates the impression of having spent a great many years nestling between the pages of an album.

We frequently find ourselves frustrated by our ignorance about Adriaen van de Velde's life. Did he travel at all, or did he prefer not to venture beyond his native Amsterdam, the Haagse Bos and the beaches of Scheveningen? *Summer landscape* in particular might so easily be a record of impressions gained during a journey in the eastern Netherlands, the region of the great rivers in Gelderland. Many seventeenth-century artists who were unable or unwilling to travel to Italy contented themselves with a more modest trip in an easterly direction, frequently with Cleves as their final destination. Such a journey involved far fewer risks than the long, hazardous journey south. Nor did it have to cost very much, since those who were sufficiently agile could undertake the entire journey on foot. M.S.

NOTES

1 "*Cette scène aussi simple qu'enchanteresse frappe au premier coupe d'œil par son naturel. Le soleil déclinant répand une couleur chaude et harmonieuse sur tous les objets, ce qui, sous le pinceau large et facile de A. van de Velde, produit le plus grande illusion; mais, comme le calme général y' est adroitement contrasté par l'incident naif de quelques oiseaux aquatiques, qui devançant tranquillement et sans méfiance la barque flottante, sont tout à-coup mis en mouvement par un chien qui les effraye*": Ploos van Amstel and Josi 1821, no.66.

2 For Ploos van Amstel's prints and the *Collection d'imitations de dessins*, see Laurentius, Niemeijer and Ploos van Amstel 1980, pp.112–31.

3 "*Een dito, daar een Schuit overvaart, getekent met Couleuren, door den zelven, hoog 7, breet 12 duym*": Jeronimus Tonneman sale, Amsterdam, 21st October 1754 and following days, Kunstboek N, lot 21.

4 "*Een uitgestrekt Land- en Akkergezigt, op den voorgrond bij een' boom ziet men twee herders en eenige schapen; verder een bezaaid akkerveld en een aangenaam verschiet. Deze Teekening, bekend onder den naam van het Akkerlandje, is uitmuntend fraai van toon, en zeer uitvoerig van behandeling*": Jonkheer Johan Goll van Franckenstein sale, Amsterdam, 1st July 1833 and following days, Kunstboek F, lot 2.

5 Neyman (Jan Danser Nijman?) sale, Paris, 8th July 1776 and following days, lot 952.

6 Alfred Beurdeley sale, Paris, 8th–10th June 1920, lot 323 (ill.).

49

Landscape with livestock crossing a river

Brush and watercolour, framing lines in pen
and dark brown ink, 15.7 × 23.6 cm
Signed and dated, lower left on the river bank:
v d Velde f. / 1666
Teylers Museum, Haarlem, inv. no.R 045

FIG.169
Adriaen van de Velde, *Hilly landscape with a
herdsman and a herdswoman by a fence*. Signed
and dated, lower left: *a.v. velde. f 1666*. Pen
and brown ink over a sketch in black chalk,
watercolour, 15.9 × 23.7 cm. Teylers Museum,
Haarlem, inv. no.R 046

Descriptions in auction catalogues from the eighteenth and nineteenth centuries are a joy to read. The more highly coveted was a work of art, the more detailed the description in the catalogue. Drawings were generally offered for sale in *kunstboeken*, as the collector had arranged them. A *kunstboek* was a blank-leaf album, bound in leather or vellum, in which the drawings were preserved between the pages. The most important drawings were always placed at the front of the album. It was standard practice for auctioneers to work from back to front, offering the last drawings first and leaving the best ones in each album until the end. This was a good way of sustaining excitement during the auction. A wonderful example of a promotional text is the one advertising Adriaen van de Velde's *Landscape with livestock crossing a river* in the catalogue of the Jacob de Vos collection, which was sold in Amsterdam on 30th October 1833 and the following days. The drawing was in Kunstboek B ("Containing coloured drawings by old Dutch Masters") and was the first sheet in the album: "This outstanding Drawing depicts a pleasant Landscape with a wide river; in the foreground a cow drinking, beside her a goat; also a herdsman who is driving a cow and some sheep through the water; to one side on an elevation a barn, trees and other staffage; in the distance a castle on a cliff. The natural tone and detailed treatment with watercolours make this Drawing exceedingly pleasant; for its rarity too, this drawing is extremely important."[1]

The price was in proportion to this encomium: the drawing fetched fl. 1,730, a sum that probably caused some of those present to gasp. The man who made the highest bid was Gerrit Jan Michaëlis, the *kastelein* – superintendent – of Teylers Museum in Haarlem, in those days the only museum in the Netherlands that purchased Old Master drawings. To be sure, the Rijksmuseum in the Trippenhuis in Amsterdam had its own Print Room, but in those days this institution confined itself – true to its name – to collecting prints. It was not until the 1870s that Amsterdam started, initially on a very small scale, to build up a collection of Old Master drawings.

The drawing that Michaëlis purchased was the second most expensive in the De Vos sale; it was surpassed only by another coloured drawing, *The Klosbaan* (*Peasants playing gallet or shuffleboard outside an inn*) by Adriaen van Ostade, another darling of art buyers in the eighteenth and early nineteenth centuries. Here too the catalogue's author pulled out all the stops in his effusive praise: "The wondrous heights of detail combine with the most superb draughtsmanship, and the limpidness and delicacy with which all has been treated with watercolours is astonishing".[2] *The Klosbaan* fetched fl. 2,405, and would eventually end up, by way of the Verstolk van Soelen collection, in the British Museum, London.[3]

Michaëlis may have suspected that in making his purchase he was reuniting two pendants, for in 1800 Wybrand Hendriks, his predecessor as *kastelein*, had bought a coloured drawing by Adriaen van de Velde with near-identical dimensions, also dated 1666 (fig.169). Hendriks purchased 'his' Van de Velde at the Ploos van Amstel sale, where the drawing was described as "A delightfully sunny Landscape in the surroundings of the House at Brederode".[4] It is not easy to recognize in the pieces of crumbling masonry

in the distance the remains of Brederode Castle, in the vicinity of Haarlem. The ruins might equally well be a fragment of a complex of Roman baths, intended to give the landscape an exotic appearance, a device to which Van de Velde had frequent resort.

Whatever the case may be, it is unlikely that the two drawings were ever intended to form a pair. In terms of technique there are substantial differences. Much of the drawing purchased by Hendriks appears to have been laid in with the brush and grey tones of ink. After that the colours were applied, and finally the entire drawing was finished in pen and brown ink. In *Landscape with livestock crossing a river* there is far less grey ink; large sections of the image appear to have been executed entirely with the brush and watercolour, and there are no penned lines in brown, so that the image as a whole gives a softer, more atmospheric impression.

Van de Velde's *Landscape with livestock crossing a river* has everything that an eighteenth- or early nineteenth-century collector would have desired. The description of it as "*aangenaam*" (pleasant) in the catalogue of the De Vos sale is no idle choice of words. Today, this adjective has paled to a fairly neutral epithet for something that is experienced as agreeable, enjoyable. But two hundred years ago the word's meaning appears to have been stronger: it was applied to something that gave one an overwhelming feeling of well-being. Everything in Van de Velde's drawing is *aangenaam*: it is spring or early summer, judging by the gentle ripples in the water of the picturesque winding river; at most there is a light breeze, with a few cumulus clouds sailing across the sky, but nothing ominous. The landscape presents an attractive mix of flat and hilly areas, but without any menacing, inhospitable high mountains. There are enough trees to give the weary traveller a brief respite in the shade, but nowhere is there any suggestion of a dense forest in which one might lose one's way. That was exactly how the denizens of the eighteenth century liked to see nature – charming, orderly, and without the slightest intimation of uncontrollable forces. Then there is of course the staffage of people and animals: besides bringing the viewer into the scene, as it were, they also provide a narrative element, and that was something that art lovers could ill do without.

The author of the De Vos catalogue also praises the drawing's "natural tone". By this he undoubtedly meant that everything depicted in it seemed uncontrived – nothing looked 'invented'. On closer inspection, however, what appears at first sight to be a simple, informal composition was meticulously constructed, the whole image carefully composed down to the smallest detail. The animals in the foreground – the drinking cow, the goat, the dog with its cheerful curly tail – are carefully placed so as to draw the viewer's gaze further and further into the landscape. Even the tiny figures such as the little horse in the background, darkly silhouetted against the light water of the river, are positioned exactly so as to produce the best possible effect.

In addition, there was of course the "detailed treatment with watercolours" that connoisseurs of the day so admired. Indeed, Van de Velde demonstrates here his mastery of just about everything that can be done with a brush and a little watercolour: the reflection of the bank on the left in the calm water of

the river is a consummate example of the brilliant rendering of surfaces
in a single square centimetre.

Josi referred to the drawing as a "*Vue du Rhin*" (View of the Rhine), while
many later publications called it an 'Italian' landscape. Both are wrong.
The essence of the work is precisely that it depicts an idealized, non-existent
landscape composed of a variety of elements, an invented Arcadia.

Just how greatly Van de Velde's drawing was admired in the eighteenth
and early nineteenth centuries is clear from the fact that it was reproduced
three times in the form of prints. First came an etching by Carl Wilhelm
Weisbrod, depicting the scene in reverse image (fig.170). Weisbrod's print
was included as a foldout plate in the catalogue of the Neyman sale that
was held in Paris in July 1776.[5] Of a rather later date was a print produced as
an etching and an engraving, the combined work of father and son Reinier
and Abraham Vinkeles (fig.171). Finally, a coloured print, made using the
technique developed by Cornelis Ploos van Amstel, was included in Josi's de
luxe edition *Collection d'imitations de dessins*, published in 1821, illustrated
on p.182, fig.168. Teylers Museum also possesses two drawn copies made
after Van de Velde's *Landscape with livestock crossing a river*, one by Johannes
Hulswit and one by Gerrit Jan Michaëlis himself.[6] M.S.

PROVENANCE

Neyman (Jan Danser Nijman?) sale, Paris, 8th July
1776 and following days, lot 950 (1,661 livres; not
sold); Jacob de Vos sale, Amsterdam, 30th October
1833 and following days, Kunstboek B, lot 1,
bought by Gerrit Jan Michaëlis for Teylers Museum
(fl. 1,730)

EXHIBITIONS

Haarlem 1986, no.39

REFERENCES

Ploos van Amstel and Josi 1821, under Adriaen van
de Velde; Scholten 1904, p.257, no.45; Plomp 1997,
p.18, pl.16; Plomp 2001, p.273, fig.183; Van den
Eerenbeemd 2006, no.20

NOTES

1 "*Deze uitmuntende Teekening verbeeldt een
aangenaam Landschap met eene breede rivier; op
den voorgrond eene drinkende koe, waarbij een bok;
verder een herder die eene koe en eenige schapen
door het water drijft; ter zijde op eene hoogte een
schuur, geboomte en verdere stoffagie; en op den
derden grond een kasteel op een rots. De natuurlijke
toon en de uitvoerige behandeling met sapverwen
maken deze Teekening hoogst aangenaam; dezelve*

is ook om de zeldzaamheid zeer belangrijk"; Jacob
de Vos sale, Amsterdam, 30tht October 1833 and
following days, Kunstboek B, lot 1.

2 "*De hoogste uitvoerigheid vereenigt zich met de
voortreffelijkste teekening, en de helderheid en
dunheid waarmede alles met sapverwen behandeld
is, zijn verwonderlijk*"; ibid., Kunstboek A, lot 1.

3 Inv. no.1847,0326.6; Hind 1931, p.17, no.64.

4 Scholten 1904, pp.257–58, no.46.

5 Neyman (Jan Danser Nijman?) sale, Paris,
8th July 1776 and following days; the print is
inserted between pp.142 and 143 of the auction
catalogue.

6 Hulswit: inv. no.Y 035a; Michaëlis: inv. no.Y 060;
see Scholten 1904, p.495, and Plomp 1997, p.18,
fig.17.

50

A herdsman with livestock and passing travellers in a southern landscape with an ancient ruin

Black chalk, brush and black ink and two tones of grey ink, 19.6 × 29.7 cm
Verso, at lower left, the mark of Jacob de Vos Jbzn (Lugt 1450) and the mark of William Pitcairn Knowles (Lugt 2643); above this, the mark of the Rijksprentenkabinet, Rijksmuseum, Amsterdam (Lugt 2228)
Rijksprentenkabinet, Rijksmuseum, Amsterdam, inv. no.RP-T-1902-A-4604

Adriaen van de Velde's paintings generally began with a *prima idea*, a cursory sketch. Several of these sketches have been preserved. Some were made in pen and brown ink, combined with brush and brown or grey ink, others in black chalk and brush in a range of grey tones. Josi gives an apt description of them in his *Collection d'imitations de dessins d'après les principaux maîtres hollandais et flamands*: "His sketches of entire compositions drawn with light contours in chalk, sometimes with pen, and shadows indicated only by an ink or bistre wash, done with such ease that the individual objects appear to have escaped, as it were, from his brush, those of this type are worth 100 to 200 guilders".[1]

Of the sketches in black chalk and grey ink, the one in the Rijksprentenkabinet is among the finest and best preserved. At first sight it appears a simple thing, but on closer inspection it proves to be quite an ambitious composition, with numerous human figures and animals. A herdsman has stopped to rest. His cow has lain down beside him, and his sheep are calmly grazing nearby. Leaning placidly on his staff, he has all the time in the world to watch a passing group of travellers – a cart weighed down with passengers and goods, two donkeys carrying heavy loads, a few figures pursuing the journey on foot, and some horsemen in the distance. In the background is an impressive ruin, a crumbling wall among tall trees; on the left is a view of a hilly landscape with a southern ambience. All this is drawn with wide brushstrokes in two tones of grey ink, with occasional darker accents, over a rough sketch in black chalk. This chalk drawing is extremely fragmentary and goes awry in places – the artist frequently diverged from it when elaborating the sketch with the brush. Even so, few viewers would want to be without those chalk lines. They add a certain vibrancy to the whole; they are the pepper in the soup.

In a world without electricity and with a limited range of artificial light sources – oil lamps and candles – artists had to make maximum use of the daylight. Daytime was for painting, which could not be done by candlelight, but the evenings could be used for drawing. Samuel van Hoogstraeten advised his readers to give free rein to their imagination in the evening and to develop their "*schikkunst*" ('art of arrangement'), which was his apt term for such compositional forays.[2] Although not many drawings of this kind have survived – rejects may well have been used as wrapping paper – it is conceivable that Van de Velde produced scores of them. Drawings made using the same technique and with the same function as the Amsterdam sketch are preserved in collections in Budapest, Göttingen, New York and elsewhere.[3] Drawings of this kind reveal yet again Van de Velde's preoccupation with the play of light. The Amsterdam drawing too, besides serving as a compositional sketch, is above all a study in rendering sunlight. As so often in Van de Velde's work, the scene is shown in strong raking light, almost backlighting, which adds expressive relief to human figures, animals and architecture.

Most of Van de Velde's sketches are unlikely to have gone beyond the stage of simple thoughts on paper. Today, we know of only one case in which a drawing of this kind actually developed into a painting.[4] M.S.

PROVENANCE

Probably Jacob de Vos sale, Amsterdam, 30th
October 1833 and following days, Kunstboek
W, under lot 12 ("*Twee stuks Landschappen, rijk
gestoffeerd met onderscheiden vee. Luchtig en
meesterlijk met o.i. inkt*"), bought by Albertus
Brondgeest (fl. 81); probably J.G. Baron Verstolk
van Soelen sale, Amsterdam, 22nd March 1847 and
following days, either lot 244, bought by De Vries
(fl. 250) or lot 255, bought by Albertus Brondgeest
(fl. 160); Jacob de Vos Jbzn, not identifiable with
certainty in his sale, Amsterdam, 22nd–24th May
1883; William Pitcairn Knowles sale, Amsterdam,
25th–26th June 1895, lot 663, bought by C.F. Roos
(fl. 21); acquired with the support of the Vereniging
Rembrandt, 1902

REFERENCES

Exh. cat. Koblenz, Göttingen and Oldenburg 2000,
under no.75; Van den Eerenbeemd 2006, p.12, fig.7,
pp.13–14, and no.4

NOTES

1 "*Ses esquisses de compositions entières d'un léger
contour au crayon, quelquefois à la plume, et puis
les ombres indiquées d'un seul lavis à l'encre,
ou au bistre, mais d'une manière si facile que
les différents objets paraissent, pour ainsi dire,
échappés à son pinceau, ceux de cette espèce valent
de 100 à 200 florins*": Ploos van Amstel and Josi
1821, unpaginated, under Adriaen van de Velde.
2 Hoogstraeten 1678, pp.191–92; see
Schapelhouman 2006, p.87.

3 Kunstsammlung der Universität Göttingen,
Sammlung Uffenbach (exh. cat. Koblenz,
Göttingen and Oldenburg 2000, no.75); Museum
of Fine Arts, Budapest, inv. no.1499 (Gerszi 2005,
no.290); Pierpont Morgan Library, New York, inv.
no.I, 152 (Turner and Stampfle 2006, no.294).
4 A drawing in Teylers Museum, Haarlem, inv.
no.R 039, and one in the C.P. van Eeghen
collection, The Hague, provided the material
for a painting dated 1662 in the Pushkin
Museum, Moscow (inv. no.3252). The drawing
in Haarlem is undoubtedly an initial version of
the composition, while the one in The Hague is
far closer to the painting. For the drawings, see
Robinson 1979, nos.B-1 and B-2; for the painting,
see Senenko 2009, p.377.

51

Herdsman and herdswoman with livestock by a stream

Pen and brown ink, brush and grey ink, over faint traces of a sketch in graphite or black chalk, 17.7 × 17.7 cm
Verso: minuscule sketch of a seated herdswoman and a recumbent herdsman, graphite; numbered at lower left: *N° 394* (pen and brown ink) and *751*
Teylers Museum, Haarlem, inv. no.R 043

52

Couple herding cows and sheep with a sleeping dog by a small stable with a horse

Pen and brush and brown ink over remnants of a sketch in graphite or black chalk, framing lines with pen and dark brown ink, 20.1 × 29.2 cm; attached along the upper edge is strip of paper measuring approx. 4.2 cm in width, which overlaps the drawing by about 1.8 cm
Verso, at lower left: *N-1879* (pen and dark brown ink, Goll van Franckenstein); below this: *N°. 546. N°880* (pencil, nineteenth-century) and the mark of the Rijksprentenkabinet, Rijksmuseum, Amsterdam (Lugt 2228)
Rijksprentenkabinet, Rijksmuseum, Amsterdam, inv. no.RP-T-1967-93

AMSTERDAM ONLY

Seventeenth-century Dutch painting bristles with specialists – artists who concentrated wholly on the production of a single genre, or who in any case had a limited repertoire. Johannes Verspronck painted only portraits, all the paintings we know by Willem Claesz Heda are still lifes, and Hendrick Avercamp turned out one winter landscape after another, to name just a few examples. Although Adriaen van de Velde ventured into numerous fields – his known works include portraits and religious scenes – it is clear that he spent most of his working life painting landscapes with figures and livestock. Since that working life spanned little more than fifteen years, his production methods must have been fast and extremely efficient. This efficiency is reflected again and again in the highly ingenious way in which he composed his works, using an array of recurrent motifs. The two drawings discussed here illustrate this technique perfectly.

A fine example is *Herdsman and herdswoman with livestock by a stream* (cat. no.51), which was Van de Velde's 'initial idea' for the painting dated 1664 in Chicago (fig.172).[1] Such a drawing was a utilitarian object, so to speak: it was intended from the outset to be used for the painting. Everything is already there – a tightly knit composition, clearly bounded on both sides, a dark foreground that provides depth, and the play of light as the cohesive element. Van de Velde had a preference for sharp raking light, almost backlighting, which lends the entire image sculptural relief. Here too he exploits the theatrical play of light and dark to maximum effect. For the grazing cow in the foreground, Van de Velde used a drawing from his stock of figure and animal studies: the creature's pose corresponds almost exactly to that of the cow in a sheet of studies in the Dutuit collection in the Petit Palais, Paris.[2] Years later, Van de Velde would use this same animal study once again for his etching *Grazing cow with two sheep*, dated 1670 (fig.173).[3]

FIG.172
Adriaen van de Velde, *Pastoral landscape with ruins*. Signed and dated, lower centre: *A.v.Velde.f. / 1664*. Oil on canvas, 67 × 78.4 cm. Art Institute of Chicago, inv. no.1894.1024

51

The first sketch was probably followed by a second, more detailed one, but
this appears not to have survived. That it must have existed seems very likely,
however, once we compare the initial sketch with the finished painting:
although many elements were adopted almost literally, the artist also made
changes – rather too many, it seems, for him not to have tried them out in a
second drawing. The bullock in the middle of the group of three, described
expressively in the 1793 sale catalogue as a "bellowing young bullock"
("*bulkend osje*"), did not survive in the painting, having been jettisoned in
favour of a white horse. This modification had another consequence. In
the initial sketch, the standing herdsman is partly hidden by the bellowing
creature; behind the much larger horse he would have become near-invisible,
and so he had to be moved a little to the left. To make room for him there,
Van de Velde adjusted the format of his painting. While the original sketch
was square, the painting became a horizontal rectangle, to give the human
figures a little more space. Interestingly, the drawing and painting exude

52

PROVENANCE

Probably anonymous (Huquier) sale, Amsterdam,
14th September 1761 and following days, lot 640
(fl. 2.15); Jonkheer Johan Goll van Franckenstein
sale, Amsterdam, 1st July 1833 and following
days, Kunstboek L, lot 7, bought by C.F. Roos
(fl. 120); Jonkheer Mr. J.A. Repelaer sale, The
Hague, 7th–8th November 1967, lot 178, bought
by the Rijksprentenkabinet (fl. 1,200)

REFERENCES

'Keuze uit de aanwinsten', *Bulletin van het
Rijksmuseum* 16 (1968), p.39, no.14

a more distinctly Italianate ambience than is customary in Van de Velde's
work. The ruins dominating the background are suggestive of the remains
of a Roman aqueduct.

The drawing of the *Couple herding cows and sheep with a sleeping dog by a
small stable with a horse* in Amsterdam (cat. no.52) was also undoubtedly a
preparatory sketch for a painting, although in this case the painted version
is apparently lost – or was never made. This drawing is considerably larger
than the one in Teylers Museum and elaborated in rather more detail, yet it
has retained the sketch-like, informal nature of an initial design, not least
because when the artist ran out of space at the top he simply pasted an
extra strip of paper along the upper edge of his sheet. Here too we see Van
de Velde at work as an efficient supplier of pleasing bucolic scenes, who
constantly recycled tried and tested motifs in imaginative ways. We have
already encountered the little goat lying in the left foreground in the Teylers
Museum drawing, where it lies in the right foreground. The cow lying in the

NOTES

1 Exh. cat. Montreal 1990, no.61.

2 Lugt 1927, p.34, no.80.

3 Hollstein 1949–2010, XXXII, p.224, no.11.

4 De Lairesse 1707, I, pp.353–54: "*Ook is het oneigen, dat een vrouw, fatsoenlyk gekleed, aan den weg of in een bosch op de grond alleen zal gaan zitten, of staan praaten met volk van veel geringer staat. Het is veel beter, dat men een man doe zitten en een vrouw voorby gaan, dan dat de vrouw zit en de man voorby gaat, of daar mede staat en praat, ten ware dat hy na den weg vraagde*"; "*De herders, herderinnen, boeren en boerinnen voegen wel bij malkander. Daar geen schaapen zyn, past past ook geen hoeder noch fluiter, noch meisjes met bloemenkranssen: want die luiden komen niet op het veld om te zitten praaten, maar om te werken. Het is beter dat men vraagt waar de herder is, als waar de schaapen zyn*"; English translation from Lairesse 1817, I, pp.237–38.

foreground with her head turned towards the viewer is very similar to the reddish-brown cow in *The Hut* (cat. no.30), so it is highly likely that both were drawn after the terracotta figurine that Van de Velde evidently had in his possession (see fig.148 on p.145). On further inspection, we discover that the cow on the far left, with her back to us, is lying in exactly the same position as the one beside her. Van de Velde simply rotated his figurine by 180°. The sheep that is lying with its raised head facing left can also be identified in one of the drawings that were used for *The Hut* (see cat. no.32).

A drawing such as *Couple herding cows and sheep* shows Van de Velde the choreographer of people, animals and natural scenery at his most brilliant. His ability to depict human figures and creatures in such a way that they form a harmonious part of the surrounding landscape must have particularly aroused the admiration of eighteenth-century art lovers. The influential art theorist Gerard de Lairesse emphasized in his *Groot schilderboek* (1707) the importance of appropriate and well-painted staffage. Those who were incapable of painting the human figures in their landscapes and who were obliged to enlist another artist's help, or to copy from prints, were not worth a penny. But even those who did possess this ability must work circumspectly, observing diverse rules of decency and decorum: "It is also improper that a woman, well dressed, should sit alone by an immodest wayside, or in a wood, or stand prattling with ordinary people. It is much more proper to make a man sitting, and a woman passing by, than the woman sitting, and the man passing by, or holding discourse, unless he be inquiring the way." Van de Velde frequently used shepherds and shepherdesses for the staffage of his landscapes, a practice that found favour with De Lairesse: "Shepherds and shepherdesses, husbandmen and women, suit well together. Where there are no sheep, a shepherd or piper, or maids with chaplets of flowers, are improper; because such people are not sent into the field to prattle, but work; it is better to inquire after the shepherd than the sheep."[4] M.S.

53

The church of Quattro Santi Coronati and adjacent buildings in Rome

Black chalk, tip of the brush and brush in brownish-grey ink, 12.3 × 16.4 cm
Verso, lower centre: *hoog 5¼ | breed 6¼ dm | A v d Velde* (graphite, in the hand of Cornelis Ploos van Amstel); at lower left *N° 878 z* (pen and brown ink) and *A v d Velde f* (graphite, faded) and *g. N° 5* (? graphite, faded)
Teylers Museum, Haarlem, inv. no. R 049

54

Hilly landscape with a ferry on a river, 1666

Pen or tip of brush and blackish-brown ink, brush and greyish-brown ink, framing lines in pen and dark brown ink, 17.3 × 24.8 cm
Signed and dated, lower left: *A.v.velde.f 1666* (pen and brown ink)
Teylers Museum, Haarlem, inv. no. R 044

There is no concrete or irrefutable evidence that Adriaen van de Velde ever visited Italy. Houbraken says nothing about any journey to southern Europe. True, his life of Van de Velde is scarcely a marvel of completeness, but one would nonetheless expect something as crucial to an artist's life as a trip to Italy to be worth mentioning. The first author to state confidently that Van de Velde must have visited the south was Alfred von Wurzbach (1846–1915). On the basis of three etchings dated 1653, he concluded that Adriaen van de Velde must undoubtedly have been in Italy in 1653.[1] It is a fact that two of six known etchings from 1653 have a southern setting, or even contain antique motifs – one displays a fragment of an antique temple – but this is very thin evidence indeed.[2] Hoogewerff too was convinced that Van de Velde had been in Italy in the years 1653–1656.[3] The artist's age in itself makes the assumption fairly implausible, since it implies that Van de Velde undertook the dangerous and expensive journey to Italy at sixteen or seventeen years of age – in other words while he was still an apprentice. That would have been highly exceptional. In the paintings or drawings by Adriaen van de Velde that might be called 'Italian' or Italianate – or even 'southern' – there is nothing that the artist must unquestionably have known from direct observation: most of these southern elements are little more than crumbling walls or round arches. Van de Velde could have found all such elements in another artist's work, or indeed simply have plucked them from his own imagination. Furthermore, in many of his Italianate paintings and drawings there is not a single antique ruin to be seen. Even the vegetation is often as Dutch as could be, and the whiff of southern ambience is evoked by the suggestion of warm sunlight and the addition of a hill in the background.

There is just one case that gives us pause. Teylers Museum possesses a small drawing in which Van de Velde drew the church of Quattro Santi Coronati (Four Crowned Saints) and adjacent buildings in Rome (cat. no. 53), apparently with topographical accuracy.[4] In his book *Vereeuwigde stad*, Van Regteren Altena ponders that "The drawing … reinforces the suspicion that Adriaen van de Velde spent some time in Rome", before immediately going on to say that the artist may naturally have worked from an existing depiction and even suggesting a possible contender, a drawing by Bartholomeus Breenbergh in the Louvre.[5] Breenbergh's drawing was almost certainly not the example that Van de Velde copied: the play of light is different from that in Van de Velde's drawing, the buildings are somewhat taller and narrower, and there are a good many differences in the details. In the seventeenth century, the complex, which looks more like an impenetrable fortress than a place of worship, rose menacingly from its virtually unbuilt surroundings. Nowadays this part of the city is almost entirely built-up. The pleasant shallow stream through which a number of country folk are wading with their livestock was entirely the product of Van de Velde's imagination.

According to the text on the verso, the drawing comes from the collection of Cornelis Ploos van Amstel. It must be identical to lot 13 in Kunstboek F in the catalogue of Ploos's sale in March 1800. According to the catalogue, lot 13 was the "*wedergaê*" – counterpart – of the previous lot number, which was described as "An Italian landscape, containing a bridge over a river; to one

53

PROVENANCE

Cornelis Ploos van Amstel sale, Amsterdam, 3rd March 1800 and following days, Kunstboek F, lot 13, bought by C.F. Roos (together with Kunstboek F, lot 12; fl. 440); possibly Jonkheer Johan Goll van Franckenstein sale, Amsterdam, 1st July 1833 and following days, Kunstboek M, lot 3 ("Adriaen van de Velde. Beside a splendid Italian Building, surrounded by trees, in the foreground herdsmen lead their livestock across a pond. As above, the light and shade strikingly well done, and more than worthy of this excellent Master"),[6] bought by Johannes Hulswit (fl. 320)

EXHIBITIONS

Haarlem 1986, no.37

REFERENCES

Scholten 1904, pp.258–59, no.49; Van Regteren Altena 1964, p.111, no.66; Roethlisberger 1969, under no.30; Van den Eerenbeemd 2006, no.22

54

PROVENANCE

Anonymous sale (Galitzine?), Amsterdam, 28th
April 1783 and following days, Konstboek A,
lot 4, bought by Heemskerk (fl. 240); M. Hoofman
sale, Haarlem, 2nd June 1846 and following days,
Kunstboek A, lot 8, bought by Gerrit Jan Michaëlis
for Teylers Museum (fl. 240)

REFERENCES

Scholten 1904, pp.256–57, no.44; Van den
Eerenbeemd 2006, no.19

side near a rising path are seen a herdsman with a mule and some sheep".[7] The two drawings were purchased at this sale by the dealer Cornelis Sebille Roos. What eventually happened to no.12 we do not know.

Hilly landscape with a ferry on a river (cat. no.54) is a characteristic example of the type of landscape that is described above: it looks vaguely southern, but it has all manner of elements that could just as well be encountered in the Low Countries, and with the kind of anecdotal staffage that was so sought after at the time, and that is accordingly described at length in the 1783 sale catalogue: "... on the Bank of a River, in the foreground is a ferry, in which we see a mounted gentleman and peasants with animals, some of which appear to be drinking from the water, a waggoner with a loaded cart who appears also to want to board the boat; for the rest we see a shepherd with sheep, some boats and a raft".[8] All this takes place against a backdrop consisting of a section of city wall with round-arched niches that one might have found in virtually every walled city in the Northern Netherlands, the ruins of a square tower with a makeshift roof that appears to consist of tree trunks laid in a criss-cross pattern, and the picturesque overgrown remains of a city gate. The only truly exotic-looking detail is the fortified town in the hills in the right background, which could easily be in Tuscany or Umbria.

The fact that the drawing is signed and dated, as well as its meticulous execution, its fairly formal composition – a classical triangular structure – and the emphatic use of the posts in the water in the foreground as a repoussoir all leave one in no doubt that the work was produced for sale to a collector. After roughly the mid-century mark, a variety of factors – economic malaise, saturation, changing tastes – combined to send the demand for easel paintings in the Northern Netherlands into decline.[9] Someone like Adriaen van de Velde, who painted primarily for the open market and whose wares – given their quality and meticulous execution – were not exactly cheap, must have suffered particularly badly from this slump. Perhaps he hoped that his independent drawings – which were naturally far less labour-intensive than easel paintings – might reach a new public. Whether he succeeded seems doubtful: the little we know of his personal circumstances is not suggestive of an easy life. By an irony of fate, when collectors were eventually prepared to pay towering prices for his work, Van de Velde had been dead for a hundred years. M.S.

NOTES

1 Wurzbach 1904–11, II, p.748.
2 The six etchings dated 1653 are: *Shepherd and shepherdess with their animals* (Hollstein 1949–2010, XXXII, no.17); *The town gate* (ibid., no.18); *Hunters resting near a ruin* (ibid., no.19); *Man on horseback* (ibid., no.21); *Woman spinning and two men near a tent* (ibid., no.23); and *Three huntsmen with hounds* (ibid., no.24). Only in Hollstein nos.18 and 19 are Italianate motifs discernible.
3 Hoogewerff 1952, pp.96–97.
4 On the church, see Buchowiecki 1974, pp.677–706.

5 Van Regteren Altena 1964, p.111, no.66. The Breenbergh drawing is inv. no.22.541 A; Lugt 1929–33, I, p.23, no.162.
6 "*Adriaen van de Velde. Nevens een prachtig Italiaansch Gebouw, met geboomte omgeven, gaan op den voorgrond eenige herders met hun vee door een waterplas. Als voren, treffend van licht en bruin, en dezen verdienstelijken Meester overwaardig*".
7 "*Een Italiaansch Landgezigt, waarin een Brug over een Rivier; ter zyde by een opgaanden Weg ziet men een Veehoeder met een Muilëzel en eenige Schaapen*": Cornelis Ploos van Amstel sale,

Amsterdam, 3rd March 1800 and following days, Kunstboek F, lot 12.
8 "*... aan den Oever van een Rivier, op de voorgrond legt een Pontschuit waar in een Heer te Paard, en Landlieden met eenig Vee, waar onder een der zelve uit het Water scheind te drinken, een Voerman met een belaaden Kar, scheind meede over te willen vaaren; verder ziet men een Herder met Schaapen, eenige Schuiten en een Houtvlot*": anonymous sale (Galitzine?), Amsterdam, 28th April 1783 and following days, Konstboek A, lot 4.
9 Bakker 2011, pp.233–34.

55

Skittle players in a clearing

Pen and brown ink, brush and brown and light purple ink, framing lines with pen and brown ink, 22.9 × 35.4 cm; strip of approximately 1 cm in width added along the lower edge
Signed(?), lower right: *A.v.d.Velde. f* (red chalk); verso: *in 't Haagsche bos* (black chalk)
Kupferstichkabinett, Staatliche Museen zu Berlin, inv. no.KdZ 2598

The simple composition and lively depiction of human figures, along with the extraordinarily suggestive rendering of the sunlight on the foliage, points to *Skittle players in a clearing* being a drawing made 'after life'. Still, whether a drawing such as this one – given its quite considerable size – was actually made on the spot is open to doubt. It would not have been physically impossible: a pen and an inkpot, a small bowl and a little water are easy to carry about. We do not know very much about the practice of open-air sketching in the seventeenth century. Little was written about it; but there was no need to write at length about matters that were commonplace and self-evident. We have a few pictorial documents, however: a drawing by Joris van der Haagen shows an artist drawing a landscape in the surroundings of Doorwerth, in the province of Gelderland, on a fairly large sheet of paper that was probably pinned to a wooden panel (fig.174).[1] Van de Velde may have sat down to draw like this. Alternatively, he may have made his drawing in the studio on the basis of small sketches produced on the spot. We scarcely have any sheets from his sketchbooks, such as those by Jan van Goyen, for example, which have survived in abundance. There are a few small images of cows drawn from life that may have originated in a sketchbook.

The inscription on the reverse of the drawing, *in 't Haagsche bos*, helps to identify the place where Van de Velde came upon this summer skittles game – the wooded region on the eastern outskirts of The Hague. Stylistically, Van de Velde's skittles alley is closely related to a drawing in the Amsterdam Museum that served as the basis for a painting dated 1666 in Berlin.[2] The drawing and painting depict the Koekamp, which forms part of the forest known as the Haagse Bos (see figs.112 and 113 on p.95). There is another, though somewhat later, indication that the drawing depicts a spot close to the Koekamp. In a large bird's-eye view of The Hague, after a drawing by Gerrit van der Giessen, entitled *'s Graven-Hage Zoo als dezelve zig in den*

FIG.174
Detail of Joris van der Haagen, *View in the vicinity of Doorwerth*. Black chalk and grey wash, pen and brown ink, 19.5 × 25.9 cm. Rijksprentenkabinet, Rijksmuseum, Amsterdam, inv. no.RP-T-1884-A-342

FIG.175
After Gerrit van der Giessen, *The Hague as it appeared in the 1730s on the side of the Haagse Bos* (detail). Etching and engraving, 42.5 × 97 cm. Rijksmuseum Research Library, Amsterdam

jaare 1730 aan de zyde van het Bosch vertoont (The Hague as it appeared in the 1730s on the side of the Haagse Bos), a skittles alley can be seen in the right foreground, adjacent to the Koekamp (fig.175).[3] While the print after a design by Van der Giessen was admittedly made some 65 years after Van de Velde's drawing, skittles alleys could have long lives, and it is entirely possible that this was the spot where Adriaen saw these men playing their game.

It is impossible to pronounce with any confidence on the original purpose of the drawing, but it may well have been produced, like the drawing in the Amsterdam Museum, in preparation for a painting that was either never made or that has been lost. It is noteworthy, however, that it bears a finely penned 'signature' at lower right, similar in kind to those on a number of Adriaen van de Velde's figure studies, suggesting that the artist or one of his descendants tried to sell it on the open market at some point (for these signatures, see cat. no.42).

Skittles alleys were often close to inns, and the game was enjoyed by people from all walks of life. The elite did not disdain it. The poet Constantijn Huygens had a skittles alley constructed at his country estate, Hofwijck. He had no time for games of chance played for money with cards or dice, which he saw as sure paths to envy and misery. He preferred activities that required a healthy physical effort. Skittles had another delightful side to them: if you lost interest you could always rest and entertain yourself by criticizing the poor play of your fellow players:

> And whosoever tires can take relief in rest,
> And stand nearby to watch or sit and act the judge,
> Pronouncing on the errors in his comrades' play.

This is what is happening in Van de Velde's drawing: only two men are still actively playing skittles, while a third looks on critically and a fourth watches from a distance, comfortably seated on a small bench. Van de Velde depicts the men playing with nine skittles, as was customary. The middle

FIG.176
Jan Steen, *Skittle players outside an inn*, c.1660–63.
Oil on panel, 33.5 × 27 cm. The National Gallery,
London, inv. no.NG2560

skittle was called the 'king', who was surrounded, as it were, by his subjects. This led Huygens to pen some melancholy contemplations:

> And thus is felled the one that has been King of eight,
> And thus a vision flits through idly sifting thoughts,
> Of Kings undone, surrounded by their people
> Who stand unmov'd as the blackest of all clouds
> That e'er obscured the Sun, [a] cloud beyond compare,
> Fells three Crowns at a single stroke with unheard thunder.[4]

Huygens is referring to the recent beheading of King Charles I after a show trial. The 'three Crowns' are those of England, Scotland and Ireland. Not everyone is a poet, and not everyone will be inspired by the sight of nine skittles to draw an analogy with regicide. Van de Velde probably saw the group of skittle players as nothing more than an attractive motif for the staffage of his landscape. Indeed, he was not alone in this: just a few years earlier, Jan Steen had chosen a small group of skittle players in a wooded landscape as the subject of one of his most appealing paintings (fig.176).[5]

M.S.

PROVENANCE

J.H. Molkenboer-Schenkhuizen sale, Amsterdam, 6th September 1853, Portefeuille A, lot 4, bought by Chapelain (fl. 20); A. van der Willigen and A. van der Willigen Pz sale, The Hague, 10th–11th June 1874, lot 267, bought by B. Suermondt; his sale, Frankfurt am Main, 5th May 1879, lot 176, bought by Amsler (DM 151)

EXHIBITIONS

Berlin 1974, no.191

REFERENCES

Zoege von Manteuffel 1927, p.59, pl.57; Bock and Rosenberg 1930, I, p.292; Lugt 1931, p.75; Möhle 1948, p.75 and fig.42; Broos and Schapelhouman 1993, under no.137

NOTES

1 Exh. cat. Amsterdam 1987–88, no.72.
2 Amsterdam Museum, inv. no.10348; Broos and Schapelhouman 1993, p.180, no.137 (ill.)
3 The print was included as a foldout illustration in J. de Riemer, *Beschryving van 's Graven-Hage*, 2 vols., Amsterdam 1730–39, I, between pp.70 and 71; see Dumas 1991, pp.142, 145 note 22. Maps of The Hague do not show the skittles alley, but they generally give only a schematic rendering of the Haagse Bos and Koekamp area and their surroundings.
4 "*En dien 't niet langer lust veraessemt sich met rusten, / En staet als kijker by, of neemt de rechtbanck waer, / En oordeelt sittende van 't naeste spelend paer: / En soo de Kegel valt die Koningh is van achten, / Soo vlieght'er wel een droom door spelende gedachten, / Van Koningen ontdaen in 't midden van haer volck, / Dat over einde staet, terwijl de swartste wolck / Die oyt de Sonn besloegh, wolck boven alle wonder, / Dry Kroonen zeffens velt met ongehoorden donder*": Huygens 1920, p.105, lines 2146–54 (translation Beverley Jackson). Ter Gouw 1871, p.333, quotes only lines 2149–50 in his passage about skittles, which obscures the point for the reader.
5 MacLaren 1991, I, pp.429–30, no.2560.

56

Plundering soldiers at a peasant's dwelling, 1669

Pen and dark brown ink, brush and grey ink, framing
lines with pen and black ink, 18.9 × 23.4 cm
Signed and dated, lower left, beneath the little bench:
a.v.velde / 1669 (pen and brown ink)
Verso, lower left: *–N. 3923* (pen and brown ink,
Goll van Franckenstein, cf. Lugt 2987)
Rijksprentenkabinet, Rijksmuseum, Amsterdam,
inv. no.RP-T-1902-A-4602

AMSTERDAM ONLY

The violence of war is not exactly a theme that one would be inclined to associate with the Arcadian, eternally sun-drenched world of Adriaen van de Velde. Yet he did produce a few drawings that display a decidedly rawer, more disturbing reality than we are accustomed to seeing in his work. This was a reality that, at the time when he was making these drawings, was not in fact so very far away, either in place or time. For much of the seventeenth century, large parts of Europe, including the southern regions of what is now the Netherlands, were embroiled in a war that seemed never-ending. All the warring parties deployed largely mercenary armies. Most of these solders came from society's underclass, and numerous criminals and semi-criminals rubbed shoulders with men for whom enlisting in an army – any army – appeared to offer the only way out of abject poverty. The pay was generally insufficient for an honest living, besides which it was only disbursed intermittently. In consequence, the countryside in particular was constantly plagued by gangs of itinerant mercenaries intent on robbery and plunder.[1]

In Van de Velde's drawing in Amsterdam, violence is about to erupt. Two men armed with a heavy tree trunk have positioned themselves outside the door of a peasant's dwelling, ready to batter down the door. An elderly inhabitant watches in dread from an upstairs window. Two mounted horsemen wait calmly for their turn to go into action; meanwhile, three others are loading their rifles. Yet – as if Van de Velde cannot resist it – this menacing scene is set in a summery, sun-drenched landscape. As always in his finished drawings, the artist has recorded the play of light and shade on the figures and objects with meticulous care.

A second drawing, in the Albertina in Vienna, depicts the sequel to this story. The violence, which was still only latent in the first scene, is here displayed in explicit, and fairly shocking, form (fig.177). Someone has already been killed. In the foreground, one of the thugs is threatening a terrified peasant with his pistol, while another is assaulting the man's wife. A third

FIG.177
Adriaen van de Velde, *Marauders attack peasants at their huts*. Pen and brown ink, brush and greyish-brown ink over traces of a sketch in black chalk, 18 × 26.3 cm. Albertina, Vienna, inv. no.10144

soldier has grabbed another peasant by the hair as the man begs for mercy, and is about to run him through with his rapier. In the middle distance two men and a woman are fleeing, pursued by two soldiers whose swords are drawn. And all this is taking place, as in the Amsterdam drawing, in an idyllic hilly landscape.

In stylistic and technical respects, the drawings in Amsterdam and Vienna are very similar, and their dimensions too are not very different. The one in Amsterdam is slightly less wide, but the rather abrupt way in which the two horsemen on the right are cut off might be an indication that a strip was cut off along the right side. The drawing in Vienna, on the other hand, measures less in height (although the difference is less than 1 cm), and this too could mean that a narrow strip of paper was cut off along the top or bottom edges, or indeed both. The evidence strongly suggests that the two drawings were once a pair.[2]

In both of his war scenes, Van de Velde drew inspiration from the work of artists from an earlier generation, most notably David Vinckboons and Esaias van de Velde. The use of a battering ram to smash a door is a motif depicted in an anonymous engraving after a design by Vinckboons, the first in a series of four that is known as *The peasant's sorrow* (fig.178).[3] The theme of this series, which was executed during the Twelve Years' Truce, is the strained relationship between peasants and soldiers in wartime. The images reflect Vinckboons's pessimistic view of the Truce, which provided only a brief respite. Pillaging and plunder abound in the drawings and paintings of Esaias van de Velde, although it must be said that his scenes are seldom as violent as the drawing by Adriaen van de Velde in Vienna.[4]

The question remains of what may have prompted Adriaen van de Velde to produce these two drawings, which are quite out of step with the rest of his oeuvre. Both drawings are carefully finished, and the one in Amsterdam is signed and dated. In all probability, then, they should be regarded as independent works of art. This means that there are two possibilities: either he produced them for the open market, simply because there was a demand for scenes of this kind, or they were commissioned by a collector. We shall probably never know the answer. M.S.

PROVENANCE

Jeronimus Tonneman sale, Amsterdam, 21st October 1754 and following days, Konstboek N, lot 9, bought by Huquier (together with lot 10; fl. 43); Neyman (Jan Danser Nijman?) sale, Paris, 8th July 1776 and following days, lot 949* (100 livres); Jonkheer Johan Goll van Franckenstein sale, Amsterdam, 1st July 1833 and following days, Kunstboek C, lot 7, bought by Albertus Brondgeest (fl. 102); J.G. Baron Verstolk van Soelen sale, Amsterdam, 22nd March 1847 and following days, lot 298, bought by Lamme (fl. 71); Herman de Kat sale, Rotterdam, 4th March 1867 and following days, lot 264, bought by William Pitcairn Knowles (fl. 41); his sale, Amsterdam, 25th–26th June 1895, lot 660, bought by H.J. Valk (fl. 82); acquired with the support of the Vereniging Rembrandt, 1902

NOTES

1 Parker 1972, pp.158–74; De Cauwer 2008, pp.169–94.
2 The fact that both drawings were still together in the Tonneman and Neyman sales seems to confirm this supposition (see the provenance listed above). In the Neyman sale the Vienna drawing was lot 949 (140 livres).
3 Fishman 1982, pp.31–44.
4 Keyes 1984, pp.103–15, pp.131–34, nos.44–58, pp.219–23, nos.D22–D35.

57

The continents of Europe and Asia

Pen and brown ink, brush and grey ink, contours indented for transfer, verso rubbed with red chalk, framing line with pen and dark brown ink, 12 × 11.6 cm
Inscribed, lower right: *A.Vande Velde.* (pen and dark brown ink, seventeenth- or eighteenth-century)
Amsterdam City Archives, inv. no.10097/555

AMSTERDAM ONLY

58

The continents of America and Africa

Brush and grey ink, contours indented for transfer, framing line with pen and dark brown ink, 12 × 10.8 cm
Amsterdam City Archives, inv. no.10097/556

AMSTERDAM ONLY

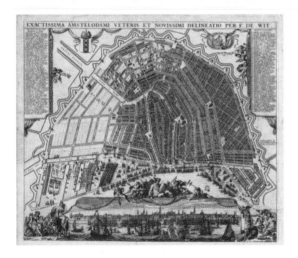

Probably in 1671, shortly before his early death, Adriaen van de Velde drew a number of designs for decorations on a map of Amsterdam and a map of the world that were published by Frederick de Wit. That dry, factual statement may possibly conceal a small misfortune. After all, however beautiful and imaginative such decorations may have been, the designer's work would not have been held in high regard. Only rarely – Nicolaes Berchem's decorations on Nicolaes Visscher's map of the world are one such exception – was the illustrator's name mentioned on a map.[1] An artist produced designs for vignettes and cartouches on maps because he had to earn a living, not as a path to fame and glory. Of Adriaen van de Velde's relations with Frederick de Wit we know nothing; it is noteworthy, however, that on 2nd August 1674 Adriaen's widow Maria Ouderkerck signed a document acknowledging a debt to De Wit for the sum of 1,000 guilders that he had lent her.[2]

The two small, almost square drawings were designed for the decorations in the lower corners of a map of Amsterdam that De Wit probably marketed between 1671 and 1675 (fig.179).[3] The scenes flank a profile view of Amsterdam over the water of the IJ bay, which spans almost the entire lower edge of the map. Europe and Asia are depicted in the lower left, and America and Africa on the right. In the drawing for the left-hand vignette, Europe appears in the guise of a young woman, seated on a bull garlanded with flowers. This is an allusion to the myth in which Jupiter, enamoured of the Phoenician princess Europa, transformed himself into a white bull and abducted her. In depicting the personifications of the continents, Van de Velde largely adhered to the *Iconologia of uytbeeldinghe des verstands* (1644) by Cesare Ripa. Thus, in the case of Asia: "A woman adorned with a beautiful garland of flowers, entwined with diverse fruits; in a rich embroidered garment, all embellished with gold, pearls and other precious stones; in her right hand branches with leaves and fruit of cassia, pepper, cloves, nutmeg etc.; in her left she holds a finely wrought Censer, from which rises a very great plume of smoke. By the side of this woman, a camel appears on its knees, or in some other manner, as the painter sees fit."[4]

In Van de Velde's depiction of America, on the left of the second drawing, he followed Ripa in showing her nude, with only a cloak slung over her shoulders, her head adorned with feathers, an arrow and a bow in her hands, and accompanied by a large lizard. He omitted the other attributes recommended by Ripa, a quiver (possibly for lack of space), and "a human head pierced with an arrow",[5] possibly because this latter detail struck him, or the publisher, as unduly gruesome. In the figure of Africa, too, the illustrator followed Ripa's prescription almost to the letter: she is nude aside from a loincloth, she is dark-skinned, and holds a cornucopia filled with ears of corn in one hand and a scorpion in the other; a lion stands beside her, and serpents coil across the ground behind her. The presence of all these

FIG.179
Map of Amsterdam published by Frederik de Wit. First edition, c.1671–75. Amsterdam City Archives, inv. no.10095/116

FIG.180
Adriaen van de Velde, *Venus and Amor with putti in a landscape*. Pen and grey ink, brush and grey ink, pen and black ink, 14.3 × 9 cm. Teylers Museum, Haarlem, inv. no.TvB T 619

creatures was deemed to require an explanation: "The cruel lion, scorpions, and other venomous beasts, indicate that many of such are to be found in Africa, being venomous beyond measure".[6]

The drawing containing the images of America and Africa was made entirely with brush and grey ink. As a result, it has a rather pale appearance in comparison to the design for Europe and Asia, which was touched up carefully with pen and brown ink. The anonymous engraver who worked for Frederick de Wit simply transferred the two designs, faithfully and scrupulously, to the copperplate.

Probably in the same year in which he produced the two designs for the map of Amsterdam, Van de Velde worked on another of Frederick de Wit's projects. A drawing in Teylers Museum in Haarlem depicting *Venus and Amor with putti in a landscape* (fig.180) has been identified as the right half of a design for the decorations in the upper left corner of a map of the world.[7] The decorations in this map depict the four seasons, dressed in a mythological sauce, and with the signs of the zodiac belonging to the season more or less concealed within the scene. In the vanished left half of the drawing were depicted putti engaging with a bull and a ram, allusions to the zodiac signs of Taurus and Aries, for spring. The designs for the other three corners, depicting summer, autumn and winter, must also have been by Adriaen van de Velde, but these drawings have been lost or are living a concealed existence somewhere. M.S.

PROVENANCE

Sale, Amsterdam, Sotheby Mak van Waay, 29th October 1979, lots 212 and 213; C.G. Boerner, Düsseldorf, 1980; collection of Jacobus A. Klaver, Amsterdam, 1988; his sale, Amsterdam, Sotheby's, 10th May 1994, lots 67 and 68, purchased by the Amsterdam City Archives

EXHIBITIONS

Amsterdam 1993, nos.66a–b; Amsterdam 2007–08, nos.38a–b

REFERENCES

Exh. cat. Amsterdam 1989, pp.82–84; Hameleers 1994a, pp.77–79; Hameleers 1994b, pp.166–71; Hameleers 2013, pp.139–40

NOTES

1 On Berchem's decorations, see exh. cat. Amsterdam 1989, pp.76–80.
2 Frensemeier 2001, p.195, Doc. 32.
3 For the map and its various editions, see Hameleers 2013, pp.139–40, no.68.
4 "*Een Vrouwe met een schoone bloemenkrans geciert, en met verscheiden vruchten doorvlochten, wesende seer rijcklijck gekleet, geheel met goud, peerlen en andere kostelijcke steenen, geciert, hebbende in de rechter hand eenige taxkens met*

blaederen en vruchten van Cassie, Peper, Nagelen, Muscaet-noten &c. in de slinker heeftse een konstigh Wieroock-vat, waer uyt een seer groote roock opstijght. By dese Vrouwe leyt een Cameel op zijne knyen, of op een andere maniere, soo 't den Schilder best dunckt geraeden." For the four continents, see Ripa/Pers 1644, pp.601–05.
5 "*... een Menschen hoofd met een Pijle doorschoten*": ibid.
6 "*De wreede Leeuw, Scorpioenen en andere venijnige beesten, betoonen dat in Africa van dit goed, veel te vinden is, zijnde boven maeten venijnigh*": ibid.
7 See C. van Tuyll van Serooskerken in exh. cat. Haarlem 1995–96, no.22; for De Wit's world map, see Shirley 1987, pp.468–69, no.451.

59

The Golden Age, 1664

Pen and brush and brown ink, 16.6 × 25.2 cm
Signed and dated, lower right: *a. v. velde. f 1664*;
verso, lower left: mark of the Rijksprentenkabinet,
Rijksmuseum, Amsterdam (Lugt 2228); lower right:
370 (pencil, early twentieth-century)
Rijksprentenkabinet, Rijksmuseum, Amsterdam,
inv. no.RP-T-1905-100

AMSTERDAM ONLY

FIG.181
Antonio Tempesta, *Aetas Aurea, The Golden Age*.
Etching, 10.5 × 11.8 cm. Rijksprentenkabinet,
Rijksmuseum, Amsterdam, inv. no.RP-P-OB-37.777

Themes derived from classical mythology are scarce in Adriaen van de Velde's oeuvre. He painted Mercury, Argus and Io, and Mercury and Battus, subjects that are essentially close to his customary landscapes featuring herdsmen with sheep and cattle, while one *Vertumnus and Pomona* has been preserved – likewise a scene with relatively small figures in a landscape.[1]

Van de Velde's most ambitious mythological scene is this drawing of the *Aetas Aurea*, the Golden Age, a composition with the remarkable number of eight nudes, both female and male, from children to adults, in a wide variety of poses amid a paradisiacal setting. The subject comes from Ovid's *Metamorphoses*. The poet describes the four ages that followed the creation of the world and mankind, the Golden, Silver, Bronze and Iron Ages. In the Golden Age of Saturn, there was eternal spring, and people lived together in love and innocence, without rulers or laws, in complete harmony with nature. After Saturn was banished and Jupiter ruled the world, in the Silver Age, the supreme deity created the four seasons. People learned to live with blistering heat and bitter cold; they built houses for shelter, and worked the land to obtain their daily bread. In the third, the Bronze Age, people took up arms against each other, but they did not yet fall prey to godlessness. This did not happen until the Iron Age, when greed drove them to mine for gold and to threaten each other's lives. Eventually the gods, disgusted by the sins of mankind, unleashed a devastating flood that engulfed the Earth.

In their representations of the Golden Age, artists have almost always drawn inspiration from these lines of Ovid: "The earth herself, without compulsion, untouched by hoe or ploughshare, of herself gave all things needful. And men, content with the food which came with no one's seeking, gathered the fruits of the arbute tree, the hillside strawberries, the cornel-cherries, the berries hanging thick upon prickly brambles, and the acorns fallen from the spreading tree of Jove. Then spring was everlasting, and gentle zephyrs with warm breath played with the flowers that sprang unplanted. Anon the earth, untilled, brought forth her stores of grain, and the fields, though unfallowed, grew white with the heavy, bearded wheat. Streams of milk and streams of sweet nectar flowed, and yellow honey was distilled from the verdant oak."[2]

Van de Velde's drawing is clearly based on an etching by Antonio Tempesta, the third print in a series of 150 Ovid illustrations, published by Pieter de Jode in Antwerp in 1603 (fig.181). The compositions are reverse images of each other, but they largely correspond. Especially the small group on the right in Van de Velde's drawing – the two men, one of whom has climbed a tree, and the woman seen from behind – displays a marked resemblance to the three figures on the left in Tempesta's print. Van de Velde did change the animals depicted in the scene, however: whereas Tempesta presented an elephant and a dromedary, Van de Velde confined himself to two cows and a goat, with a few chickens scratching around in the foreground. His Arcadia, aside from the hills in the background, is a very Dutch Arcadia.

The meticulous care lavished on details, combined with the fact that the drawing is signed and dated, suggests that *The Golden Age* was an independent work of art, and may well have been commissioned. M.S.

PROVENANCE

Samuel Woodburn sale, London, 12th–14th June 1860, lot 1536 (£2 12s 6d); Edward Habich sale, Stuttgart, 27th April 1899 and following days, lot 688, bought by Scheltema (? 76); René della Faille de Waerloos sale, Amsterdam, 19th January 1904, lot 370 (fl. 140); acquired from Jean H. Odink, 1905

NOTES

1 Frensemeier 2001, nos.13a–c (*Mercury, Argus and Io*, with the accompanying drawings), 14 (*Vertumnus and Pomona*, with the accompanying drawings) and 15 (*Mercury and Battus*, with the accompanying drawings).
2 Ovid, *Metamorphoses*, pp.8–11 (Book I, 101–22).

60

The Angel appearing to the Shepherds

Brush and brown ink over black chalk, 17.2 × 20.2 cm
At lower right the mark of the Marquis de Lagoy
(Lugt 1710)
British Museum, London, inv. no.1895,0915.1329

FIG.182
Pieter van Laer, *The Angel appearing to the Shepherds*. Oil on panel, 60 × 47.5 cm. Museum Bredius, The Hague, inv. no.219-1946

It will come as no surprise that a good many seventeenth-century Dutch artists who were not primarily known for their history paintings nonetheless chose occasionally to depict the subject of the angel appearing to the shepherds at the Nativity. The story provides a splendid opportunity to present miscellaneous animals and a number of human figures in a nocturnal landscape. In addition, the fact that the scene can bathe in a heavenly glow gives the artist an opportunity to indulge in the virtuoso depiction of spectacular light effects. The very brevity of the Bible story – fewer than a dozen sentences – and the relative paucity of details allow for a personal interpretation on the artist's part. The passage in question follows immediately after the equally succinct account of the birth of Jesus:

> And there were in the same country shepherds abiding in the field, keeping watch over their flock by night. And, lo, the angel of the Lord came upon them, and the glory of the Lord shone round about them: and they were sore afraid. And the angel said unto them, Fear not: for, behold, I bring you good tidings of great joy, which shall be to all people. For unto you is born this day in the city of David a Saviour, which is Christ the Lord. And this shall be a sign unto you; Ye shall find the babe wrapped in swaddling clothes, lying in a manger. And suddenly there was with the angel a multitude of the heavenly host praising God, and saying, Glory to God in the highest, and on earth peace, good will toward men.
> (Luke 2: 8–14)

Artists generally opted for one of two moments – the central scene with the angel delivering his heavenly tidings to the dumbfounded shepherds, or the passage immediately after it, in which the angel is surrounded by a heavenly host praising the Lord. The other details, such as the number and kind of creatures tended by the shepherds, as well as the number of shepherds and the nature of the landscape, were all subject to near-infinite variation. David Vinckboons chose the first of the two key moments for his drawing dated 1604, with three shepherds – possibly by analogy with the three Magi – watching over a large flock of sheep and a few goats.[1] Pieter van Laer, a painter of cattle pieces and scenes of everyday life in Italy, produced a small painting in the early 1630s depicting four shepherds accompanied by just three cows and a horse (fig.182).[2] Van Laer's version is the least 'celestial' of all those mentioned here: rather than hovering on the clouds, as is customary, his angel has already landed and stands with both feet on the ground. His scene appears to be illuminated less by the 'glory of the Lord' than by the light of a full moon veiled by the clouds. Nicolaes Berchem must have known Van Laer's painting: the shepherd seen from behind with folded hands, who features prominently in the foreground in his large painting of 1656 in Bristol (fig.183), is an almost exact quotation, in reverse, of his shepherd.[3] Berchem depicted the Annunciation to the Shepherds in several paintings and drawings; he often included the figure of a shepherd tumbling backwards in fright in the same characteristic pose.[4] A number of *Annunciation*s by Philips Wouwerman, known for his paintings of Dutch

landscapes with cattle, have also been preserved: each one includes the animal that virtually became Wouwerman's trademark, a white horse.[5] Two curious exceptions merit a brief mention here: both Cornelis Saftleven and Adam Pynacker painted an Annunciation to the Shepherds in which there is no angel to be seen. In Saftleven's painting, the heavenly tidings take the form of a wide beam of light from the sky that falls on the earth, while in Pynacker it is a powerful streak of lightning.[6] These iconographical oddities may perhaps have been intended for orthodox Calvinist clients, who considered representations of God, Jesus or any heavenly being – mindful of Calvin's words on the subject – to be improper.[7]

In the meantime, Rembrandt van Rijn, the only dyed-in-the-wool history painter in this company, had also applied his powers to the subject, with – as one would expect – spectacular results. In most of the interpretations, it is the people who are overcome, entirely in accordance with the biblical text, by great fear at the sight of the heavenly apparition: "and they were sore afraid". The livestock generally undergo the apparition with equanimity. This does not apply in Rembrandt: in his 1634 etching, human figures and animals alike flee in unbridled panic in response to the display of divine power (fig.184).[8]

Adriaen van de Velde appears to have incorporated elements from several of his predecessors into his drawing. His angel, who brings the glad tidings with raised right hand, resembles the celestial beings of Rembrandt and Berchem. Here the angel is not the source of the heavenly light; the source is behind him, so that his face and body remain largely in the shade. Much the same applies in the painting by Berchem, and to a lesser extent in Rembrandt's print. Like Van Laer, Van de Velde depicts the event from close by, which has the effect of involving the viewer in what is happening. Van de Velde has drawn only two shepherds actually beholding the miracle, besides which a few sleeping figures, one of them clearly a woman, can be made out in the semi-darkness in the middle distance. Van Laer too depicts a shepherd who sleeps right through the wondrous event. One of the two shepherds in Van de Velde's drawing has sunk to his knees; arms outstretched, he gazes up at the miraculous messenger. The other shepherd seems to have been about to flee, but to have changed his mind, and is looking over his shoulder at the angel. His pose – feet wide apart, hands raised and folded before his breast – is quite similar to that of the shepherds seen from behind in Van Laer and Berchem, except that here we see him from the front. It is clear that Van de Velde has quoted both these predecessors here – in a way that is both brilliant and original. Like Van Laer and Wouwerman, Van de Velde limits the number of creatures: he depicts two cows and a calf, a few sheep and a lamb, and a little goat. Only the goat appears startled by what is taking place above. It has scrambled to its feet to take flight; its back legs are already extended, while the front legs are still bent. This reflects the pose of one of the cows in Rembrandt's etching, which also seems frozen in an attempt to flee.

Since the only light source in the scene is behind the angel, Van de Velde was able to take his love for backlighting to extremes, rendering every detail with unremitting consistency. With uncommon virtuosity, Van de Velde

allows the glittering light to play across his human figures and creatures. The cow lying in the left foreground falls just outside the light; her dark bulk functions here as a repoussoir that lends the scene depth. The shadows of people and animals, too, add depth and cohesiveness to the composition.

Van de Velde drew his *Angel appearing to the Shepherds* over an initial sketch in black chalk using only the brush and a rich array of brown hues. The clouds that surround the angel have been splashed on to the paper in wide strokes, wet-in-wet, whereas details in human figures and animals have been drawn with extreme care using the point of the brush, and the artist has cleverly exploited the white of his paper to suggest brightly illuminated spots, leaving carefully calculated spots blank against a dark or semi-dark background in the dog's light, raised snout, in the goat's back, and in the back and ears of the sheep lying behind the small goat. Intentionally or otherwise, Van de Velde's technique here is more than ever akin to that in some of Nicolaes Berchem's most virtuoso drawings from the 1650s.[9]

The purpose for which Adriaen van de Velde produced this *tour de force* is unknown. Since the drawing is neither signed nor dated, it cannot have been intended as an independent piece for a collector. The most logical explanation is that it was made in preparation for a small painting. No painting of this scene by Adriaen van de Velde is known, but fortunately we do have this drawing, which, for all its modest dimensions, ranks among the finest works in this master's oeuvre. M.S.

PROVENANCE

Marquis de Lagoy (1764–1829); John Heywood Hawkins (1802/3–1877); John Malcolm of Poltalloch (1805–1893); purchased from Col. John Wingfield Malcolm, 1895

REFERENCES

Hind 1931, p.28, no.24; Bernt 1957–58, II, no.591

NOTES

1 Rijksprentenkabinet, Rijksmuseum, Amsterdam, inv. no.RP-T-1935-22; Schapelhouman 1987, no.93.
2 Blankert 1991, no.90; Blankert 2004, pp.93–98.
3 Exh. cat. Washington, Detroit and Amsterdam 1980–81, no.50.
4 For example, in a drawing that probably dates from the late 1650s or early 1660s; sale, Amsterdam, Sotheby's, 13th November 1991, lot 306.
5 For example, private collection, New York (exh. cat. Washington, Detroit and Amsterdam 1980–81, no.78), and an interesting drawing, rightly attributed to Philips Wouwerman, in the Morgan Library & Museum, New York (inv. no.III, 199; Turner and Stampfle 2006, p.216, no.350).
6 Saftleven (whereabouts unknown; Schulz 1978, no.550); Pynacker (The Weldon Collection sale, New York, Sotheby's, 22nd April 2015, lot 15).
7 Manuth 1993–94, pp.240–48; Joby 2007, pp.4–13.
8 Exh. cat. Amsterdam and London 2000–01, no.21.
9 For example, *Shepherd family travelling at night*, dated 1655, in the British Museum, London (inv. no.Oo.10-200; Hind 1926, p.29, no.13).

BIBLIOGRAPHY

ADLER ET AL. 1981
W. Adler, E. Herzog, F. Lahusen and J.M. Lehmann, *Gemäldegalerie Alte Meister Schloss Wilhelmshöhe*, Braunschweig 1981

ANDREWS 1985
K. Andrews, *Catalogue of the Netherlandish drawings in the National Gallery of Scotland*, 2 vols., Edinburgh 1985

APOSTOOL 1825
[C. Apostool], *Catalogus der schilderijen, oudheden, enz. op 's Rijks Museum te Amsterdam berustende*, 6th ed., Amsterdam [1825?]

BAILEY 2002
C.B. Bailey, *Patriotic taste: collecting modern art in pre-revolutionary Paris*, New Haven and London 2002

BAKKER 2011
P. Bakker, 'Crisis? Welke crisis? Kanttekeningen bij het economisch verval van de schilderkunst in Leiden na 1660', *De Zeventiende Eeuw* 27 (2011), pp.232–69

BARTSCH 1803–21
A. Bartsch, *Le peintre graveur*, 21 vols., Vienna 1803–21

BASTIDE 1766
J.-F. de Bastide, *Le temple des arts ou le cabinet de M. Braamcamp*, Amsterdam 1766

BECKER 1923
F. Becker, *Handzeichnungen holländischen Meister aus der Sammlung Dr. C. Hofstede de Groot im Haag: fünfzig ausgewählte Zeichnungen Rembrandts, seines Kreises und seiner Zeit*, Leipzig 1923

BENSON 1927
R.H. Benson, *The Holford collection, Dorchester House*, 2 vols., Oxford 1927

BERGVELT 1992
E. Bergvelt, 'Koning Willem I als verzamelaar, opdrachtgever en weldoener van de Noordnederlandse musea', in C.A. Tamse and E. Witte, eds., *Staats- en natievorming in Willem I's Koninkrijk (1815–1830)*, Brussels and Baarn 1992, pp.261–85

BERGVELT 1998
E. Bergvelt, *Pantheon der Gouden Eeuw: van Nationale Konst-Gallerij tot Rijksmuseum van Schilderijen (1798–1896)*, Zwolle 1998

BERGVELT, MEIJERS AND RIJNDERS 1993
E. Bergvelt, D.J. Meijers and M. Rijnders, eds., *Verzamelen: van rariteitenkabinet tot Kunstmuseum*, Heerlen 1993

BERNT 1957–58
W. Bernt, *Die Niederländischen Zeichner des 17. Jahrhunderts*, 2 vols., Munich 1957–58

BILLE 1961
C. Bille, *De Tempel der Kunst of Het Kabinet van den Heer Braamcamp*, 2 vols., Amsterdam 1961

BIONDA 1986
R.W.A. Bionda, 'De Amsterdamse verzamelaar J.A. Brentano (1753-1821) en de inrichting van zijn "zaal" voor Italiaanse kunst', *Bulletin van het Rijksmuseum* 34 (1986), pp.135–76

BLANC 1857–58
C. Blanc, *Le trésor de la curiosité tiré des catalogues de vente, avec diverses Notes et Notices historiques et biographiques*, 2 vols., Paris 1857–58

BLANC 1861
C. Blanc, *Histoire des peintres de toutes les écoles: Ecole hollandaise*, 2 vols., Paris 1861

BLANKERT 1967–68
A. Blankert, 'Stechow: addenda', *Simiolus* 2 (1967–68), pp.103–08

BLANKERT 1968A
A. Blankert, 'Over Pieter van Laer als dier- en landschapschilder', *Oud Holland* 83 (1968), pp.117–34

BLANKERT 1968B
A. Blankert, 'Adriaen van de Velde', in G. Bazin *Kindlers Malerei Lexikon*, V, Zurich 1968, pp.646–48

BLANKERT 1991
A. Blankert, *Museum Bredius: catalogus van de schilderijen en tekeningen*, Zwolle 1991

BLANKERT 2004
A. Blankert, *Selected writings on Dutch painting: Rembrandt, Van Beke, Vermeer and others*, Zwolle 2004

BLANKERT AND RUURS 1979
A. Blankert and R. Ruurs, *Amsterdams Historisch Museum: schilderijen daterend van voor 1800, voorlopige catalogus*, Amsterdam 1979

BOCK 1996
H. Bock *et al.*, *Gemäldegalerie Berlin Gesamtverzeichnis*, Berlin 1996

BOCK AND ROSENBERG 1930
E. Bock and J. Rosenberg, *Die niederländischen Meister: beschreibendes Verzeichnis sämtlicher Zeichnungen*, 2 vols., Berlin 1930

BODE 1900
W. Bode, 'Die Gemäldegalerie Alfred Thieme in Leipzig', *Zeitschrift für bildende Kunst* N.S. 11 (1900), pp.97–105 and 129–43

BODE 1906
W. von Bode, 'Adriaen van de Velde', *Die Graphischen Künste* 29 (1906), pp.14–24

BODE 1917
W. von Bode, *Die Meister der holländischen und flämischen Malerschulen*, Leipzig 1917

BOL 1973
L.J. Bol, *Die holländische Marinemalerei des 17. Jahrhunderts*, Braunschweig 1973

BOON 1955
K.G. Boon, 'De tekenkunst in de zeventiende eeuw', in H.E. van Gelder, ed., *Kunstgeschiedenis der Nederlanden van de middeleeuwen tot onze tijd*, II, Utrecht, Antwerp, Brussels, Ghent and Leuven 1955, pp.134–51

BORGHERO 1981
G. Borghero, *Thyssen-Bornemisza Collection: catalogue of the exhibited works of art*, Castagnola 1981

BORGHERO 1986
G. Borghero, *Thyssen-Bornemisza Collection: catalogue raisonné of the exhibited works of art*, Milan 1986

BÖRSCH-SUPAN 1964
H. Börsch-Supan, *Die Gemälde im Jagdschloss Grunewald*, Berlin 1964

BREDIUS 1912
A. Bredius, 'De nalatenschap van Jan van der Heyden's weduwe', *Oud Holland* 30 (1912), pp.129–51

BRENNINKMEYER-DE ROOIJ 1976
B. Brenninkmeyer-de Rooij, 'De schilderijengalerij van Prins Willem V op het Buitenhof te Den Haag (2)', *Antiek* 11 (1976), pp.138–76

BROOS 1987
B. Broos, *Meesterwerken in het Mauritshuis*, The Hague 1987

BROOS 1989
B. Broos, 'Improving and Finishing Old Master Drawings: an Art in Itself', *The Hoogsteder-Naumann Mercury* 8 (1989), pp.34–55

BROOS AND SCHAPELHOUMAN 1993
B. Broos and M. Schapelhouman, *Oude tekeningen in het bezit van het Amsterdams Historisch Museum, waaronder de collectie Fodor, 4 Nederlandse tekenaars geboren tussen 1600 en 1660*, Zwolle 1993

BRUYN 1987
J. Bruyn, 'Toward a Scriptural Reading of Seventeenth-Century Dutch Landscape Paintings', in exh. cat. Amsterdam, Boston and Philadelphia 1987–88, pp.84–103

BUCHANAN 1824
W. Buchanan, *Memoirs of painting, with a chronological history of the importation of pictures by the great masters into England since the French revolution*, 2 vols., London 1824

BUCHOWIECKI 1974
W. Buchowiecki, *Handbuch der Kirchen Roms, 3. Band: Die Kirchen innerhalb der Mauern Roms (S. Maria della Neve bis S. Susanna)*, Vienna 1974

BUVELOT 2004
Q. Buvelot, *Royal Picture Gallery Mauritshuis: a summary catalogue*, The Hague and Zwolle 2004

CAT. AMSTERDAM 1855
Catalogus der schilderijen van het Museum Van der Hoop te Amsterdam, Amsterdam 1855

CAT. AMSTERDAM 1863
Beschrijving der schilderijen, teekeningen, prenten, prentwerken en boeken, in het Museum Fodor te Amsterdam, Amsterdam 1863

CAT. LEIPZIG 1916
Die Galerie Alfred Thieme im Museum der Bildenden Künste zu Leipzig: Neuerwerbungen vom Jahre 1916, Leipzig 1916

CAT. PARIS 1905
Illustrated Catalogue of the ninth series of 100 paintings by old masters of the Dutch, Flemish, Italian, French, and English schools, being a portion of the Sedelmeyer Gallery which contains about 1500 original Pictures by ancient and modern Artists, Paris 1905

CAUSID 1783
S. Causid, *Verzeichnis der Hochfürstlich-Hessischen Gemälde-Sammlung in Cassel*, Kassel 1783

DE CAUWER 2008
P. De Cauwer, *Tranen van bloed. Het beleg van 's-Hertogenbosch en de oorlog in de Nederlanden, 1629*, Amsterdam 2008

CHARINOWA-ZAYNOWSKA 1923
E. Charinowa-Zaynowska, [article devoted to Dutch and Flemish paintings at the Pavlovsk Palace Museum, St Petersburg], in *Gorod* (January 1923), p.94

DAALDER 2016
R. Daalder, *Van de Velde & Zoon, zeeschilders: het bedrijf van Willem van de Velde de Oude en Willem van de Velde de Jonge, 1640–1707*, Leiden 2016

DIBBITS, VERSLYPE AND WALLERT 2008
T. Dibbits, I. Verslype and A. Wallert, 'Paulus Potters "Herders met vee": Rijksmuseum versus Woburn Abbey', *Bulletin van het Rijksmuseum* 56 (2008), pp.66–81

VAN DER DOES 1668
J. van der Does, *'s Graven-Hage, Met de Voornaemste Plaetsen en Vermaecklijckheden*, The Hague 1668

DROSSAERS AND LUNSINGH SCHEURLEUR 1974–76
S.W.A. Drossaers and T.H. Lunsingh Scheurleur, *Inventarissen van de inboedels in de verblijven van de Oranjes en daarmede gelijk te stellen stukken, 1567–1795*, 3 vols., The Hague 1974–76

DUBOURCQ 1858
P.L. Dubourcq, *Beschrijving der schilderijen op 's Rijks Museum te Amsterdam met fac simile der naamteekens*, Amsterdam 1858

DUBREUIL 2001
M.-M. Dubreuil, 'Le Catalogue du Muséum Français (Louvre) en 1793', *Bulletin de la société d'histoire de l'art français* (2001), pp.125–65

DUMAS 1991
C. Dumas, in collaboration with J. van der Meer, *Haagse stadsgezichten 1550–1800 topografische schilderijen van het Haags Historisch Museum*, Zwolle 1991

DUPARC 1980
F.J. Duparc, *Mauritshuis. Hollandse schilderkunst: landschappen 17e eeuw*, The Hague 1980

DUPARC 2012
F.J. Duparc, 'Een onbekend ruiterportret door Adriaen van de Velde', in E. Buijsen, C. Dumas and V. Manuth, eds., *Face Book: Studies on Dutch and Flemish Portraiture of the 16th–18th Centuries. Liber Amicorum Presented to Rudolf E.O. Ekkart on the Occasion of his 65th Birthday*, Leiden 2012, pp.331–34

VAN ECK 1999
X. van Eck, 'The Artist's Religion: Paintings Commissioned for Clandestine Catholic Churches in the Northern Netherlands, 1600–1800', *Simiolus* 27 (1999), pp.70–94

VAN ECK 2008
X. van Eck, *Clandestine splendor: paintings for the catholic church in the Dutch Republic*, Zwolle 2008

EDWARDS 1996
J. Edwards, *Alexandre-Joseph Paillet: expert et marchand de tableaux à la fin du XVIIIe siècle*, Paris 1996

VAN EEGHEN 1971
I.H. van Eeghen, 'De verzamelaar Nicolaas Doekscheer', *Bulletin van het Rijksmuseum* 19 (1971), pp.173–82

VAN DEN EERENBEEMD 2006
A. van den Eerenbeemd, 'De Italianiserende tekeningen van Adriaen van de Velde', *Delineavit et Sculpsit* 30 (2006), pp.1–64

VAN EIJNDEN AND VAN DER WILLIGEN 1816–40
R. van Eijnden en A. van der Willigen, *Geschiedenis der vaderlandsche schilderkunst*, 4 vols., Haarlem 1816–40

EISELE 2000
K. Eisele, *Jan Wijnants (1631/32–1684): ein niederländischer Maler der Ideallandschaft im Goldenen Jahrhundert*, Stuttgart 2000

EXH. CAT. ALMELO 1961
D. Hannema, exh. cat. *Oude tekeningen uit de verzameling Victor de Stuers*, Almelo (Kunstkring de Waag) 1961

EXH. CAT. AMSTERDAM 1845
exh. cat. *Tentoonstelling van schilderijen door oude meesters*, Amsterdam (Koninklijke Akademie van Beeldende Kunsten) 1845

EXH. CAT. AMSTERDAM 1876
D.C. Meijer and P.H. Witkamp, eds., exh. cat. *Historische Tentoonstelling van Amsterdam*, Amsterdam (Oudemannenhuis) 1876

EXH. CAT. AMSTERDAM 1934
exh. cat. *Nederlandsche italianiseerende schilders, 16de en 17de eeuw*, Amsterdam (Arti et amicitiae) 1934

EXH. CAT. AMSTERDAM 1956
I.Q. van Regteren Altena and L.C.J. Frerichs, exh. cat. *De verzameling van Dr. A. Welcker, I: Nederlandse tekeningen der zestiende en zeventiende eeuw*, Amsterdam (Rijksprentenkabinet) 1956

EXH. CAT. AMSTERDAM 1973
P. Schatborn, ed., exh. cat. *Hollandse genre-tekeningen uit de zeventiende eeuw*, Amsterdam (Rijksmuseum) 1973

EXH. CAT. AMSTERDAM 1975–76
L.C.J. Frerichs and P. Schatborn, exh. cat. *De verzameling van H. van Leeuwen*, Amsterdam (Rijksprentenkabinet) 1975–76

EXH. CAT. AMSTERDAM 1983
M. Schapelhouman, exh. cat. *Het beste bewaard: een Amsterdamse verzameling en het ontstaan van de Vereniging Rembrandt*, Amsterdam (Rijksprentenkabinet) 1983

EXH. CAT. AMSTERDAM 1987–88
M. Schapelhouman and P. Schatborn, exh. cat. *Land & water: Hollandse tekeningen uit de 17de eeuw in het Rijksprentenkabinet / Dutch drawings from the 17th century in the Rijksmuseum Print Room*, Amsterdam (Rijksprentenkabinet) 1987–88

EXH. CAT. AMSTERDAM 1989
J.F. Heijbroek and M. Schapelhouman, eds., exh. cat. *Kunst in kaart. Decoratieve aspecten van de cartografie*, Amsterdam (Rijksprentenkabinet) 1989

EXH. CAT. AMSTERDAM 1993
M. Schapelhouman and P. Schatborn, exh. cat. *Tekeningen van oude meesters. De verzameling Jacobus A. Klaver*, Amsterdam (Rijksprentenkabinet) 1993

EXH. CAT. AMSTERDAM 1997–98
W. Loos *et al.*, exh. cat. *On country roads and fields: the depiction of 18th- and 19th-century landscape*, Amsterdam (Rijksmuseum) 1997–98

EXH. CAT. AMSTERDAM 1997
E. de Jongh and G. Luijten, exh. cat. *Mirror of everyday life: genreprints in the Netherlands 1550–1700*, Amsterdam (Rijksmuseum) 1997

EXH. CAT. AMSTERDAM 2000A
J. Kiers and F. Tissink: exh. cat. *The glory of the Golden Age: Dutch art of the 17th century: painting, sculpture and decorative art*, Amsterdam (Rijksmuseum) 2000

EXH. CAT. AMSTERDAM 2000B
E. Runia, exh. cat. *The glory of the Golden Age: Dutch art of the 17th century: drawings and prints*, Amsterdam (Rijksmuseum) 2000

EXH. CAT. AMSTERDAM 2004–05
E. Bergvelt *et al.*, exh. cat. *De Hollandse meesters van een Amsterdamse bankier: de verzameling van Adriaan van der Hoop (1778–1854)*, Amsterdam (Rijksmuseum and Amsterdams Historisch Museum) 2004–05

EXH. CAT. AMSTERDAM 2007–08
B. Bakker and E. Schmitz, exh. cat. *Het aanzien van Amsterdam. Panorama's, plattegronden en profielen uit de Gouden Eeuw*, Amsterdam (Stadsarchief) 2007–08

EXH. CAT. AMSTERDAM AND LONDON 2000–01
E. Hinterding, G. Luijten and M. Royalton-Kisch *et al.*, exh. cat. *Rembrandt the printmaker*, Amsterdam (Rijksmuseum) and London (British Museum) 2000–01

EXH. CAT. AMSTERDAM AND WASHINGTON 1981–82
P. Schatborn, exh. cat. *Dutch figure drawings from the seventeenth century*, Amsterdam (Rijksprentenkabinet) and Washington (National Gallery of Art) 1981–82

EXH. CAT. AMSTERDAM, BOSTON
AND PHILADELPHIA 1987–88
P.C. Sutton et al., exh. cat. *Masters of 17th-century Dutch landscape painting*, Amsterdam (Rijksmuseum), Boston (Museum of Fine Arts) and Philadelphia (Philadelphia Museum of Art) 1987–88

EXH. CAT. ANN ARBOR 1964
W. Stechow, exh. cat. *Italy through Dutch eyes: Dutch 17th century landscape artists in Italy*, Ann Arbor (University of Michigan Museum of Art) 1964

EXH. CAT. ARNHEM 1958
A.J. de Lorm and J.M. Cochius, exh. cat. *Collectie J.C.H. Heldring te Oosterbeek*, Arnhem (Gemeentemuseum) 1958

EXH. CAT. BERLIN 1974
W. Schulz, exh. cat. *Die Holländische Landschaftszeichnung 1600–1740 Hauptwerke aus dem Berliner Kupferstichkabinett*, Berlin (Kupferstichkabinett) 1974

EXH. CAT. BOLSWARD 1950
exh. cat. *Catalogus van de tentoonstelling van 17de eeuwse kunstschatten uit het Rijksmuseum te Amsterdam*, Bolsward (Stadhuis) 1950

EXH. CAT. BONN, SAARBRÜCKEN
AND BOCHUM 1968–69
I.M. Nelissen and B.W. Meijer, exh. cat. *Niederländische Zeichnungen des 17. bis 19. Jahrhunderts aus der Sammlung Hans van Leeuwen, Utrecht*, Bonn (Rheinisches Landesmuseum), Saarbrücken (Saarländisches Museum) and Bochum (Städtische Kunstgalerie) 1968–69

EXH. CAT. BOSTON AND KANSAS CITY 2015–16
R. Baer et al., exh. cat. *Class Distinctions. Dutch Painting in the Age of Rembrandt and Vermeer*, Boston (Museum of Fine Arts) and Kansas City (Nelson-Atkins Museum of Art) 2015–16

EXH. CAT. BOSTON AND SAINT LOUIS 1980–81
C.S. Ackley, exh. cat. *Printmaking in the age of Rembrandt*, Boston (Museum of Fine Arts) and Saint Louis (Art Museum) 1980–81

EXH. CAT. BREMEN, BRAUNSCHWEIG
AND STUTTGART 1979–80
H. van Leeuwen, exh. cat. *Meisterzeichnungen aus drei Jahrhunderten. Niederländische Handzeichnungen des 17. Bis 19. Jahrhunderts aus der Sammlung Hans van Leeuwen*, Bremen (Kunsthalle), Braunschweig (Städtisches Museum) and Stuttgart (Galerie der Stadt Stuttgart) 1979–80

EXH. CAT. BRUSSELS 1961
exh. cat. *Dessins hollandais du siècle d'or*, Brussels (Bibliothèque Royale Albert Ier) 1961

EXH. CAT. BRUSSELS 1971
H.R. Hoetink and P.J.J. van Thiel, exh. cat. *Rembrandt en zijn tijd*, Brussels (Paleis voor Schone Kunsten) 1971

EXH. CAT. BRUSSELS, ROTTERDAM,
PARIS AND BERN 1968–69
C. van Hasselt, exh. cat. *Dessins de Paysagistes Hollandais du XVII Siècle de la Collection particulière conservée à l'Institut Néerlandais de Paris*, Brussels (Bibliothèque Albert I), Rotterdam (Museum Boijmans Van Beuningen), Paris (Institut Néerlandais) and Bern (Kunstmuseum) 1968–69

EXH. CAT. CHANTILLY 2001–02
D. Mandrella, exh. cat. *Arcadie du Nord: dessin hollandais du Musée Condé à Chantilly*, Chantilly (Musée Condé) 2001–02

EXH. CAT. CHAPEL HILL, ITHACA
AND WORCESTER 1999–2001
F.W. Robinson and S. Peck, exh. cat. *Fresh Woods and Pastures New. Seventeenth-century Dutch landscape drawings from the Peck Collection*, Chapel Hill (Ackland Art Museum), Ithaca (Herbert F. Johnson Museum of Art) and Worcester (Worcester Art Museum) 1999–2001

EXH. CAT. COLOGNE 1954
exh. cat. *Meisterwerke holländischer Landschaftsmalerei des 17. Jahrhunderts*, Cologne (Wallraf-Richartz-Museum) 1954

EXH. CAT. DETROIT 1939
exh. cat. *Loan Exhibition of Dutch Landscape Paintings*, Detroit (Institute of Arts) 1939

EXH. CAT. DIJON 1993
E. Starcky et al., exh. cat. *L'age d'or flamand et hollandaise: collections de Catherine II, Musée de l'Ermitage, Saint-Pétersbourg*, Dijon (Musée des Beaux-Arts) 1993

EXH. CAT. DORDRECHT 1949–50
L.J. Bol, exh. cat. *Catalogus van de Kersttentoonstelling in Dordrechts Museum: 17de eeuwse meesters uit de collectie Leendert Dupper wz (Rijksmuseum Amsterdam) en Scheffer intime*, Dordrecht (Dordrechts Museum) 1949–50

EXH. CAT. DORDRECHT 1964
L.J. Bol, exh. cat. *Zee-, rivier- en oevergezichten, Nederlandse schilderijen uit de 17e eeuw*, Dordrecht (Dordrechts Museum) 1964

EXH. CAT. DORDRECHT AND LEEUWARDEN 1988–89
C. Boschma et al., exh. cat. *Meesterlijk vee: Nederlandse veeschilders 1600–1900*, Dordrecht (Dordrechts Museum) and Leeuwarden (Fries Museum) 1988–89

EXH. CAT. DÜSSELDORF 1970–71
W. von Kalnein exh. cat. *Die Sammlung Bentinck-Thyssen*, Düsseldorf (Kunstmuseum) 1970–71

EXH. CAT. EDINBURGH AND LONDON 2004–05
C. Lloyd, exh. cat. *Enchanting the eye: Dutch paintings of the Golden Age*, Edinburgh (Queen's Gallery) and London (Queen's Gallery) 2004–05

EXH. CAT. EDINBURGH, LONDON AND BARNARD
CASTLE 2010–12
D. Shawe-Taylor and J. Scott, exh. cat. *Dutch landscapes*, Edinburgh (Queen's Gallery), London (Queen's Gallery) and Barnard Castle (Bowes Museum) 2010–12

EXH. CAT. EINDHOVEN 1948
exh. cat. *Nederlandse landschapskunst in de zeventiende eeuw*, Eindhoven (Stedelijk Van Abbe-Museum) 1948

EXH. CAT. ENSCHEDE 1998–99
E. Koolhaas-Grosveld and E. van Uitert, exh. cat. *Wouter van Troostwijk 1782–1810 schilder, tekenaar en etser*, Enschede (Rijksmuseum Twenthe) 1998–99

EXH. CAT. GREENWICH AND AMSTERDAM 2006–07
P.C. Sutton et al., exh. cat. *Jan van der Heyden (1637–1712)*, Greenwich (Bruce Museum of Arts and Science) and Amsterdam (Rijksmuseum) 2006–07

EXH. CAT. HAARLEM 1986
M.C. Plomp, exh. cat. *'In Italiën Geteekent' Nederlandse 17de-eeuwse tekeningen uit het bezit van Teylers Museum*, Haarlem (Teylers Museum) 1986

EXH. CAT. HAARLEM 1995–96
M. Menalda et al., exh. cat. *Een kunstkast gaat open: tekeningen uit de verzameling Teding van Berkhout*, Haarlem (Teylers Museum) 1995–96

EXH. CAT. HAARLEM AND PARIS 2001–02
M. van Berge-Gerbaud et al., exh. cat. *Collectionner, passionnément. Les plus beaux dessins dans les collections hollandaises du XVIII siècle*, Haarlem (Teylers Museum) and Paris (Institut Néerlandais) 2001–02

EXH. CAT. THE HAGUE 1936–37
exh. cat. *Oude Kunst uit Haagsch bezit*, The Hague (Gemeentemuseum) 1936–37

EXH. CAT. THE HAGUE 1948
exh. cat. *Zeven eeuwen Den Haag*, The Hague (Gemeentemuseum) 1948

EXH. CAT. THE HAGUE 1994–95
A. Walsh, E. Buijsen and B. Broos, exh. cat. *Paulus Potter. Schilderijen, tekeningen en etsen*, The Hague (Mauritshuis) 1994–95

EXH. CAT. THE HAGUE 2001–02
A. van Suchtelen et al., exh. cat. *Holland frozen in time: the Dutch winter landscape in the Golden Age*, The Hague (Mauritshuis) 2001–02

EXH. CAT. THE HAGUE 2002
Q. Buvelot and H. Buijs, exh. cat. *A choice collection: seventeenth-century Dutch paintings from the Frits Lugt Collection*, The Hague (Mauritshuis) 2002

EXH. CAT. THE HAGUE AND CAMBRIDGE 1981–82
S. Slive, exh. cat. *Jacob van Ruisdael*, The Hague (Mauritshuis) and Cambridge (Fogg Art Museum) 1981–82

EXH. CAT. THE HAGUE AND LONDON 1970–71
A.G.H. Bachrach, exh. cat. *Shock of recognition: the landscape of English Romanticism and the Dutch seventeenth-century school*, The Hague (Mauritshuis) and London (Tate Gallery) 1970–71

EXH. CAT. THE HAGUE AND WASHINGTON 2008–09
A. van Suchtelen and A.K. Wheelock et al., exh. cat. *Dutch cityscapes of the Golden Age*, The Hague (Mauritshuis) and Washington (National Gallery of Art) 2008–09

EXH. CAT. HULL 1961
exh. cat. *Dutch painting of the seventeenth century*, Hull (Ferens Art Gallery) 1961

EXH. CAT. KASSEL AND THE HAGUE 2009–10
F. Duparc and Q. Buvelot et al., exh. cat. *Philips Wouwerman 1619–1668*, Kassel (Gemäldegalerie Alte Meister) and The Hague (Mauritshuis) 2009–10

EXH. CAT. KOBLENZ, GÖTTINGEN
AND OLDENBURG 2000
G. Unverfehrt, ed., exh. cat. *Zeichnungen von Meisterhand: die Sammlung Uffenbach aus der Kunstsammlung der Universität Göttingen*, Koblenz (Mittelrhein-Museum), Göttingen (Kunstsammlung der Universität) and Oldenburg (Landesmuseum für Kunst und Kulturgeschichte) 2000

EXH. CAT. LAREN 1963
exh. cat. *Nederlandse tekeningen: collectie Hans van Leeuwen*, Laren (Singer Museum) 1963

EXH. CAT. LEEUWARDEN 1966
exh. cat. *Oude Tekeningen uit Drie Eeuwen, Collectie Hans van Leeuwen*, Leeuwarden (Museum Princessehof) 1966

EXH. CAT. LEEUWARDEN,
DEN BOSCH AND ASSEN 1979–80
C. Dumas, exh. cat. *In het zadel: het Nederlands ruiterportret van 1550 tot 1900*, Leeuwarden (Fries Museum), Den Bosch (Noordbrabants Museum) and Assen (Provinciaal Museum van Drenthe) 1979–80

EXH. CAT. LEIPZIG 1914
exh. cat. *Ausstellung Alter Meister aus Leipziger Privatbesitz*, Leipzig (Leipziger Kunstverein) 1914

EXH. CAT. LEIPZIG 1916
exh. cat. *Die Galerie Alfred Thieme in Leipzig*, Leipzig (Leipziger Kunstverein) 1916

EXH. CAT. LONDON 1871
exh. cat. *Exhibition of the Works of the Old Masters, associated with Works of Deceased Masters of the British School*, London (Royal Academy of Arts) 1871

EXH. CAT. LONDON 1877
exh. cat. *Exhibition of Works by the Old Masters, and by Deceased Masters of the British School*, London (Royal Academy of Arts) 1877

EXH. CAT. LONDON 1879
exh. cat. *Exhibition of Works by the Old Masters, and by Deceased Masters of the British Shool, including Oil Paintings, Miniatures, and Drawings*, London (Royal Academy of Arts) 1879

EXH. CAT. LONDON 1887
exh. cat. *Exhibition of Works by the Old Masters, and by Deceased Masters of the British School*, London (Royal Academy of Arts) 1887

EXH. CAT. LONDON 1890
exh. cat. *Exhibition of Works by the Old Masters, and by Deceased Masters of the British School*, London (Royal Academy of Arts) 1890

EXH. CAT. LONDON 1929
exh. cat. *Exhibition of Dutch Art, 1450–1900*, London (Royal Academy of Arts) 1929

EXH. CAT. LONDON 1938
exh. cat. *Catalogue of the exhibition of 17th century art in Europe*, London (Royal Academy of Arts) 1938

EXH. CAT. LONDON 1946–47
A. Blunt *et al.*, exh. cat. *Catalogue of the exhibition of the King's pictures*, London (Royal Academy of Arts) 1946–47

EXH. CAT. LONDON 1952–53
exh. cat. *Dutch pictures, 1450–1750*, London (Royal Academy of Arts) 1952–53

EXH. CAT. LONDON 1962
exh. cat. *Treasures from the Royal collection*, London (Queen's Gallery) 1962

EXH. CAT. LONDON 1971–72
O. Millar, exh. cat. *Dutch Pictures from the Royal Collection*, London (Queen's Gallery) 1971–72

EXH. CAT. LONDON 1975–76
exh. cat. *Landscapes: paintings and drawings from the Royal collection*, London (Queen's Gallery) 1975–76

EXH. CAT. LONDON 1978
exh. cat. *Old master paintings: recent acquisitions*, London (Thos. Agnew and Sons Ltd) 1978

EXH. CAT. LONDON 1988–89
exh. cat. *Treasures from the Royal Collection*, London (Queen's Gallery) 1988–89

EXH. CAT. LOS ANGELES AND BOSTON 1981–82
J. Walsh and C.P. Schneider, exh. cat. *A mirror of nature: Dutch paintings from the collection of Mr. and Mrs. Edward William Carter*, Los Angeles (County Museum of Art) and Boston (Museum of Fine Arts) 1981–82

EXH. CAT. LOS ANGELES, PHILADELPHIA AND LONDON 2005–06
S. Slive, exh. cat. *Jacob van Ruisdael: master of landscape*, Los Angeles (Los Angeles County Museum of Art), Philadelphia (Philadelphia Museum of Art) and London (Royal Academy of Arts) 2005–06

EXH. CAT. MADRID 1994
P.C. Sutton, exh. cat. *The golden age of Dutch landscape painting*, Madrid (Museo Thyssen-Bornemisza) 1994

EXH. CAT. MELBOURNE AND KOBE 2005–06
R. Priem, exh. cat. *Dutch masters from the Rijksmuseum Amsterdam*, Melbourne (National Gallery of Victoria) and Kobe (Hyogo Prefectural Museum of Art) 2005–06

EXH. CAT. MILWAUKEE 2005–06
Marjan Bisanz-Prakken, exh. cat. *Rembrandt and His Time. Masterworks from the Albertina, Vienna*, Milwaukee (Milwaukee Art Museum) 2005–06

EXH. CAT. MONTREAL 1990
F.J. Duparc and L.L. Graif, exh. cat. *Italian Recollections: Dutch Painters of the Golden Age*, Montreal (Museum of Fine Arts) 1990

EXH. CAT. MUNICH 1930
R. Heinemann-Fleischmann, exh. cat. *Sammlung Schloss Rohoncz*, Munich (Neue Pinakothek) 1930

EXH. CAT. MUNICH 1972–73
W. Koschatzky and H. Pée, exh. cat. *Das Aquarel 1400–1950*, Munich (Haus der Kunst) 1972–73

EXH. CAT. NEW YORK AND FORT WORTH 1995
Marian Bisanz-Prakken, exh. cat. *Drawings from the Albertina: landscape in the age of Rembrandt*, New York (Drawing Center) and Fort Worth (Kimbell Art Museum) 1995

EXH. CAT. NEW YORK AND PARIS 1977–78
C. van Hasselt, exh. cat. *Rembrandt and his Century: Dutch Drawings of the seventeenth Century*, New York (Pierpont Morgan Library) and Paris (Institut Néerlandais) 1977–78

EXH. CAT. NEW YORK, CHICAGO, BOSTON AND AMSTERDAM 1972–73
P. Schatborn, *Dutch genre drawings of the seventeenth century*, New York (Pierpont Morgan Library), Chicago (Art Institute of Chicago), Boston (Museum of Fine Arts) and Amsterdam (Rijksprentenkabinet) 1972–73

EXH. CAT. NEW YORK, TOLEDO AND TORONTO 1954–55
exh. cat. *Dutch Painting: the Golden Age*, New York (Metropolitan Museum of Art), Toledo (Museum of Art) and Toronto (Art Gallery) 1954–55

EXH. CAT. NIJMEGEN 1965
M. van Boven, exh. cat. *Tekeningen uit de collectie Hans van Leeuwen*, Nijmegen (Waag) 1965

EXH. CAT. NOVOSIBIRSK 1988
exh. cat. *Shedevry Zapadnoevropeiskoi Zhivopisi XVI–XVIII vv. iz sobraniya Tissen-Bornemisa*, Novosibirsk (Picture Gallery) 1988

EXH. CAT. OBERLIN 1948
W. Stechow, exh. cat. *A Loan Exhibition of Dutch and Flemish Paintings: The Collection of the Late Adolf Mayer*, Oberlin (Allen Memorial Art Museum) 1948, published as an issue of the *Bulletin of the Allen Memorial Art Museum* 5 (1948)

EXH. CAT. OSLO 1959
S. Willoch and R. Jørgensen, exh. cat. *Fra Rembrandt til Vermeer*, Oslo (Nasjonalgalleriet) 1959

EXH. CAT. PARIS 1950–51
J. Bruyn *et al.*, exh. cat. *Le paysage Hollandais au XVIIe siècle*, Paris (Musée de l'Orangerie) 1950–51

EXH. CAT. PARIS 1960
exh. cat. *Bestiaire hollandais: exposition de tableaux, aquarelles, dessins, et gravures par des artistes hollandais des XVIIe–XVIIIe siècles, et d'un choix de livres de la même période*, Paris (Institut Néerlandais) 1960

EXH. CAT. PARIS 1970A, G. Monnier and F. Viatte *et al.*, exh. cat. *Rembrandt et son temps. Dessins des collections publiques et privées conservées en France*, Paris (Musée du Louvre) 1970

EXH. CAT. PARIS 1970B
exh. cat. *Choix de la collection Bentinck: en souvenir de l'ambassadeur des Pays-Bas*, Paris (Institut Néerlandais) 1970

EXH. CAT. PARIS 1974
A.W.F.M. Mey *et al.*, exh. cat. *Dessins flamands et hollandais du dix-septième siècle. Collections des Musées de Belgique, Musée Boymans-van Beuningen Rotterdam, Institut Néerlandais, Paris*, Paris (Institut Néerlandais) 1974

EXH. CAT. PARIS 1983
S. Nihom-Nijstad, exh. cat. *Reflets du siècle d'or: tableaux hollandais du dix-septième siècle, collection Frits Lugt, Fondation Custodia*, Paris (Institut Néerlandais) 1983

EXH. CAT. PARIS 1986
B. Broos *et al.*, exh. cat. *De Rembrandt à Vermeer: les peintres hollandais au Mauritshuis de La Haye*, Paris (Grand Palais) 1986

EXH. CAT. PARIS 2004
S. Alsteens *et al.*, exh. cat. *Regards sur l'art hollandais du XVIIe siècle: Frits Lugt et les frères Dutuit, collectionneurs*, Paris (Institut Néerlandais) 2004

EXH. CAT. PARIS 2009–10
R. Priem *et al.*, *L'âge d'or hollandais: de Rembrandt à Vermeer avec les trésors du Rijksmuseum*, Paris (Pinacothèque de Paris) 2009–10

EXH. CAT. PARIS 2012
exh. cat. *'Un Univers intime': Paintings from the Frits Lugt Collection*, Paris (Institut Néerlandais) 2012; online catalogue: www.fondationcustodia.fr/ununiversintime

EXH. CAT. PARIS AND HAARLEM 1997–98
M. van Berge-Gerbaud, exh. cat. *Rembrandt en zijn school: tekeningen uit de collectie Frits Lugt*, Paris (Institut Néerlandais) and Haarlem (Teylers Museum) 1997–98

EXH. CAT. PARIS, ANTWERP, LONDON AND NEW YORK 1979–80
F. Stampfle, exh. cat. *Rubens and Rembrandt in their century: Flemish and Dutch drawings in the 17th century from the Pierpont Morgan Library*, Paris (Institut Néerlandais), Antwerp (Koninklijk Museum voor Schone Kunsten), London (British Museum), New York (Pierpont Morgan Library) 1979–80

EXH. CAT. PROVIDENCE 1938
W. Stechow, exh. cat. *Dutch painting in the 17th century*, Providence (Rhode Island School of Design) 1938

EXH. CAT. RHEYDT 1971
exh. cat. *Niederländische Zeichnungen des 17. bis 19. Jahrhunderts aus der Sammlung Hans van Leeuwen, Utrecht*, Rheydt (Städtisches Museum Schloss Rheydt) 1971

EXH. CAT. ROME 1956–57
exh. cat. *Il Seicento Europeo: Realismo, Classicismo, Barocco*, Rome (Palazzo delle esposizioni) 1956–57

EXH. CAT. ROME AND MILAN 1954
A.B. de Vries *et al.*, exh. cat. *Mostra di pittura olandese del seicento*, Rome (Palazzo delle Esposizione) and Milan (Palazzo Reale) 1954

EXH. CAT. ROTTERDAM 1945–46
exh. cat. *Tentoonstelling van Nederlandsche zee en riviergezichten uit de XVIIde eeuw*, Rotterdam (Museum Boymans) 1945–46

EXH. CAT. ROTTERDAM AND AMSTERDAM 1961–62
C. van Hasselt, exh. cat. *150 Tekeningen uit vier eeuwen uit de verzameling van Sir Bruce en Lady Ingram*, Rotterdam (Museum Boijmans Van Beuningen) and Amsterdam (Rijksmuseum) 1961–62

EXH. CAT. ROTTERDAM AND BERLIN 1996–97
J. Giltaij and J. Kelch, exh. cat. *Praise of ships and the sea: the Dutch marine painters of the 17th centruy*, Rotterdam (Museum Boijmans Van Beuningen) and Berlin (Gemäldegalerie) 1996–97

EXH. CAT. ROTTERDAM AND FRANKFURT 1999–2000
A. Blankert *et al.*, exh. cat. *Dutch classicism in seventeeth-century painting*, Rotterdam (Museum Boijmans Van Beuningen) and Frankfurt (Städelsches Kunstinstitut) 1999–2000

EXH. CAT. SACRAMENTO AND POUGHKEEPSIE 2010–11
W. Breazeale *et al.*, exh. cat. *A pioneering collection: master drawings from the Crocker Art Museum*, Sacramento (Crocker Art Museum) and Poughkeepsie (Frances Lehman Loeb Art Center) 2010–11

EXH. CAT. SALZBURG AND VIENNA 1986
R. Trnek, exh. cat. *Die Niederländer in Italien: italianisante Niederländer des 17. Jahrhunderts aus österreichischem Besitz*, Salzburg (Residenzgalerie) and Vienna (Akademie der Bildenden Künste) 1986

EXH. CAT. SCHAFFHAUSEN 1949
exh. cat. *Rembrandt und seine Zeit. Zweihundert Gemälde der Blütezeit der holländischen Barockmalerei des 17. Jahrhunderts aus deutschen, holländischen und schweizerischen Museums- und Privatbesitz*, Schaffhausen (Museum zu Allerheiligen) 1949

EXH. CAT. SHANGHAI 2007–08
R. Priem, exh. cat. *Rembrandt and the Golden Age: highlights from the Rijksmuseum Amsterdam*, Shanghai (Shanghai Museum) 2007–08

EXH. CAT. TILBURG 1953
exh. cat. *De Gouden Eeuw, een keuze uit het werk van onze 17e eeuwse schilders: schilderijen uit de collecties van het Rijk*, Tilburg (Paleis-Raadhuis) 1953

EXH. CAT. UTRECHT 1959–60
exh. cat. *Catalogus der tentoonstelling van tekeningen uit de collectie van de heer Hans van Leeuwen te Amsterdam. Utrechtse meesters uit de 17e t.e.m. de 19e eeuw en bladen van andere meesters uit de collectie*, Utrecht (Genootschap Kunstliefde) 1959–60

EXH. CAT. UTRECHT 1960
M.E. Houtzager, exh. cat. *Collectie J.C.H. Heldring te Oosterbeek*, Utrecht (Centraal Museum) 1960

EXH. CAT. VANCOUVER 2009
R. Priem *et al.*, exh. cat. *Vermeer, Rembrandt and the Golden Age of Dutch art: masterpieces from the Rijksmuseum*, Vancouver (Vancouver Art Gallery) 2009

EXH. CAT. VENICE 1993
A. Bettagno, exh. cat. *Francesco Guardi: vedute capricci feste*, Venice (Fondazione Giorgio Cini) 1993

EXH. CAT. VIENNA 1993
M. Bisanz-Prakken, exh. cat. *Die Landschaft im Zeitalter Rembrandts. Niederländische Zeichnungen des 17. Jahhunderts aus der Graphischen Sammlung Albertina*, Vienna (Graphische Sammlung Albertina) 1993

EXH. CAT. VIENNA 2009
K.A. Schröder and M. Bisanz-Prakken, exh. cat. *Das Zeitalter Rembrandts*, Vienna (Graphische Sammlung Albertina) 2009

EXH. CAT. WASHINGTON 1998
A.K. Wheelock, exh. cat. *A collector's cabinet*, Washington (National Gallery of Art) 1998

EXH. CAT. WASHINGTON AND DETROIT 2004–05
A.K. Wheelock *et al.*, exh. cat. *Gerard ter Borch*, Washington (National Gallery of Art) and Detroit (Detroit Institute of Arts) 2004–05

EXH. CAT. WASHINGTON ETC. 1958–59
exh. cat. *Dutch Drawings: Masterpieces of Five Centuries*, Washington (National Gallery of Art), New York (Pierpont Morgan Library), Minneapolis (Minneapolis Institute of Arts), Boston (Museum of Fine Arts), Cleveland (Cleveland Museum of Art), Chicago (Art Institute of Chicago) 1958–59

EXH. CAT. WASHINGTON ETC. 1959–60
exh. cat. *Old master drawings from the collection of Sir Bruce Ingram, circulated by the Smithsonian Institution*, Washington (Smithsonian Institution) etc. 1959–60

EXH. CAT. WASHINGTON, DETROIT AND AMSTERDAM 1980–81
A. Blankert *et al.*, exh. cat. *Gods, saints and heroes : Dutch painting in the age of Rembrandt*, Washington (National Gallery of Art), Detroit (Detroit Institute of Arts) and Amsterdam (Rijksmuseum) 1980–81

EXH. CAT. ZURICH 1947
exh. cat. *Petit Palais, musée de la ville de Paris*, Zurich (Kunsthaus) 1947

EXH. CAT. ZURICH 1953
exh. cat. *Holländer des 17. Jahrhunderts*, Zurich (Kunsthaus) 1953

EXH. CAT. ZURICH 1987
P. ten Doesschate-Chu *et al.*, exh. cat. *Im Lichte Hollands: holländische Malerei des 17. Jahrhunderts aus den Sammlungen des Fürsten von Liechtenstein und aus schweizer Besitz*, Zurich (Kunsthaus) 1987

FAIRFAX MURRAY 1905–12
C. Fairfax Murray, *Collection J. Pierpont Morgan: Drawings by the Old Masters Formed by C. Fairfax Murray*, 5 vols., London 1905–12

FILEDT KOK ET AL. 2001
J.P. Filedt Kok *et al.*, *Netherlandish art in the Rijksmuseum 1600–1700*, Zwolle and Amsterdam 2001

FIOZZI 2004
D. Fiozzi, *Les tableaux hollandais des XVIIe et XVIIIe siècles du musée des Augustins: catalogue raisonné*, Toulouse 2004

FISHMAN 1982
J.S. Fishman, *Boerenverdriet: Violence between Peasants and Soldiers in Early Modern Netherlands Art*, Ann Arbor 1982

FOUCART 2009
J. Foucart, *Catalogue des peintures flamandes et hollandaises du Musée du Louvre*, Paris 2009

FRANSEN 1997
H. Fransen *et al.*, *Michaelis Collection, the Old Town House, Cape Town: Catalogue of the Collection of Paintings and Drawings*, Zwolle 1997

FRENSEMEIER 2001
M. Frensemeier, *Studien zu Adriaen van de Velde (1636–1672)*, Aachen 2001

FRERICHS 1966
L.C.J. Frerichs, 'Strandgezicht, Adriaan van de Velde (1636–1672)', *Openbaar Kunstbezit* 10 (1966), pp.16a–16b

FROMENTIN 1984
E. Fromentin 'Carnets dus voyage en Belgique et en Hollande et pages abandonnées des "Maîtres d'autrefois (Julliet 1875)"', in E. Fromentin *Oeuvres complètes*, Paris 1984, pp.1121–1215

FURNÉE 2011
J.H. Furnée, 'A Dutch Idyll? Scheveningen as a Seaside Resort, Fishing Village and Port, c.1700–1900', in P. Borsay and J.K. Walton, eds., *Resorts and Ports: European Seaside Towns since 1700*, Bristol, Tonawanda and Ontario 2011, pp.33–49

FUSCONI ET AL. 1992
G. Fusconi *et al.*, *Il disegno: i grandi collezzionisti*, Turin 1992

GASKELL 1990
I. Gaskell, *The Thyssen-Bornemisza Collection: Seventeenth-century Dutch and Flemish painting*, London 1990

VAN GELDER 1958
J.G. van Gelder, *Prenten en tekeningen (De schoonheid van ons land*, vol.15), Amsterdam 1958

VAN GELDER 1959
H.E. van Gelder, *Holland by Dutch artists in paintings, drawings, woodcuts, engravings and etchings*, Amsterdam 1959

GERSON 1952
H. Gerson, *De Nederlandse schilderkunst: Het tijdperk van Rembrandt en Vermeer*, Amsterdam 1952

GERSON 1953
H. Gerson, 'Dutch Landscape', *The Burlington Magazine* 95 (1953), pp.47–53

GERSON 1960
H. Gerson, *Catalogue of Paintings in the Fitzwilliam Museum, Cambridge, Vol. I: Dutch and Flemish*, Cambridge 1960

GERSZI 2005
T. Gerszi, *17th-Century Dutch and Flemish Drawings in the Budapest Museum of Fine Arts: A Complete Catalogue*, Budapest 2005

GIBSON 2000
W.S. Gibson, *Pleasant places: the rustic landscape from Bruegel to Ruisdael*, Berkeley 2000

GILTAIJ AND LAMMERTSE 2001
J. Giltaij and F. Lammertse, 'Maintaining a Studio Archive. Drawn Copies by the De Bray Family', *Master Drawings* 39 (2001), pp.367–94

GOLDSCHEIDER 1936
L. Goldscheider, *Fünfhundert Selbstporträts von der Antike bis zur Gegenwart (Plastik, Malerei, Graphik)*, Vienna 1936

VAN GOOL 1750/51
J. van Gool, *Antwoordt op den zoo genaemden brief aen een vrient, mitsgaders noch op de intrërede voor het eerste deel der catalogus van schilderijen, beide in druk uitgegeven door Gerard Hoet, ter afwissinge van den laster en schendtael, in die beide geschriften uitgespoogen ...*, n.p. 1750/51?

TER GOUW 1871
J. ter Gouw, *De volksvermaken*, Haarlem 1871

GOWER 1875
R. Gower, *A pocket guide to the public and private galleries of Holland and Belgium*, London 1875

GROENENDIJK 2008
P. Groenendijk, *Beknopt biografisch lexicon van Zuid- en Noord-Nederlandse schilders, graveurs, glasschilders, tapijtwevers et cetera van ca.1350 tot ca.1720*, Utrecht 2008

HAAK 1984
B. Haak, *Hollandse schilders in de Gouden Eeuw*, Amsterdam 1984

VAN HALL 1963
H. van Hall, *Portretten van Nederlandse beeldende kunstenaars / Portraits of Dutch painters and other artists of the Low Countries*, Amsterdam 1963

HAMELEERS 1994A
M. Hameleers, 'Adriaen van de Velde ontwierp decoraties voor Frederick de Wit's kaart van Amsterdam', *Caert-Thresoor* 13 (1994), pp.77–79

HAMELEERS 1994B
M. Hameleers, 'Ontwerptekeningen van Adriaen van de Velde voor de kaart van Amsterdam van Frederick de Wit', *Maandblad Amstelodamum* 81 (1994), pp.166–71

HAMELEERS 2013
M. Hameleers, *Kaarten van Amsterdam I: 1538–1865*, Bussum and Amsterdam 2013

HANNEMA 1955
D. Hannema, *Catalogue raisonné of the pictures in the collection of J.C.H. Heldring*, Rotterdam 1955

HASSE 1969
M. Hasse, *Die Zeichnungen alter Meister in der Lübecker Graphiksammlung*, Lübeck 1969

HEINEMANN 1937
R. Heinemann, *Stiftung Sammlung Schloss Rohoncz*, 3 vols., Lugano-Castagnola 1937

HEPPNER 1948
A. Heppner, 'Religieuze kunst in Holland's bloeitijd', *Maandblad voor Beeldende Kunsten* 24 (1948), pp.77–82 and 113–20

HERZOG 1969
E. Herzog, *Die Gemäldegalerie der Staatlichen Kunstsammlungen Kassel. Geschichte der Galerie*, Hanau 1969

HIND 1926
A.M. Hind, *Catalogue of Drawings by Dutch and Flemish Artists preserved in the Department of Prints and Drawings in the British Museum, Vol. III: Dutch Drawings of the XVII Century (A–M)*, London 1926

HIND 1931
A.M. Hind, *Catalogue of Drawings by Dutch and Flemish Artists preserved in the Department of Prints and Drawings in the British Museum, Vol. IV: Dutch Drawings of the XVII Century (N–Z and Anonymous)*, London 1931

HIRSCHMANN 1917
O. Hirschmann, 'Die Handzeichnungen-Sammlung Dr. Hofstede de Groot im Haag III (Schluss): Die Rembrandt-Schüler', *Cicerone* 9 (1917), pp.199–211

HOETINK 1985
H.R. Hoetink, ed., *The Royal Picture Gallery Mauritshuis*, Amsterdam 1985

HOFSTEDE DE GROOT 1892
C. Hofstede de Groot, 'Schilderijenverzamelingen van het geslacht Slingelandt: Bijdrage tot de wordingsgeschiedenis van het Koninklijk Kabinet van Schilderijen', *Oud Holland* 10 (1892), pp.229–37

HOFSTEDE DE GROOT 1899
C. Hofstede de Groot, 'Kritische opmerkingen omtrent eenige schilderijen in 's Rijksmuseum', *Oud Holland* 17 (1899), pp.163–70

HOFSTEDE DE GROOT 1912
C. Hofstede de Groot, *A catalogue raisonné of the works of the most eminent Dutch painters of the seventeenth century*, 8 vols., London 1907–27, IV (Jacob van Ruisdael, Meindert Hobbema, Adriaen van de Velde, Paulus Potter), London 1912

HOFSTEDE DE GROOT 1923
C. Hofstede de Groot, *A catalogue raisonné of the works of the most eminent Dutch painters of the seventeenth century*, 8 vols., London 1907–27, VII (Willem van de Velde, Jan van de Cappelle, Ludolf Backhuysen, Aert van der Neer), London 1923

HOLLSTEIN 1949–2010
F.W.H. Hollstein's Dutch and Flemish etchings, engravings and woodcuts ca.1450–1700, Amsterdam; Roosendaal; and Rotterdam 1949–2010

HOOGENBOOM 1993–94
A. Hoogenboom, 'Art for the Market: Contemporary Painting in the Netherlands in the First Half of the Nineteenth Century', *Simiolus* 22 (1993–94), pp.129–47

HOOGEWERFF 1952
G.J. Hoogewerff, *De Bentvueghels*, The Hague 1952

HOOGSTRAETEN 1678
S. van Hoogstraeten, *Inleyding tot de hooge schoole der schilderkunst*, Rotterdam 1678

HOUBRAKEN 1718–21
A. Houbraken, *De groote schouburgh der Nederlantsche konstschilders en schilderessen*, 3 vols., Amsterdam 1718–21

HÜBNER 1856
J. Hübner, *Verzeichniss der königlichen Gemälde-Gallerie zu Dresden: Mit einer historischen Einleitung und Notizen über die Erwerbung der einzelnen Bilder*, Dresden 1856

HUYGENS 1920
H.J. Eymael, ed., *Constantijn Huygens' Hofwyck (Vitaulium)*, Zutphen 1920

IMMERZEEL 1842–43
J. Immerzeel, *De levens en werken der Hollandsche en Vlaamsche kunstschilders, beeldhouvers, graveurs en bouwmeesters, van het begin der vijftiende eeuw tot heden*, 3 vols., Amsterdam 1842–43

INGAMELLS 1992
J. Ingamells, *The Wallace Collection. Catalogue of Pictures, IV: Dutch and Flemish*, London 1992

JAMESON 1844
A. Jameson, *Companion to the most celebrated private galleries of art in London*, London 1844

JOBY 2007
C.R. Joby, *Calvinism and the Arts: A Re-Assessment*, Leuven 2007

DE JONGH 1986
E. de Jongh, exh. cat. *Portretten van echt en trouw: huwelijk en gezin in de Nederlandse kunst van de zeventiende eeuw*, Haarlem (Frans Halsmuseum) 1986

JUFFINGER 2010
R. Juffinger, *Residenzgalerie Salzburg: Gesamtverzeichnis der Gemälde*, 2 vols., Salzburg 2010

KEYES 1984
G.S. Keyes, *Esaias van den Velde 1587–1630*, Doornspijk 1984

KILIAN 2005
J.M. Kilian, *The paintings of Karel Du Jardin, 1626–1678*, Amsterdam 2005

KLEINMANN 1913
H. Kleinmann, *Handzeichnungen alter Meister der holländischen Malerschule*, 2nd ed., 6 vols., Leipzig 1913

DE KLERCK 2009
B. de Klerck, 'Italiaans ijs', *Kunstschrift* 53/6 (2009), pp.20–25

KRAMM 1857–64
C. Kramm, *De levens en werken der Hollandsche en Vlaamsche kunstschilders, beeldhouwers, graveurs en bouwmeesters*, 6 vols. and suppl., Amsterdam 1857–64

LAIRESSE 1707
G. de Lairesse, *Het groot schilderboek*, 2 vols., Amsterdam 1707

LAIRESSE 1817
G. de Lairesse, *A Treatise on the Art of Painting, in all branches, by Gerard de Lairesse. Revised, corrected and accompanied with an essay, by W.M. Craig*, 2 vols., London 1817

LAPAUZE 1907
H. Lapauze, *Palais des Beaux-Arts de la ville de Paris: catalogue sommaire des collections Dutuit*, Paris 1907

LAPAUZE 1910
H. Lapauze, *Le palais des Beaux-Arts de la ville de Paris (Petit Palais)*, Paris 1910

LAPAUZE, GRONKOWSKI AND FAUCHIER-MAGNAN 1925
H. Lapauze, C. Gronkowski.and A. Fauchier-Magnan, *Palais des Beaux-Arts de la ville de Paris: catalogue sommaire des collections Dutuit*, Paris 1925

LAURENTIUS, NIEMEIJER AND PLOOS VAN AMSTEL 1980
Th. Laurentius, J.W. Niemeijer en G. Ploos van Amstel, *Cornelis Ploos van Amstel 1726–1798. Kunstverzamelaar en prentuitgever*, Assen 1980

LAUTS 1966
J. Lauts, *Staatliche Kunsthalle Karlsruhe, Katalog alte Meister bis 1800*, 2 vols., Karlsruhe 1966

LONDON 1854
[Anonymous], *The works of eminent masters, in painting, sculpture, architecture, and decorative art*, 2 vols., London 1854

LUGT 1927
F. Lugt, *Les Dessins des Écoles du Nord de la Collection Dutuit au Musée des Beaux-Arts de la Ville de Paris (Petit Palais)*, Paris 1927

LUGT 1929–33
F. Lugt, *Musée du Louvre: inventaire général des dessins des écoles du nord: école hollandaise*, 3 vols., Paris 1929–33

LUGT 1931
F. Lugt, 'Beiträge zu dem Katalog der Niederländischen Handzeichnungen in Berlin', *Jahrbuch der Preuszischen Kunstsammlungen* 52 (1931), pp.36–80

LUGT 1956
F. Lugt, *Les Marques de Collections de Dessins & d'Estampes, Supplément*, The Hague 1956

MACLAREN 1991
N. MacLaren, *National Gallery Catalogues: The Dutch School, 1600–1900*, rev. and expanded by C. Brown, 2 vols., London 1991

MANUTH 1993–94
V. Manuth, 'Denomination and iconography, the choice of subject matter in the biblical paintings of the Rembrandt circle', *Simiolus* 22 (1993–94), pp.235–52

MARTIN 1936
W. Martin *De Hollandsche schilderkunst in de zeventiende eeuw*, 2 vols., Amsterdam 1936

MARTIN 1950
W. Martin *De schilderkunst in de tweede helft van de 17e eeuw*, Amsterdam 1950

MELLAART 1926
J.H.J. Mellaart, *Dutch drawings of the 17th century*, London 1926

MICHEL 1888
E. Michel, 'Les Van de Velde', *Gazette des Beaux-Arts* 38 (1888), pp.265–84

MICHEL 1892
E. Michel, *Les Van de Velde*, Paris 1892

MIDDELKOOP 2008
N. Middelkoop, *De oude meesters van de stad Amsterdam: schilderijen tot 1800*, Bussum 2008

MOES 1905–06
E.W. Moes, *Oude teekeningen van de Hollandsche en Vlaamsche school in het Rijksprentenkabinet te Amsterdam*, 2 vols., The Hague 1905–06

MOES 1913
E.W. Moes, 'Het Kunstkabinet van Valerius Röver te Delft', *Oud Holland* 31 (1913), pp.4–24

MÖHLE 1948
H. Möhle, *Holländische Zeichnungen*, Berlin 1948

MÜLLENMEISTER 1973–81
K.J. Müllenmeister, *Meer und Land im Licht des 17. Jahrhunderts*, 3 vols., Bremen 1973–81

MURRAY 1824
[J. Murray], *Tour in Holland in the Year 1819*, London [1824]

NAGLER 1835–52
G.K. Nagler, *Neues allgemeines Künstler-Lexicon; oder Nachrichten von dem Leben und den Werken der Maler, Bildhauer, Baumeister, Kupferstecher etc.*, 22 vols., Munich 1835–52

NICOLAISEN 2012
J. Nicolaisen, *Niederländische Malerei 1430–1800 Museum der bildenden Künste Leipzig*, Leipzig 2012

NIEUWENHUYS 1834
C.J. Nieuwenhuys, *A review of the lives and works of some of the most eminent painters: with remarks on the opinions and statements of former writers*, London 1834

OLTMANS 1845–46
A. Oltmans, 'Tentoonstelling van schilderijen door oude meesters, in het lokaal der Koninklijke Akademie van Beeldende Kunsten te Amsterdam', *Kunstkronijk* 6 (1845–46), pp.4–12

OVID, *METAMORPHOSES*
Ovid, *Metamorphoses*, transl. F.J. Miller, 3rd ed. revised by G.P. Gould (*The Loeb Classical Library*), 2 vols., Cambridge, MA and London 1974

PARKER 1938
K.T. Parker, *Catalogue of the collection of drawings in the Ashmolean Museum, I: Netherlandish, German, French and Spanish Schools*, Oxford 1938

PARKER 1972
G. Parker, *The army of Flanders and the Spanish Road, 1567–1659 the logistics of Spanish victory and defeat in the Low Countries' Wars*, Cambridge 1972

PARTHEY 1863–64
G. Parthey, *Deutscher Bildersaal: Verzeichniss der in Deutschland vorhandenen Ölbilder verstorbener Maler aller Schulen*, 2 vols., Berlin 1863–64

PIKE 1869
W.B. Pike, 'Fitzwilliam Museum', *Cambridge University Gazette*, 12th May 1869, pp.158–59

PITA ANDRADE AND BOROBIA GUERRERO 1992
J.M. Pita Andrade and M.M. Borobia Guerrero, *Old masters Thyssen-Bornemisza Museum*, Barcelona 1992

PLIETZSCH 1916
E. Plietzsch, 'Nebenwerke holländischer Maler des 17. Jahrhunderts, II', *Zeitschrift für bildende Kunst* 51 (1916), pp.129–42

PLOMP 1997
M.C. Plomp, *The Dutch drawings in the Teyler Museum*, Haarlem, Ghent and Doornspijk 1997

PLOMP 2001
M.C. Plomp, *Collectionner, passionément. Les collectionneurs hollandais de dessins au XVIII siècle*, Paris 2001

PLOOS VAN AMSTEL AND JOSI 1821
C. Ploos van Amstel and C. Josi, *Collection d'imitations de dessins d'après les principaux maîtres hollandais et flamands*, London 1821

PRESTON 1937
L. Preston, *Sea and river painters of the Netherlands in the seventeenth century*, London 1937

PRIEM 1997
R. Priem, 'The "Most Excellent Collection" of Lucretia Johanna van Winter: The Years 1809–22, with a Catalogue of the Works Purchased', *Simiolus* 25 (1997), pp.103–230

VAN REGTEREN ALTENA 1948
I.Q. van Regteren Altena, *Holländische Meisterzeichnungen des 17. Jahrhunderts*, Basel 1948

VAN REGTEREN ALTENA 1964
I.Q. van Regteren Altena, *Vereeuwigde stad: Rome door Nederlanders getekend 1500–1900*, Amsterdam 1964

VAN REGTEREN ALTENA 1972
I.Q. van Regteren Altena, *100 dessins du Musée Teyler Haarlem*, Paris 1972

TE RIJDT 1990
R.J. te Rijdt, 'Figuurstudies van het Amsterdamse particuliere tekengenootschap "Zonder Wet of Spreuk" (ca.1808–1819)', *Bulletin van het Rijksmuseum* 38 (1990), pp.223–44

RIPA/PERS 1644
C. Ripa, *Iconologia, of uytbeeldingen des Verstands [...] uyt het Italiaens vertaelt door D.P. Pers*, Amsterdam 1644

ROBINSON 1979A
W.W. Robinson, 'Preparatory Drawings by Adriaen van de Velde', *Master Drawings* 17 (1979), pp.3–23 and 57–69

ROBINSON 1979B
W.W. Robinson, 'Family Portraits of the Golden Age', *Apollo* 110 (December 1979), pp.490–97

ROBINSON 1990
M.S. Robinson, *Van de Velde: a catalogue of the paintings of the Elder and the Younger Willem van de Velde*, 2 vols., London 1990

ROETHLISBERGER 1969
M. Roethlisberger, *Bartholomäus Breenbergh: Handzeichnungen*, Berlin 1969

ROWELL 2013
C. Rowell, ed., *Ham House: 400 years of collecting and patronage*, New Haven and London 2013

ROYALTON-KISCH, CHAPMAN AND COPPEL 1996
M. Royalton-Kisch, H. Chapman and S. Coppel, *Old Master Drawings from the Malcolm Collection*, London 1996

SADKOV 2010
V. Sadkov *et al.*, *The Pushkin State Museum of Fine Arts: Netherlandish, Flemish and Dutch drawings of the XVI–XVIII centuries, Belgian and Dutch drawings of the XIX–XX centuries*, Amsterdam 2010

SAUNDERS AND KIRBY 1994
D. Saunders and J. Kirby, 'Light-induced Colour Changes in Red and Yellow Lake Pigments', *National Gallery Technical Bulletin* 15 (1994), pp.79–97

SCHAPELHOUMAN 1987
M. Schapelhouman, *Nederlandse tekeningen omstreeks 1600 / Netherlandish drawings circa 1600*, The Hague 1987

SCHAPELHOUMAN 2006
M. Schapelhouman, *Rembrandt and the Art of Drawing*, Zwolle and Amsterdam 2006

SCHATBORN 1975
P. Schatborn, 'De Hut van Adriaen van de Velde', *Bulletin van het Rijksmuseum* 23 (1975), pp.159–65

SCHNACKENBURG 1996
B. Schnackenburg, *Gesamtkatalog Gemäldegalerie Alte Meister, Kassel*, 2 vols., Mainz 1996

SCHNEIDER 1927
H. Schneider in H. Thieme en F. Becker, *Allgemeines Lexicon der bildenden Künstler von der Antike bis zur Gegenwart*, XX, Leipzig 1927, pp.240–41

SCHOLTEN 1904
H.J. Scholten, *Musée Teyler à Haarlem: catalogue raisonné des dessins des écoles française et hollandaise*, Haarlem 1904

SCHULZ 1978
W. Schulz, *Cornelis Saftleven, 1607–1681 Leben und Werke: mit einem kritischen Katalog der Gemälde und Zeichnungen*, Berlin 1978

SCOTT 1994
C.R. Scott *et al.*, *Paintings from Europe and the Americas in the Philadelphia Museum of Art. A concise catalogue*, Philadelphia 1994

SEBAG MONTEFIORE AND ARMSTRONG-TOTTEN 2013
C. Sebag Montefiore with J.I. Armstrong-Totten, *A dynasty of dealers: John Smith and successors 1801–1924. A study of the art market in nineteenth-century London*, Arundel 2013

SENENKO 2009
M. Senenko, *The Pushkin State Museum of Fine Arts: Collection of Dutch Paintings XVII–XIX Centuries*, Moscow and Amsterdam 2009

ŠEVČÍK 2012
A.K. Ševčík, ed., *National Gallery in Prague: Dutch paintings of the 17th and 18th centuries*, Prague 2012

SHIRLEY 1987
R.W. Shirley, *The Mapping of the World. Early Printed World Maps 1472–1700*, London 1987

SINT NICOLAAS AND STEVENS 2006
E. Sint Nicolaas and H. Stevens, 'Kolders. Van modieus militair kledingstuk tot slagveldreliek', *Bulletin van het Rijksmuseum* 54 (2006), pp.267–89

SLIVE 1956
S. Slive, 'Notes on the relationship of protestantism to seventeenth century Dutch painting', *Art Quarterly* 19 (1956), pp.3–15

SLIVE 1995
S. Slive, *Dutch painting, 1600–1800*, New Haven and London 1995

SLIVE 2001
S. Slive, *Jacob van Ruisdael: a complete catalogue of his paintings, drawings and etchings*, New Haven and London 2001

SMITH 1834
J. Smith, *A catalogue raisonné of the works of the most eminent Dutch, Flemish, and French painters*, 9 vols., London 1829–42, V (Nicholas Berchem, Paulus Potter, Adriaen van de Velde, Karel Dujardin, Aelbert Cuyp, Jan van der Heyden), London 1834

SMITH 1835
J. Smith, *A catalogue raisonné of the works of the most eminent Dutch, Flemish, and French painters*, 9 vols., London 1829–42, VI (Jacob van Ruisdael, Meindert Hobbema, Jan and Andries Both, Jan Wijnants, Adam Pynacker, Jan Hackaert, Willem van de Velde, Ludolf Backhuysen, Jan van Huysum, Rachel Ruysch), London 1835

SMITH 1842
J. Smith, A catalogue raisonné of the works of the most eminent Dutch, Flemish, and French painters, 9 vols., London 1829–42, IX (Supplement), London 1842

STECHOW 1966
W. Stechow, *Dutch Landscape Painting of the Seventeenth Century*, London and New York 1966

STECHOW 1967
W. Stechow, 'A Painting and a Drawing by Adriaen van de Velde', *Bulletin of the Cleveland Museum of Art* 54 (1967), pp.30–35

STEENGRACHT VAN OOSTKAPELLE 1826–30
J. Steengracht van Oostkapelle, *De voornaamste schilderijen van het Koninklijk Kabinet te 's Gravenhage, in omtrek gegraveerd, met derzelver beschrijving*, 4 vols., The Hague 1826–30

SUTTON 1992
P.C. Sutton, *Dutch & Flemish seventeenth-century paintings: the Harold Samuel Collection*, London 1992

TAYLOR 2008
P. Taylor, 'Flatness in Dutch Art: Theory and Practice', *Oud Holland* 121 (2008), pp.153–84

TERWESTEN 1770
P. Terwesten, *Catalogus of naamlyst van schilderyen met derzelver pryzen*, The Hague 1770

TEXIER 1857
E. Texier, *Voyage pittoresque en Hollande et en Belgique*, Paris 1857

VAN THIEL 1976
P.J.J. van Thiel, *All the paintings of the Rijksmuseum in Amsterdam: a completely illustrated catalogue*, Amsterdam and Maarssen 1976

VAN THIEL ET AL. 1992
P.J.J. van Thiel *et al.*, *All the paintings of the Rijksmuseum in Amsterdam: a completely illustrated catalogue. First supplement: 1976–91*, Amsterdam and The Hague 1992

THIEME 1900
U. Thieme, ed., *Galerie Alfred Thieme in Leipzig*, Leipzig 1900

THORÉ-BÜRGER 1858–60
W. Bürger [E.-J.-T. Thoré], *Musées de la Hollande*, 2 vols., Paris 1858–60

THORÉ-BÜRGER 1859
W. Bürger [E.-J.-T. Thoré], *Galerie d'Arenberg à Bruxelles avec le catalogue complet de la collection*, Paris 1859

TURNER AND STAMPFLE 2006
J.S. Turner, with contributions by F. Stampfle, *Dutch Drawings in the Pierpont Morgan Library: Seventeenth to Nineteenth Centuries*, New York 2006

VETH 1890
G.H. Veth, 'Aanteekeningen omtrent eenige Dordrechtsche schilders', *Oud Holland* 8 (1890), pp.23–28

VAN VLOTEN 1874
J. van Vloten, *Nederlands schilderkunst van de 14e tot de 18e eeuw, voor het Nederlandsche volk geschetst*, Amsterdam 1874

DE VRIES AND BUVELOT 2012
A. de Vries, with Q. Buvelot, *Passie voor schilderijen: de verzameling Steengracht van Duivenvoorde*, Leiden 2012

WAAGEN 1838
G.F. Waagen, *Works of art and artists in England*, 3 vols., London 1838

WAAGEN 1854
G. Waagen, *Treasures of art in Great Britain being an account of the chief collections of paintings, drawings, sculptures, illuminated mss., &c. &c.*, 3 vols., London 1854

WAAGEN 1857
G. Waagen, *Galleries and cabinets of art in Great Britain, being an account of more than forty collections of paintings, drawings, sculptures, mss., &c. &c. visited in 1854 and 1856, and now for the first time described, forming a supplemental volume to the Treasures of Art in Great Britain*, London 1857

WAAGEN 1860
G. Waagen, *Handbook of painting. The German, Flemish, and Dutch schools. Based on the Handbook of Kugler. Enl. and for the most part re-written*, 2 vols., London 1860

WADDINGHAM AND KLEMM 1988
M.R. Waddingham and C. Klemm, *The paintings of the Betty und David M. Koetser Foundation*, Zurich and Doornspijk 1988

WAIBOER 2005
A. Waiboer, 'The early years of Gabriel Metsu', *The Burlington Magazine* 147 (2005), pp.80–90

WAIBOER 2012
A.E. Waiboer, *Gabriel Metsu. Life and work. A catalogue raisonné*, New Haven and London 2012

WALSH 1996
J. Walsh, *Jan Steen: the drawing lesson*, Malibu 1996

WEGNER 1973
W. Wegner, *Katalog der Staatlichen Graphischen Sammlung München, 1 Die niederländischen Handzeichnungen des 15.-18. Jahrhunderts*, 2 vols., Berlin 1973

VAN DE WETERING 2015
E. van de Wetering, *Rembrandt's Paintings revisited. A complete Survey (A Corpus of Rembrandt Paintings, VI)*, Dordrecht 2015

WHEELOCK ET AL. 2000
A.K. Wheelock *et al.*, *The Golden age of Dutch and Flemish painting: the Edward and Sally Speelman Collection*, Houston and The Hague 2000

WHITE 1982
C. White, *The Dutch pictures in the collection of Her Majesty the Queen*, Cambridge 1982

WHITE 2015
C. White, *Dutch Pictures in the Collection of Her Majesty The Queen*, with technical notes supplied by R. de Sancha, London 2015

WIERSUM 1910
E. Wiersum, 'Het schilderijen-kabinet van Jan Bisschop te Rotterdam', *Oud Holland* 28 (1910), pp.161–86

WIERSUM 1922
E. Wiersum, 'Uit het dagboek van Gerrit van der Pals', *Rotterdams Jaarboekje* (1922), pp.3–17

WOERMANN 1887
K. Woermann, *Katalog der königlichen Gemäldegalerie zu Dresden*, Dresden 1887

DE WOLF 1967
H.C. de Wolf, 'Kunst uit de schuilkerkentijd', *Antiek* 1 (1967), no.9, pp.3–10

WOLTMANN AND WOERMANN 1888
A. Woltmann and K. Woermann, eds., *Geschichte der Malerei, III: Die Malerei von der Mitte des Sechzehnten bis zum Ende des achtzehnten Jahrhunderts*, 2 vols., Leipzig 1888

WURZBACH 1904–11
Alfred von Wurzbach, *Niederländisches Künstler-Lexikon*, 3 vols., Leipzig and Vienna 1904–11

DE ZEEUW 1979
J.W. de Zeeuw, 'De Gouden Eeuw uit turf geboren', *Spieghel Historiael* 14 (1979), pp.524–31

ZOEGE VON MANTEUFFEL 1927
K. Zoege von Manteuffel, *Die Künstlerfamilie van de Velde*, Bielefeld and Leipzig 1927.

PHOTOGRAPHIC CREDITS

AUSTRIA
Albertina, Vienna: cat. no.36; fig.177; KHM – Museumsverband: fig.39; Liechtenstein. The Princely Collections, Vaduz–Vienna: fig.105; © Residenzgalerie Salzburg, Fotostudio Ghezzi, Oberalm: figs.58, 90

BELGIUM
© Lukas – Art in Flanders VZW, photo Hugo Maertens: fig.128

DENMARK
National Gallery of Denmark, Copenhagen © SMK Photo: figs.13, 141

FRANCE
Bibliothèque Municipale de Lyon: fig.127; Fondation Custodia, Collection Frits Lugt, Paris: cat. nos.27, 37, 40, 47; Photo © RMN-Grand Palais (Domaine de Chantilly) / René-Gabriel Ojéda: fig.156; © Musées d'Angers: fig.99; Musée des Beaux-Arts de Caen, Martine Seyve Photographe: fig.79; Photo © RMN-Grand Palais (Musée du Louvre): fig.104; Photo © RMN-Grand Palais (Musée du Louvre) / Gérard Blot: cat. no.6; figs.22, 132; Photo © RMN-Grand Palais (Musée du Louvre) / René-Gabriel Ojéda: fig.142; Photo © Musée du Louvre, Dist. RMN-Grand Palais / Pierre Philibert: fig.148; Honfleur, Musée Eugène Boudin © Photo Henri Brauner: fig.78; © Petit Palais / Roger-Viollet: cat. nos.12, 44; figs.20, 163

GERMANY
bpk / Bayerische Staatsgemäldesammlungen: fig.65; © die Lübecker Museen, Museum Behnhaus Drägerhaus: fig.160; bpk / Museum der bildenden Künste, Leipzig / Ursula Gerstenberger: fig.72; Photo © Museum der bildenden Kunste, Leipzig : cat. no.3; bpk / Museum der bildenden Künste Leipzig: figs.32, 34(a); © Museumslandschaft Hessen Kassel, Gemäldegalerie Alte Meister: cat. no.5; figs.21, 52(a), 77(a), 123; Staatliche Graphische Sammlung München, Inv. 2034 Z: fig.161; bpk / Staatliche Kunsthalle Karlsruhe / Annette Fischer / Heike Kohler: figs.40, 154 ; bpk / Staatliche Kunstsammlungen Dresden / Hans-Peter Klut: cat. no.26; fig.71; bpk / Staatliche Kunstsammlungen Dresden / Herbert Boswank: fig.150; bpk / Gemäldegalerie, SMB: fig.140; bpk / Gemäldegalerie, SMB / Jörg P. Anders: figs.5, 66, 113, 115; bpk / Kupferstichkabinett, SMB / Dietmar Katz: cat. no.21; fig.153; bpk / Kupferstichkabinett, SMB / Jörg P. Anders: cat. no.48; bpk / Kupferstichkabinett, SMB / Volker-H. Schneider: cat. no.55; bpk / Staatliches Museum Schwerin / Elke Walford: figs.8, 35

ITALY
Galleria Luigi Caretto, Turin, Italy: fig.97

THE NETHERLANDS
Amsterdam City Archives: cat. nos.57, 58, fig.179; Amsterdam Museum: figs.41, 76, 77(b), 80(b), 81(b), 109, 138; Amsterdam Museum, legaat C.J. Fodor: cat. nos.32, 33, 38, 46; figs.112, 162, 164; Collectie Six, Amsterdam: fig.69; Leiden University Library, PK-T-AW-294: fig.159; © Mauritshuis, The Hague: cat. nos.8; figs.14, 44, 52(b), 60, 158; Museum Boijmans Van Beuningen, Rotterdam: fig.120; Museum Boijmans Van Beuningen, Rotterdam / photographer: Studio Tromp, Rotterdam: figs.17, 55; Museum Bredius, The Hague: figs.89, 182; Photograph courtesy RKD-Netherlands Institute for Art History, The Hague: figs.1, 3, 4, 12, 16, 19, 25, 26, 37, 48, 54, 88, 94, 103, 108, 111, 129, 130, 137, 139, 151; Rijksmuseum, Amsterdam: cat. nos.19, 30, 42, 43, 45, 50, 52(d), 56; figs.6, 9, 10, 33, 34(b), 46, 47, 52, 70, 110(a), 144, 146, 147(a), 167, 168, 170, 171, 174, 175, 178, 181; Rijksmuseum, Amsterdam. Dupper Wzn. Bequest, Dordrecht: cat. no.10; Rijksmuseum, Amsterdam. Mr and Mrs De Bruijn-van der Leeuw Bequest, Muri, Switzerland: fig.184; Rijksmuseum, Amsterdam. On loan from the City of Amsterdam (A. van der Hoop Bequest): cat. nos.22, 29; Rijksmuseum, Amsterdam. Purchased with the support of the Vereniging Rembrandt: cat. nos.23, 39, 59; fig.114; Rijksmuseum, Amsterdam. F.G. Waller Bequest, Amsterdam: fig.173; Teylers Museum, Haarlem, The Netherlands: cat. nos.49, 51, 53, 54; figs.100, 136, 165, 169, 180

POLAND
National Library of Poland, Warsaw: fig.86

RUSSIA
The Pushkin State Museum of Fine Arts: figs.24, 29, 106; The State Hermitage Museum, St. Petersburg. Photography © The State Hermitage Museum/ photo by Vladimir Terebenin: figs.93, 95, 96(b)

SOUTH AFRICA
© Iziko Museums of South Africa Art Collections. Photograph by Carina Beyer: fig.98

SOUTH AMERICA
Donación Mario HIRSCH, Sara Saavedra Guari de Hirsch, Claudia Caraballo de Quentin y Octavio Caraballo, 1983 Colección Museo Nacional de Bellas Artes, Argentina: fig.83

SPAIN
© Museo Thyssen-Bornemisza. Madrid: cat. no.13,

SWEDEN
Photo: Gothenburg Museum of Art, Sweden: fig.118

SWITZERLAND
© 2016 Kunsthaus Zürich: fig.57; Kunsthaus Zürich, Betty and David Koetser Foundation, 1986: fig.92

UK
© Ashmolean Museum, University of Oxford: cat. no.20; © His Grace, the Duke of Bedford, and the Trustees of the Bedford Estates: figs.7, 145; © Bristol Museum and Art Gallery, UK / Purchased, 1954. / Bridgeman Images: fig.183; © The Trustees of the British Museum: cat. nos.35, 41, 60; figs.38, 62(b), 101, 124, 125; © Christie's Images Limited: figs. (2014) 43, (2007) 155, (1993) fig.152, (1994) fig.107; © Art Image Library: fig.64; By permission of the Trustees of Dulwich Picture Gallery, London: figs.45, 122; © The Fitzwilliam Museum, Cambridge: cat. nos.15, 24; figs.75, 110(b), 166; © Guildhall Art Gallery, City of London / Harold Samuel Collection / Bridgeman Images: fig.131; Courtesy Johnny van Haeften Ltd, London: fig.143; © The National Gallery, London: cat. nos.1, 2, 25; figs.49, 62(a), 85, 116; © The National Gallery, London. Salting Bequest, 1910: figs.67, 176; © The National Gallery, London. Wynn Ellis Bequest, 1876: fig.15, 82(b); © The National Gallery, London. Bought with a special grant and contributions from The Art Fund and The Pilgrim Trust, 1959: fig.68; © National Maritime Museum, Greenwich, London: fig.73; © National Trust Images: figs.42, 157; Raveningham Hall, Norfolk / © Fisheye Images: fig.121; Royal Collection Trust / © Her Majesty Queen Elizabeth II 2016: cat. nos.7, 16, 28; figs.11, 80(a), 81(a), 82(a), 117, 147(b); The Schroder Collection: cat. no.11; fig.96(a); © Sotheby's London: figs.51, 53; Purchased with assistance from the Friends of the Tate Gallery, the Art Fund, the Pilgrim Trust and subscribers 1977 © Tate, London 2016: fig.126; © The Wallace Collection, London: figs.27, 31, 50; Private collections: Photograph by Matthew Hollow Photography: cat. no.4; Photograph by Antonia Reeve, Edinburgh: cat. no.18; Private Collection / Photo © Christie's Images / Bridgeman Images: fig.87, 135; Private Collection / Bridgeman Images: fig.59

USA
In loving memory of Harold T. Martin from Eloise W. Martin, wife, and Joyce Martin Brown, daughter; Charles H. and Mary F.S. Worcester Collection; Lacy Armour Endowment; through prior gift of Frank H. and Louise B. Woods 1997.336. Photography © The Art Institute of Chicago: fig.2; Sidney A. Kent Fund, 1894.1024. Photography © The Art Institute of Chicago: fig.172; © The Cleveland Museum of Art: fig.30; Crocker Art Museum, E. B. Crocker Collection, 1871.186: fig.36; Harvard Art Museums/Fogg Museum, Gift of Maida and George S. Abrams in memory of Jakob Rosenberg, 1980.75: fig.28; Indianapolis Museum of Art, James E. Roberts Fund, 40.253: figs.52(c), 56; Digital image courtesy of the Getty's Open Content Program. © J. Paul Getty Trust: figs.18, 149; Los Angeles (CA), Los Angeles County Museum of Art (LACMA). Gift of Mr. and Mrs. Edward William Carter (M.2009.106.14). © 2016. Digital Image Museum Associates/LACMA/Art Resource NY/ Scala, Florence. © Photo SCALA, Florence 2016: fig.84; Los Angeles (CA), Los Angeles County Museum of Art (LACMA). Gift of Mr. and Mrs. Edward William Carter (M.2009.106.12). © 2016. Digital Image Museum Associates/LACMA/Art Resource NY/Scala, Florence. © Photo SCALA, Florence 2016: fig.91; From the Collection of Rita and Frits Markus, Bequest of Rita Markus, 2005. © 2000–2016 The Metropolitan Museum of Art. All rights reserved: fig.74; The Museum of Fine Arts, Houston, Museum Purchase funded by the Agres Cullen Arnold Endowment Fund, 2009.556: fig.61; The Museum of Fine Arts, Houston, The Edward and Sally Speelman Collection, TR:1644-2005: cat. no.17; The Museum of Fine Arts, Houston, The Edward and Sally Speelman Collection, TR:1636-2005: fig.134; Philadelphia Museum of Art, John G. Johnson Collection, 1917: figs.63, 119, 133; Peck Collection, Boston: cat no.31; The Pierpont Morgan Library, New York. I,149. Purchased by Pierpont Morgan (1837–1913) in 1909: cat. no.14; Private collection © Lee Ewing: fig.102